RICKY BROWN

The Great Awakening in Columbus, Ohio (1895)

Historical Account of Late 19th Century Revival Meetings

SONS OF PROPHETS

Sons of Prophets Publishing
PO Box 575 | Pickerington, OH 43147
sonsofprophets.com

| 10 9 8 7 6 5 4 3 2 1 |

Published in the United States of America

Second edition

ISBN (paperback): 978-1-966354-35-2
ISBN (hardcover): 978-1-966354-36-9

Contents

IV   Part Four

V   Scans of Original Publication Pages

Preface

Excited to dust off this old, typewritten publication of "The Great Awakening in Columbus, Ohio," as many are unaware of its existence - this republishing of original work is presented to you, the reader, as a bridge between centuries of generations contending for revival. Historical documentation bridges the yearnings of the past, the contending of the present, and the outpourings of the future as pursuit of God's desire overtakes His followers to establish His Kingdom in their city, state, and nation.

Thrilled to read old sermons of messages preached by leaders who have gone before us, we've reproduced this content to pass it along to our brothers and sisters in the faith to be stirred with God's destiny for the city of Columbus, Ohio. When reading through, I urge you to peek into that destiny, root yourself in God's purposes, and be established in the preaching, contending, and praying in faith that has gone before us.

I would remind the readers that over time - politics, political parties, governmental systems, and cultural contexts have changed. Therefore, it is important to have eyes of grace, not pulling apart any detail one may disagree with at the cost of losing a chance to see the heart and the spirit in which these sermons were written and preached. Just as we are not to worship our perspectives of the "letter of the law" while denying the Spirit in which that law was written.

As you read, may hunger be stirred. May we apprehend the gospel that will carry this generation, and may we document the mighty moves of God that are upon us now and those that are soon to come. May our prayers be generations ahead of us just as the prayers of the men and women of "The Great Awakening" in 1985 have laid a path for today's generation of believers who contend for revival, and for the knowledge of the Glory of God to rise in Columbus, Ohio.

-Ricky Brown

The Great Awakening in Columbus, Ohio (1895)

Originally edited by Henry Stauffer.
Introduction by Washington Gladden.

The Great Awakening in Columbus, Ohio

Henry Stauffer, Washington Gladden

Committees in charge of the Mills Meetings

EXECUTIVE COMMITTEE

A. A. E. Taylor, D. D, *Chairman*, Rev. Henry Stauffer, *Secretary*, N. B. Abbott, W. A. Mahony, William Price, Rodney Nelson, O. C. Hooper, J. A. Jeffrey, Rev. W. L. Lemon, Rev. W. J. Russell, J L. Hampton, A. W. Field, A. R. Markel, L. B. Lewis, J. R. Hughes, Rev. D. F. Harris, Rev. P. A. Baker, Rev. A. E. Davis

COMMITTEE ON FINANCE

Walter Crafts, *Chairman*, Robert Candy, Joseph Dunn

COMMITTEE ON ADVERTISING

Howard H. Russell, *Chairman*, Frank Frankenberg, Henry a. Morgan, Charles F. Guthridge

COMMITTEE ON CANVASSING

F. W. Wallis, *Chairman*, Horace J. Maynard, E. D. Bancroft, Charles H. Lewis

COMMITTEE ON USHERS

Secretary W. T. Perkins, *Chairman*, William H. Hughes, J. E. Huff

COMMITTEE ON MUSIC

O. H. Perry, Chairman, A. S. Humphrys, J. F. Blair

LADIES' COMMITTEE

Mrs. H. M. Petit, *Chairman*, Mrs. E. L. Harris, Miss Maud Dye, Mrs . R. M. Rownd, Mrs. A. N. Fox. Mrs. Jennie E. Hurlbut, Mrs. N. C. Helfrich

DEVOTIONAL COMMITTEE
Rev. W. L. Lemon, *Chairman*, Rev. William Macafee, Rev. W. H. Fishburn, D. D, Rev. J. C. Jackson, Jr., D. D.

COMMITTEE ON CHRISTIAN CONVENTION
Rev. Washington Gladden, D. D., Rev. William Macafee, Rev. J. C. Watt, D. D, Rev. W. L. Lemon, Rev. W. J. Russell

COMMITTEE ON MIDWEEK SABBATH
W. A. Mahony, Foster Copeland, John Estill, J. H. Dunn, W. H. Hughes, Geo. M. Peters, R. M. Rownd, J. A. Jeffrey, Z. L. White, Robert Candy, N. F. Mcmanigal, Rev. Washington Gladden, D. D., Rev. F. E. Marsten, D. D., W. D. Park, Rev. William Macafee, Dr. F. F. Lawrence, C. E. Munson, C. H. Miller, W. R. Walker, E. W. Seeds

I

Part One

The New Evangelism, Rev. Washington Gladden, D. D

I HAVE been asked to contribute a few prefatory words to this report of the meetings in Columbus. The papers and addresses speak for themselves; what I should be glad to do would be to give some idea of the spirit of the whole work of Mr. Mills and his associates in our city, of which this convention was an important episode. This, however, is an extremely difficult thing to do. The spirit of an occasion like this is the one unreportable thing. But something of its significance may be suggested.

I have ventured to speak of Mr. Mills as a new type of evangelist. To this he makes no claim; he does not assume that his doctrine or his method possesses any novelty. As to the doctrine, the substance. of it was very familiar sixteen or eighteen hundred years ago. In the words of Clement of Alexandria and Athanasius and Origen, a view of Christianity, almost identical with the view presented in these meetings, may be found. It is really the oldest orthodoxy which reappears in the impassioned words of this evangelist. Yet the conception of Christ of his relation to God and to the race, of the nature of His kingdom, of the meaning of His gospel, is certainly quite unlike the conception which has been current for the past three centuries in Reformed churches.

If the substance of Evangelical truth is loyalty to Christ, there can be no question about the soundness of the doctrine of Mr. Mills. A more passionate devotion to Him, as Son of God and Son of Man, as Saviour and Captain and Deliverer and King of Men, does not often find utterance.

Nor is there any hesitation in affirming that men need a Saviour. That sin is something more than misfortune or immaturity is clearly seen; the tragedy of the evil will is not concealed.

But the Fatherhood of God is with Mr. Mills not a mere figure of speech; it is an eternal fact. Every man is a child of God; that relation can never be annulled; the prodigal has no legal barriers to overcome; he has only to come home. Jesus Christ is our Elder Brother: He has shown us what God is and what man may be.

In every man there are divine and Christly elements; what Christ wants to do for us is to deliver us from the sins that are demoralizing us and to restore our souls. The kingdom of God is here; it is not to be awaited, it has come. Already it is taking possession of every department of human life; all that is needed is that the work should be carried on to completion. It comes only as every man learns to do habitually the loving thing. Love is the only law; its force is irresistible; it solves all social problems; it reclaims the felon; it rehabilitates the pauper; it binds capital and labor together with the golden bands. of fraternity; it brings the happy day of good will and peace.

I am not trying to reproduce the essential teaching of Mr. Mills; I am only reciting a few of the truths which he has been enforcing. I am sure that no one has listened to the noonday sermons, devoted to the Gospel of the Kingdom, without being profoundly stirred by the power and nobility of the presentation. Day, after day we have confessed with swelling hearts that this is a glorious world to be in-a world that Christ has redeemed; and that this is a good time to live brightest of all the days since time began.

For one, I desire to record my deepest gratitude for the uplifting and inspiring message of this prophet and leader of men.

-WASHINGTON GLADDEN, December 4, 1895

The Mills Meeting

GREAT results often grow out of small beginnings. The great evangelistic movement which has produced so profound an effect on this city, commenced in the hearts of a few ministers early in May of the present year. The first meeting held to counsel in regard to inviting Rev. B. Fay Mills to conduct a union evangelistic meeting in this city, was held in the Young Men's Christian Association building, on Friday, May 17th, Rev. F. E. Marsten, D. D., acting as Chairman, and Rev. Henry Stauffer as Secretary.

It was first proposed to ask Mr. Mills to spend ten days among us at the beginning of the tent meeting campaign, which was carried on under the auspices of the young people's organizations during the summer in different sections of the city; and the first meeting was called with a view to securing the sanction of the pastors to such a plan. But the more the matter was discussed, the more it became apparent that it would be vastly better to arrange for special meetings, not during the hot summer months, but at such a season of the year as would be most favorable for such a work.

The outcome of this first meeting was the appointment of the following committee of five to confer with Mr. Mills in regard to coming to this city to labor: Rev. James Haig, Rev. Henry Stauffer, Rev. J. C. Jackson, Jr., D. D., Rev. B. F. Patt, and Rev. D. F. Harris.

The committee had an interesting conference with Mr. Mills the next day at the Young Men's Christian Association Building and were deeply impressed by the personality of the man and the originality and practical value of his plans.

The feeling was general among the pastors present on that now historic occasion that our city was in sad need of a general and aggressive religious campaign by all the churches, and it was the unanimous opinion that Mr. Mills was the man best fitted to lead in such a movement. The deliberations of this meeting resulted in a motion on the part of the pastors to recommend to their respective churches that they cooperate in calling Mr. Mills to work in this city in November.

At a meeting called a few days later to hear reports from the churches to which the matter had been referred for final action, it was found that eighteen had endorsed the recommendations of their pastors and voted to cooperate. On May 27th, at a large and enthusiastic meeting of the pastors, over which Rev. Washington Gladden, D. D., presided, fifteen additional churches responded favorably, and it was voted to call Mr. Mills, and the committee of five having the matter in charge was instructed to complete the arrangements with him.

The success of the movement seemed now to be fully assured. Some, however, still stood aloof because they did not believe it possible for so many different denominations to work together successfully, however desirable it might be that they should do so. Others withheld their support because they feared that the reaction that would follow in the wake of such a great religious awakening as was. contemplated would largely neutralize its apparently good effects.

On the other hand, many of those who are praying and living for the moral welfare of others deplored the fact that there was a great, unnecessary and unpardonable waste of energy because of a lack of union in the moral and religious forces of the city. The most earnest Christians in all the churches were sighing because of the moral condition of the city and yearning to see the kingdom of God come with prevailing power. It became more and more evident that the Protestant churches of Columbus had come to a new self-consciousness. A wholesome discontent with the existing state of things, a sense of insufficiency if working alone, and a desire for a widespread revival of religion gradually took possession of the minds of the members of the various churches. The only logical result of such a condition was that which has actually come to pass, namely the union of the churches that were moved by a common impulse, under one management and under the leadership of a preeminently successful specialist. By the time the meetings began on November 19th, the following thirty-eight churches had voted to cooperate and had elected delegates to represent them in the General Committee:

- *Baptist* - First, Hildreth, Memorial, Tenth Avenue, Russell Street.
- *Congregational* - First, St. Clair Avenue, South, Mayflower, Eastwood, Washington Avenue, Welsh, Plymouth, North.
- *Christian* - Central, King Avenue.
- *Methodist Episcopal* - Miller Avenue, Glenwood Heights, Gift Street, Wesley Chapel, Third Avenue, Third Street, German, Broad, Neil Avenue, Mt. Vernon Avenue.
- *Presbyterian* -West Broad Street, St. Clair Avenue, Westminster, Broad Street, First, Fifth Avenue, Oliver, Nelson Memorial, Welsh.
- *Reformed* - Wilson Avenue.
- *Evangelical*-Emanuel.
- *United Brethren* -Grace.
- *Lutheran*-Monroe Avenue.

Walter Crafts
Chairman Finance Committee

W. T. Perkins, General Secretary of the Y. M. C. A.
And Chairman of the Ushers' Committee

Rev. A. A. E. Taylor, D. D., LL D.
Chairman of the Executive Committee

F. W. Wallis
Chairman Canvassing Committee

O. H. Perry
Chairman Music Committee

The Union Mission Association and Young Men's Christian Association also voted to support the meeting. While Second Presbyterian Church, and King Avenue, North Columbus and Town Street Methodist Churches did not come into the alliance by official action, they have, nevertheless, gone heartily into the movement; both pastors and people working harmoniously and energetically to make the meeting a success.

The great union meeting which has just been closed is as yet a matter of too recent occurrence to be accurately estimated; but it is evident that the old epoch of religious history has forever closed and the new one has begun. The conditions had for some time been gradually ripening for an advance movement, and some rapid strides forward have been taken during the last few weeks. Thousands of people have of late been thinking greater thoughts about man, God and His kingdom than had ever entered their minds before. To all these the church, life, and duty will never again be what they formerly were, because a great change has been wrought within. Multitudes of well-disposed men of the world have been led to think more highly of Christ and His work in the world and for the world because of the strong and manly appeals to which they have listened day after day. Many individual conversions have been secured. Pastors have received inspiration and enlargement, whose value is simply immeasurable, and which must entirely change the nature of their preaching. Multitudes in the city and all over the central portion of the State who could not attend the meetings read the daily reports of them in the papers and were thus greatly benefited. Many of the dwellers in the slums have had new hopes and purer desires awakened in them. To all who have in any way felt the influence of the meeting there has come a new sense of the essential sacredness of every phase of life, domestic, political, social, industrial, commercial, professional and religious.

The unity which had all along existed among Christians of different denominations has now been clearly disclosed. In the consciousness of this oneness there is new inspiration and power for every good work that is to be undertaken in the future. There are very few pessimists sitting under juniper trees hereabouts at the present; for a boundless hope for the world has laid hold of all that have been reached by the meetings. The large and long - sustained attendance at the noonday services was something never witnessed before in this city even by the oldest inhabitants.

Through the Christian Convention held from December 3rd to 6th, inclusive, the good influence of the meeting was spread throughout all Central Ohio. One hundred and twenty - seven newspapers were asked to publish the program of this unique gathering, and nine-hundred and seventy ministers residing in this section of the State were invited to attend its sessions. The program was remarkable for the wide range and practical character of the subjects discussed. The topics were so arranged and treated as to produce at first intense conviction and sorrow for social sins, but passing finally into the inspiration of a new and stronger faith in Christ as the only sufficient Savior of the individual and of society.

The midweek Sabbath which was observed Friday, December 13th, produced a most salutary effect on the entire city. As silence is sometimes more eloquent than speech, so the stopping of the mighty machinery of trade for a half day in the busy holiday season was a most convincing proof of man's reverence for God and genuine respect for a great religious movement even in these modern days.

It is utterly impossible to compress spiritual facts and forces into statistical form. A long church roll may mean much or little. We rejoice in the many accessions that will be made to the churches as a result of these meetings, but these will constitute but one portion of the many good fruits of the Mills meeting. Through their united efforts to help others the Christian people of this city have gained. new strength for themselves. They have come to their stronger selves. They have discovered their real power for good in the community. They believe in themselves and respect themselves as never before.

The way has now been opened in a perfectly natural way for a federation of all Protestant churches and a consequent economical expenditure of strength, hitherto squandered in the very midst of a perishing world. Every moral reform conceived in the conscience of man and born of his faith, hope and love, has received a fresh and powerful impulse.

The timid have become bold and outspoken against the vice and lawlessness that prevails about us.

The evangelist's sublime conception of the kingdom of God on earth has taken deep root in a great company of persons who heretofore had a vague idea that their particular denomination was the great All.

In such facts as these the spiritually minded see the seeds of a future harvest inexpressibly rich and glorious.

The Mills meeting, with its great audiences, inspiring singing, eloquent and powerful preaching, deep feeling, and blending of hearts, is over. But all who love God. man, and righteousness have received an inspiration which they will never lose and which will necessarily influence them in all future conduct. Columbus will never again be what it has been. That which is to be will be infinitely better than that which has been.

Biographical Sketches of the Evangelists

Leading Producers of "The Great Awakening"

The Men Who Took a Leading Part

REV. B. FAY MILLS

Rev. B. Fay Mills was born in Rahway, NJ., in 1857, and is therefore 38 years of age. He is the son of Dr. Thornton A. Mills, a well-known Presbyterian minister, and is himself at present a member of the Presbytery of Albany, He graduated from Lake Forest University, Illinois, in 1879. His first pastorate was with the Congregational Church at Granite Falls, Minn. From there he went to serve the Congregational Church at Cannon Falls, in the same State. In 1883 he accepted a call to a

Congregational Church at Rutland, VT. Here he found a very discouraging field. The church of which he was pastor had been weakened by dissensions and had become a repellant instead of an attractive force in the community. Here his powers were taxed to the utmost; his burning zeal, his hopefulness, his rare tact, his wonderful talent for organization, his faith in God, and, above all, his complete consecration to his chosen work soon wrought a marvelous change on his congregation. He turned the thoughts of his people from the less to the greater; from themselves and their grievances to God and the great, hungry, perishing world. Under the influence of his inspiring preaching and tactful pastoral care the church was once more united and filled with enthusiasm for work.

In this church he developed his evangelistic plans and methods, which he has since used so successfully in his larger field. Because of his conspicuous success in this difficult field many pastors, whose hearts were burdened for the salvation of men, wrote to him, inviting him to assist them in special services. But he resolutely declined all such calls, having no desire to leave the regular pastorate.

At last, however, he consented to go to Middlebury, VT for a few days. Being a college town, this has naturally become one of the New England centers of culture, and as such offered the severest test of the ability of the evangelist. Only fifty attended his first service, but the audience grew fast from the very first, until he and his addresses were the talk of the town. The candor, earnestness, and above all, the reasonable and severely ethical and practical character of his sermons at once drew the students to him. His success as an evangelist of the highest grade was now fully assured. He stayed not only many days, but even weeks, and it was the result of this first evangelistic effort away from his own church which led him to believe that he was called to become a specialist in this line of work.

When finally he went home it was to ask his congregation to release him so that he might devote his whole time to the evangelistic work. His people naturally refused to grant his release, but were willing to compromise by allowing him to devote three months of each year to work in the wider sphere. So great was his success now that his people felt that it would be wrong to insist on his staying with them any longer, so they released him from the pastorate with much regret. During the ten years which have elapsed since that time he developed intellectually and spiritually until he is now recognized as the foremost evangelist of the day.

Although Mr. Mills believes in himself and his own plans, as all successful men do, the distinction which he has attained has not made him proud or vain, as will be seen by the following incident: Two years ago when the degree of doctor of divinity was conferred on him by the trustees of Iowa College, he promptly declined the honor in such an excellent spirit as not to cast reflection on any of his brethren who can see no sufficient reason for declining a well merited honor. In his letter of declination he said: "I have a sincere wish to refrain from anything like a critical impulse concerning others, but for myself I cannot but interpret the spirit of the Master's words, 'Be not ye called Rabbi for one is your master, even Christ, and all ye are brethren,' as indicating to me that I ought not to be called by any title of honor that is not owned by all of my faithful brethren in the ministry of Christ. So, please let me remain a plain minister of Christ till the end of my pilgrimage."

Great success is a very complex result, into which many streams of good fortune enter. Mr. Mills was exceptionally fortunate in his marriage. Mrs. Mills is regarded by those who know her best as a woman of bright intellect, great force of character, rare eloquence and beauty. She is the happy mother of six children and presides over her home with pleasing grace and gentleness. When her husband was in San Francisco she assisted him ably by holding services for women only, which were largely attended and productive of great good.

Mr. Mills' marvelous success is due to his entire consecration to his work; his thorough conviction that those who are living un-Christ-like lives are losing themselves; to his firm faith in God; to his strong faith in the possibility of saving men from sin; faith in himself as one through whom God will produce great results in the building up of his kingdom; to his rare talent as an organizer and leader of men; the modernness of the gospel he preaches. He uses no "back number" theology in his sermons. He goes directly to the roots of things and is severely practical in all his preaching. Mr. Mills is in hearty sympathy with the recent hopeful tendency among the evangelical churches toward a more distinctively social gospel than has yet been preached. By his eloquent and powerful noon-day sermons during the last month he has caused men to see as never before that it is impossible to save the individual entirely until many of the existing social hindrances are removed. It has sometimes been said that narrowness is essential to intense earnestness, but Mr. Mills is a living and growing denial of that libelous statement. His work in this city proves that at least one man can preach both a personal and a social gospel with equal earnestness and power.

REV. W. E. BIEDERWOLF

Rev. W. E. Biederwolf was born at Monticello, Ind., in February, 1867, of poor but honest German parents. He took the High School course in his native town; was converted at the age of 19, and so strong was his impulse to preach, that he dedicated himself to the ministry on the very day of his conversion. After spending four years in Wabash College, located at Crawfordsville, IN., he entered Princeton College, in New Jersey, from which he graduated in 1892. He finished his theological course in Princeton Seminary with the highest honors in 1895. While a student in Princeton he labored very efficiently in the old Jerry McAuley Mission, on Water street, New York, and had charge, during that time, of several missions. As a student Mr. Biederwolf was an active member of Princeton Athletic Association, and is himself a good specimen of muscular Christianity. Since his graduation he has had the very rare opportunity of being associated with Mr. Mills in his labors. He is exceptionally well endowed and finely balanced; and multitudes in this city love him because of the benefit they have derived from his ministry.

JOHN P. HILLIS

John P. Hillis was born at Greencastle, IN, twenty-seven years ago. He took a musical course in DePauw University, which is located in his native town. At the age of 18 he was engaged by one of the best minstrel troupes in the country. He had not been on the stage long, however, till the early training he had received asserted itself. The life he was living seemed empty and almost useless. He became a thoroughly Christian man, and decided to use his great talents not to entertain, but to save men. In 1891 he joined Dr. S. A. Keen, the noted evangelist, now deceased. In November, 1892, Mr. Hillis became associated with Mr. Mills, with whom he has labored in Albany, Providence, Montreal, Kansas City, Omaha, St. Paul, Minneapolis, Milwaukee, and Chicago. Mr. Hillis possesses a very rare combination of musical qualities. He has a rich and strong baritone voice that is very well suited to leading a great congregation; yet it is so fine and flexible as to be capable of the most delicate expression. Mr. Hillis has been highly appreciated in Columbus and has made a host of friends during his stay here. REV. JOHN H. MURRAY. Rev. John H. Murray was born in this city November 15, 1866. He lost his father when four years of age. He finished the grammar school course in the Rich street building, of which Miss Mattie Simonton was then principal. During his boyhood he attended Third Street Methodist Sunday School. At the age of 14 he ran away from home and fell into the worst possible company. He tramped all over the country seeing the sights and learning to steal and gamble. In 1884 he was convicted of aiding and abetting shooting with intent to kill and was sentenced to serve a term in the Ohio Penitentiary. While in prison, sick, helpless and hopeless, he picked up an old Bible lying on a stool in his cell. He soon became deeply interested in the character and life of Jesus. Before he knew it he had fallen in love with Him; and when he read of His cruel crucifixion he found himself weeping. He knelt and gave himself to Christ. Thus he was converted from a sinful to a truly Christian life. After serving one year and thirteen days of his sentence he secured a pardon. After his release he at once became an earnest Christian worker in this city and in New York City, where he joined Col. H. H. Hadley in his famous rescue mission work.

Mr. Murray has been very successful in winning men to Christ wherever he has labored. No one can meet him or hear him preach without having a new sense of the power of Christ to cleanse from all sin.

REV. NATHANIEL NICOLAI

Rev. Nathaniel Nicolai was born in Riga, Russia, in 1866, and was educated at Stuttgart, Wurtemberg. He came to America at the age of 20. He is an Episcopal clergyman and for the last two years has been the agent of the Brooklyn City Mission and Tract Society. Mr. Nicolai is an earnest worker and a very fluent and interesting German speaker.

HARRY L. MAXWELL

Harry L. Maxwell was born in 1866 at Crawfordsville, Ind., where he spent his boyhood days. He was converted at the age of 20. He studied at DePauw University six years, three of which were devoted to music. In 1887 he organized the DePauw Male Quartet and traveled with it four years. He sang with the Schuman Quartet, of Chicago, six months. He left Chicago in October, 1893, to enter evangelistic work. In chorus work Mr. Maxwell is a superior trainer and leader. His kind, winning ways quickly draw all hearts to him. Mr. Maxwell has a tenor voice of rare sweetness and power. He enters deeply into the spirit of the music and words he renders in song, and is thus able to inspire others with the same enthusiasm that fires his own soul.

P. P. BILHORN

P. P. Bilhorn, who led the singing in connection with the German services on the South Side, is a composer of wide fame. He is endowed by nature with a rare voice which he has improved to the highest point of perfection.

* * *

The following six sermons were delivered by Rev. B. Fay Mills during the meeting held in Columbus, Ohio, from November 19th to December 16th, 1895: "The Heart that Heart that is not Right."

II

Sermons by Rev. B. Fay Mills

The Heart that is not Right

"Thy heart is not right in the sight of God." -Acts 8:21.

An Atheistic Heart is not Right in God's Sight.

An atheistic heart is not right in the God's sight. There are very few men who have atheistic heads, and a great many who have atheistic hearts. I cannot see how a man can have common sense and say in his mind that there is no God: and there are not many men, who give any thought to the matter at all, who have come to the conclusion that there is no personal God. Very frequently it depends upon what the definition of God may be as to the question whether certain men would say that there is a God or not. The tendency today of all devotees of that school of science that has been in the habit of denying the existence of a personal God has grown almost entirely away from the theoretical atheism into agnosticism; and now the tendency of all scientific thought is clearly toward the acknowledgment that there must be a personal Creator and Governor of the universe.

But there are thousands and hundreds of thousands of men who have atheistic hearts. "The fool hath said in his heart, "There is no God." "The psalmist did not mean to apply an opprobrious epithet to any man when he said that. He simply meant to say that the man was a very foolish man who should wish there were no God, because for a man to say in his heart that there is no God is to desire that there should be no God. For the heart is the seat of the desires, it is the seat of the impulses; "out of the heart are the issues of life." And very frequently the impulse of the heart will go entirely contrary to all reason; and it does so in the case of the man who says, "I would there were no God." How could a man be more foolish than that? I have heard of an insurrection in a hospital where those who were being treated by the physicians rose up and wanted to throw off all restraint and care that was laid upon them. Even suppose they had been able to do it, suppose they had been able to banish all the physicians and every restraint that had been kindly laid upon them, how much worse they would be than before they had accomplished their foolish action! And I think it was something of this thought that was in the mind of the psalmist when he said that a man was very foolish who should wish there were no God. But the man that has a heart that does not want a God, the man that does not love the ways of God, the man of whom it can be said, "God is not in all or in any of his thoughts," that man is practically an atheist. Adam and Eve were practically atheists when they ignored God's command and were ready to partake of the forbidden fruit; and no man ever committed a sin from that day until now that was not, in a sense, an atheist, and said in his heart, "I wish there were no law over me, and no restraint upon me." O man, if there is any law of God that is irksome to you, you are cherishing the seeds of atheism. If there is any law you would not gladly cherish and welcome and love because it is God's law, to that extent you are an atheist in your heart, and your heart is not right in the sight of God. Every man is a man without God in his heart except he who has learned to love the will of God and the laws of God. "Great peace have they that love Thy law: and nothing shall offend them." An Idolatrous Heart is not Right in God's Sight. An idolatrous heart is not right in God's sight. That was the trouble with the man to whom this text was spoken by Peter. He was a man who thought more of worldly power and money than he did of the Holy Ghost. Having formerly been a magician, and his trade having been taken away from him by the great revival in Samaria, occurring in connection with the labors of Philip, Peter and John, this man came to Peter and asked him if he would tell him the secrets of his trade, so that he might be as great a magician as

Peter or John, and share the power with them. I suppose his idea was that the time had come when they were about to close the revival meetings and go away from the city, and he wanted to know how to do the marvelous things they did through the inspiration they had, so that he could still retain his place and his great influence over the minds of men he had formerly deceived. Peter said to him this: "Thy money perish with thee, because thou has thought that the gift of God may be purchased with money. Thou hast neither part nor lot in this matter: for thy heart is not right in the sight of God." He did not care for the spiritual blessing; all that he cared for was the marvelous power.

Now there are a great many idolaters of this kind today. There are many men who do not begin to keep the first commandment, "Thou shalt have no other gods before Me." I believe that if a man keeps that commandment he will do all that God will ever ask of him. A man that keeps the first commandment perfectly will be able to learn all that God can teach him, and will learn to do all that God wants him to do, and will become all that God wants him to be. The man that puts God first has found the key that will unlock every perplexity concerning the development of character and the attainment of power and influence. The man who puts anything before God is an idolater.

I heard of a man who had been a whaling captain, and when he was asked to give his heart to God, he said, "Give God my heart? I have no heart. If you were able to dig down to the place where my heart ought to be you would find the image of a whale." And there are many men that, if you could dig down to the place where God ought to be, you would find some idol-money, worldly ambition, the desire for fame, something that in itself was an injury to them and had been taking the place of God. Mr. Finney tells a story about a business man who said to a minister that he desired to be a Christian. They knelt together, and after the minister had prayed he asked this man to offer prayer. The other replied that he had never prayed in his life and he did not know how to do it. Whereupon the minister asked if he would repeat a prayer after him, and upon receiving an affirmative response he commenced somewhat as follows: "O God, I desire to consecrate myself to

Thee." And the man said, "O God, I desire to consecrate myself to Thee." "I will give Thee my life." "I will give Thee my life." "I will give Thee my talents." "I will give Thee my talents." "I will give Thee my friends." "I will give Thee my friends." "I will give Thee my business." "Why don't you go on?" said the minister. And the man replied, "I am afraid the Lord does not want my business." This man had been putting the wrong thing that was in his business before his duty to God. He was a practical idolater, whose heart was not right in the sight of God.

An Unbelieving Heart is not Right in God's Sight.

An unbelieving heart is not right in God's sight. By that I mean a heart that does not believe in Jesus Christ. A man that is a righteous man wants to be a Christian. A man could not love right and righteousness and hate wrong without wanting to be a Christian. Why? Jesus Christ is incarnate righteousness, He is practical righteousness; and if a man loves righteousness he will love Jesus. We hear a good deal of talk in these days about loving practical righteousness and rejecting Jesus Christ. The statement is contradictory in itself. The man who says it means that he loves theoretical righteousness; but he does not love practical righteousness unless he loves Jesus, for Christ is the only practically righteous thing that ever existed upon this earth. It is really nonsense, it is unthinkable, for a man truly to love righteousness in theory and not love righteousness when it comes to us in the form of a human being.

Jesus Christ is concrete righteousness, righteousness put in a practical form, so that our eyes may see it, and our hands may handle it, and our minds may apprehend it. And if a man wants to do right he loves it; or, in other words, he will love Him. The man that has hungerings in his heart for righteousness finds here the food that satisfies him. The man that is thirsting and panting for that which is noble and true and good finds here the water of eternal life that quenches every thirst. There is no yearning of a human soul, as it reaches out after the good, the true, and the beautiful, that is not perfectly satisfied by Jesus Christ. And that is the reason why a man cannot want to do right and turn his back on Christ. It is a self-evident truth that a man that wants to do right will love Christ, and a man that does not want to do right will turn his back on Him. This is the great test of the ages. As some one says, "Jesus is the touchstone of character." Belief in Jesus Christ is no more a condition than it is an evidence of a man's salvation. I have heard a great many people preach on Christ's conversation with Nicodemus, and a great many comments made on the new birth. There is nothing I believe in more than the new birth, and I know something of what it means; but I only know what it means because of the experience that I have had of it. Christ was very careful not to mention it in this philosophical language. He never mentioned it in those terms but once in all His career, and then he was talking to a philosopher who, He thought, might comprehend what he had to say to him. Most of the time he talked in plain English and did not use metaphors, and all the other terms He did use were exceedingly simple, in order that men might see clearly just what God wanted them to do. If you should study the Scriptures and take the words of Christ and study them, in order that you might find out just what he wanted from men, you might be exceedingly surprised. He does not ask from men any intellectual process; He does not even ask from them in any instance what is sometimes called "faith," if by that you mean an intellectual assent to any sort of doctrines or truths. He is continually asking men to do good things and stop doing bad things, and presenting himself as the only power on earth that can help men to turn away from the bad and do the good, and make them what they ought to be. This conversation with Nicodemus that is recorded in the third chapter of John is no exception. Christ preached this marvelous sermon to this one man; and when He came to the place where He used the familiar passage concerning the lifting up of the serpent, and what is called the "little gospel"-the marvelous verse that says, "God so loved the world that He gave His only begotten Son, that whosoever believeth in Him should not perish, but have everlasting life"-that was not the application; He had not yet come to the practical part of it. He comes to it just after that, when he says, "God sent not His Son into the world to condemn the world; but that the world through Him might be saved. He that believeth on Him is not condemned."

He has made here a statement of the principle of a fact that the man whose heart has gone out toward Christ is the man that is free from condemnation; that the man that loves Christ is the man that is attracted toward what is righteous: that is the man that is not condemned. It would be more exact, in the sense in which He meant it, if He should say, "The man that is not condemned believes on Jesus Christ." The one is the natural consequence of the other; it would be hard to say which is first and which is last; it would be hard to say which is cause and which is effect. The one has an effect on the other, a direct effect and a reflex effect; so that the more a man comes into a pure nature and character the more he loves Christ, and the more he loves Christ the more his nature is purified; the better he is the more he believes, and the more he believes the better he becomes. And these two principles of spiritual character and appreciation go on acting and reacting upon each other, until at last a man becomes like Jesus and knows even as He is known. "He that believeth on Him is not condemned: but he that believeth not is condemned already, because he hath not believed in the name of the only begotten Son of God." See the statement. The man that has not believed is condemned already, because he has not believed. A man that can see Christ and not believe on Him is condemned in that very fact, because a good man would want to believe on Him. That is the reason a man is condemned already if he does not believe on Jesus. There is no strange, mysterious rule about this that we cannot comprehend.

I was talking to a man one day who had been a consumptive for years. He was one who had very bright prospects in the possession of a marvelous voice. A wealthy man, hearing him sing, sent him abroad in order that his voice might be cultivated, and he spent some time in the great centers of voiceculture in the Old World. And then consumption laid its terrible hand upon him, and he came back to die. He suffered excruciating pain. When I went to see him one day he said that although he had sung in churches and read the Bible some, he never could understand about this matter. It did not seem to him that it was necessary for a man, in order to do right, to be a Christian. "All a man has to do is to believe on Jesus Christ; and he can do wrong as much as he pleases and God will save him." He confounded opinion with faith-a theological crime of the ages. He had an idea that Christ suffered a great deal, and he said, "If the Bible is true and God wanted Christ to suffer for sin, He ought to be satisfied with me, as I have suffered as much as any man could." I referred him to the place where Christ said clearly and distinctly that the only reason a man is condemned is because his heart is wrong, because he does not want to do right; he does not believe, because he wants to do wrong. This man said, "Why, I think I see that. You mean that the trout must necessarily live in clear waters, but that the flounder wants to go down and live in the mud?" And I said, "Yes, that is true in every case." Just as soon as a man makes up his mind entirely that he wants to do what is right, Christ is the very thing he wants. He is provided for men that make up your minds to do right. Listen to the rest of it-the sermon on the new birth: "And this is the condemnation, that light is come into the world, and men loved darkness rather than light, because their deeds were evil. For every one that doeth evil hateth the light, neither cometh to the light, lest his deeds should be reproved" -the flounder must live in the mud, where the trout would die. "But he that doeth truth cometh to the light, that his deeds may be made manifest, that they are wrought in God"-the trout must live in the clear water, where the flounder would perish. Man, if you do not believe in Jesus Christ you are self-condemned; if you do not find in Him what your soul is hungering after it is because your soul is not hungering after truth and righteousness. He is the way, and the truth, and the life. Jesus Christ is practical righteousness, and you cannot love righteousness and turn your back on Him. "This is the condemnation, that light is come into the world, and men loved darkness rather than light, because their deeds were evil." If you will make up your mind that you want to do right with all your heart you will accept Christ this very night. If you are not a whole-hearted, earnest, outspoken, confessed believer in Jesus it is because your life is wrong and your heart is not right in the sight of God. You may refuse to taste and see that the Lord is good; you may be like the philosophers who disputed the existence of Jupiter's satellites and would not look through the telescope that Galileo had invented, for fear they should see them; but if, closing your eyes against the light, you go out into the darkness and lose your soul it will be because you would not yield yourself to the right, because your heart was wrong in the sight of God, and you would not come unto Jesus because your deeds were evil.

A Heart that is Wrong in the Sight of One's Fellow-men is Wrong in the Sight of God.

A heart that is wrong in the sight of one's fellow-men is wrong in the sight of God. There is a very suggestive incident that occurred in connection with the young man who came to Christ and said, "Master, what good thing must I do to inherit eternal life?" Christ told him he must keep the commandments, and the young man said, "Which commandment?" And Christ said to him - now notice them: "Do not commit adultery" -one;" Do not kill"-two; "Do not steal"-three; "Do not bear false witness" -four; "Honor thy father and thy mother"-five. Where are the other five? There are four commandments that refer to one's duty to God; there are six commandments that refer to one's duty to our fellow-men. And Christ practically told this young man that if he performed his duty to his fellow-men he would be all right in the sight of God. A man cannot perform his duty to his fellow-men until he is right in the sight of God. A man's performance of his duty toward his fellows is conditioned upon his being right with God. A man can never treat his brother right until he recognizes the fact that his brother is his brother, until he realizes that God is the Father of us all. Universal brotherhood implies universal Fatherhood, and a man will never be right with any other man until he comes to see in him a brother-perhaps an imperfect brother, but his own brother, and in a certain sense the brother of the Lord Jesus Christ, with all the possibilities in him that dwelt in Christ. And it is only when a man has come to be himself right in the sight of God that he can love his unlovely neighbor, and be willing to do for another what Christ has done for them both. Now there are men that seem to think they can be all right in God's sight and all wrong in the sight of men; there are men that seem to think they can be selfish and be Christians. There is no such thing as a selfish Christian. A man cannot swindle his fellow-men and be a

Christian. You could not wrong your brother without wronging God. He is God's child. God made him just as truly as He made you, and God will hold you to account for the way that you treat him. You will have to reckon for every injury you do to a man on earth; not with that man, but with that man's Father. God will take up the question of his injury. If you have injured any man in this world you have been injuring God. If you are not right with your fellow-men you are wrong with God. You could not have the slightest hatred rankling in your heart toward a human being, you could not have one sin against you which was unforgiven, and have your heart right in the sight of God. What right have you to hate your neighbor? What right have to act toward your neighbor in any way God has not acted toward you? Why was it that the only comment Jesus made upon the Lord's prayer was this: "For if ye forgive men their trespasses, your Heavenly Father will also forgive you"? Why did not Christ not say that the honest man would be forgiven by God? Why did He not say that the pure man would be forgiven? Why did He not say that the generous man would be forgiven? Why did He say that the man that forgave his enemy should be forgiven, and the man that would not forgive his enemy should never be forgiven? There is one test by which God and our fellow-men and we ourselves can know whether we are Christians or not, and it is the same test. But here we are face to face with this fact, that this is the test that God gives us by which He can tell whether we are Christians or not, and it is whether we have love to our fellow-men who have injured us. God tells us that the man who has any evil in his heart toward his neighbor has committed murder. God looks at the heart. He looks at the heart just as much as He looks at the deed. He sees what deeds the hearts of men would produce if they had the opportunity. I would say very frankly to -night that I believe this one thing of cherishing an unkind spirit keeps as many people out of the kingdom of God as any other cause in the world-I have thought, sometimes, as all other causes put together.

I met once six persons, I think within ten days, who were being kept out of the kingdom of God from this cause. I remember one woman who came to the kingdom of God from this cause. I remember one woman who came

31

to church and sat there and looked as though she was in torture all the time. I thought she must be sick or in great anguish. One day she came to see me, and I asked her what the trouble was; and she said she did not know. I asked if she wanted to become a Christian, and she said she had been trying, but had about made up her mind that there was no hope for her and she would never be saved. She said she was willing to give up all her sin, and was willing to do every known duty. "Well," I said, "that settles it; if you are willing to do that God will save you." She said, "There is something that is keeping me back." Finally, I said, "Is there anybody in this world that you have a grudge against?" "Yes," she said, "there is." I said, "You will have to give that up." "O Mr. Mills," she said, "if you knew what that was you would not ask me to do it." "I do not ask you to do it," I said "God asks you to do it; and the wound cannot be healed while you keep that old poisoning thorn in your flesh. There is no other way for you." She said, "I can't forgive that injury." I said, "Is it a case of can't or won't?" She said, "I won't, anyway." I said, "I thought that was the trouble. My sister, why do you wish to cling to this bitterness in your heart? Does it make you a truer woman or a better wife or mother? Do you sleep better at night on account of it, and wake up brighter and with more peace in your heart in the morning?" "No," she said, "it makes me miserable." I said, "You do not seem to act very sensibly in clasping this thorn to you, and pressing it into your heart and letting it fester there, and turning it around to add to your agony, and then saying, 'I won't let go of this thorn; I won't let go of this thorn. '" "Well," she said, "I would give it up if I could, but I can't." I said, "Let us kneel down and tell that to God." We knelt together in prayer, and after I had prayed I asked her to pray; and she told the Lord that if she could she would forgive this injury, and that she would like to get the bitterness out of her heart. And you know what the Lord did: He opened the flood-gates of His infinite love and poured His forgiving spirit through her heart until it was cleansed of its blackness and was filled with the beauty of the spirit of Christ. And when we rose up she said she would go out and write a letter to this friend and forgive her heartily; and almost immediately she came into the liberty and beauty and peace of a child of God. I saw her afterward in the congregation, where, as I looked into her shining eyes, it seemed to me that I had a vision of a soul in heaven. A few days after that I was on a railway-train and was introduced to a lady with whom I took a seat, and in a few moments I asked her if she was a Christian. She said, "No," but she wanted to be. She was an intelligent young woman, a teacher in one of the schools, and she had the most expressive eyes I have ever seen-great windows-and when you looked at her you could see into her soul. I asked her if she was willing to give up everything that was wrong, and she said, "Yes," she thought she was. "Now," said I, "what will you abandon?" And she mentioned some pleasures and habits she thought were wrong. I said, "Will you give them up?" She said, "I would if I thought I would get peace." And I said, "That is just the trouble. What you need to do is to give them up in order to get right, and then the peace will come in its natural order." Finally she said she would give up these sinful things. I said, "Are you willing to do anything God wants you to do?" And she said, "Yes," she thought she was if she knew what it was. She had always said she would never confess Christ in public, but if that was necessary she would do that. She said there were some other things that she thought she ought to do, and I said, "Will you do them?" And again she said. "I would if I thought I would get peace." And I said, "My sister, that is only one way of trifling with God. He is not trying to make you comfortable while you are sick, but what He wants to do is to make you well, and then you will be at peace." Finally she said she would do what she thought Christ would have her do. I said, "That is grand. Now what is the trouble with you?" "I don't know," she said. After a conversation of perhaps twenty minutes I said, "Are you at perfect peace with all the world?" And she answered, "No, sir." I said, "Then that is the trouble. You will have to be before you can be at peace with God." She replied, "It was an awful injury. Then I can never be saved." And she shut her teeth together and pressed her lips, and said it was so terrible that no one could forgive it. I said to her that it did not begin to be such an injury as was inflicted on Christ when He was hung on the cross, and He said, "Father, forgive them." "If any man have not the spirit of Christ, he is none of His." "Now," I said, "I will tell you right here, in God's name, that if you will forgive those that have injured you God will forgive you. If I have authority to say anything I have authority to say that. And I want to say also, in God's name, if you cannot forgive this injury God cannot forgive you. It is the test by which God can tell whether you are a Christian or not." Talk about a man being honest! If a man will forgive an injury that is done by his enemy cannot you trust him to treat his neighbors honestly? A man that can hold in check his pride when he is injured, and when his whole nature quivers under the mutilation that comes to him through an injury inflicted by a human being-a man that can conquer all that and love his enemy, cannot we trust that man to hold in check all his evil lust and passion? I said, "That is the reason why God has selected this one thing, and it will be the test of your sincerity; you can never, never be forgiven unless you can forgive this injury." "Then I can never be forgiven, she said; and the tears came into her great eyes and rolled down her cheeks as she sat there, and people looked at her and wondered what affected her so. It almost made the other people weep to see her seeming anguish. She rose to leave the train when we came to the station, and the tears were still on her cheeks and a hard look settling on her face. Many a time after that have I seen that woman sitting in the congregation, and I could look down through those great open windows into her soul, and I have seen a picture of a soul in hell. She was in hell. The spirit of hell was in her. O friend, if there be one unkind thought in your heart that you persist in cherishing against a human being, God can never forgive you; but if you will let it go the peace of God will come in and fill your soul. "Thy heart is not right in the sight of God," but it may be made right to-night if you will give up the bitterness that you have been cherishing toward some human being, and will make up your mind that you will forgive any injury, even with the sacrifice of your own life. That is what it means to be a Christian.

A proud, self-willed heart is not right in the sight of God. Sometimes we say it is very easy and sometimes it is very hard to become a Christian. It is both. Some one says, "It may be very easy to do, but it is very hard to understand." You have stated that in the wrong way. It is very easy to understand, but very hard to do. It is so easy to understand that the simplest child in this room to-night can understand it. The way of holiness is so plain that a wayfaring man, though a fool, could not err therein. And it is the first principle of human existence. "One and one make two" is a complicated proposition when compared with the reasonableness of the surrender of man's will to the will of God. But it is so hard to do that there are men here to-night whose hairs are turning gray who have never done it, and people go down to the grave without hope because they are not willing to render this reasonable service in the surrender of their wills to the will of God. It is not hard to live after you have become a Christian, but it is hard for a man to surrender entirely to God. It is hard. It was so with your little child in your discipline of him. If you have been a good parent there may have been a time when you have had a real struggle with your child; and if you let that child be the master I am afraid you have made a terrible mistake that you may regret for years. If you very kindly and firmly led the child to do what you thought was right in this emergency you helped that child through all his life in helping to give him a spirit that should lead him into obedience to his Heavenly Father. It may have been a simple little thing. I remember when one of my children made a request of me and I suggested he should say "please." The little fellow was determined he would not. He said, "I can't say ' please,' " and perhaps he said it a dozen times in declaring that he could not say it, and over and over again he would say that he would not say it, and that he could not say it. I tried gentle measures with him and other measures, and he kept insisting that he could not say "please." But finally he said it. And then he could not say it often enough. He wanted to say it all the time; it would come out on every occasion, appropriate or inappropriate "please," "please," "please." He could not say it enough to please him. He would say it where he ought to say "good-morning," or "good-night," or "thank you"; just "please," "please," "please"-he did not seem to know any other word so well. And yet how hard it was for that little fellow to give up his will and make up his mind to say "please"! O friend, the trouble with you has been that you have not been willing to say "please" to God. Just in that way it is very hard for a man to make up his mind to surrender to God; but it is the easiest thing in the world for him to know how to do it - it is the simplest thing. Man, if you will not say "please" to God, if you will not commence to do what God wants you to do, your heart is not right in the sight of God; and until you are ready to forsake your way and your thoughts, and receive God's ways and God's thoughts, your heart can never be made right in the sight of God.

A Divided, Variable Heart is not Right in the Sight of God

A divided, variable heart is not right in the sight of God. Here is a man who is trifling with God: now he is serious, and now he is thoughtless; now he is earnest, and now he seems dead and unmoved; now he is awakened, and now he seems drowsy; now his heart is sensitive, and now it has grown hard again; now he is starting heavenward, and now he is turning back.

A Hard, Impenitent Heart is not Right in God's Sight

A hard, impenitent heart is not right in God's sight. The devil makes people proud of very strange things. He makes men proud that they are lustful and brutal and selfish and mean and avaricious and cruel. He makes men proud that they are proud, and he also makes people proud that they are not proud. I think some of the proudest people I have ever seen have been those who seem to be proud of their humility. But I think the strangest thing of all is that he is able to make people proud that they have hard hearts, hearts that are unconcerned about sin and righteousness and judgment and the mercy of God and the love and service of God and man. A man draws himself up and says, "I am not concerned about these things. I have such an independent character, my intellect is so great, my culture has been so extensive, that I have lost my interest in spiritual things." Friend, you have the wrong name for that which makes you unconcerned about the things of God. It is sin itself. I heard of a woman who was ill, who took five grains of morphine when she meant to take five grains of quinine. She immediately became very sleepy and begged her friends to let her sleep. Something in her appearance so alarmed them that they sent for a physician, and he discovered the error and joined with the husband and other friends in endeavoring to arouse the woman. They shook her and sprinkled water upon her, but she begged them to leave her alone. She said, "If I only get to sleep I will get well." But the doctor said, "If she gets fairly to sleep she will never wake up," and lifting her from the couch, the physician, on one side, and the husband, on the other, walked with her up and down the room through all that night, until when the morning light was breaking signs of consciousness came back to her, and the doctor said, "Now I think she may live." You have the wrong name for the thing that has made you unconcerned about the way of life. It is sin itself, some deadening form of sin-a sin of avarice, a sin of selfishness, a sin of pride; and if you have come to the place where the terror of the law of God will not move you, and where the tenderness of God's love and mercy will not melt you, this in itself is an indication that your heart is not right in the sight of God. Brother, if your heart is not right you are all wrong; if you do not want good things and love good things, and have not that yearning after God that you ought to have and that can be satisfied alone by God, you are all wrong. "Man looketh on the outward appearance, but God looketh on the heart." "Out of the heart are the issues of life."

A Careless, Procrastinating Heart is not Right in the Sight of God

And, finally, a careless, procrastinating heart is not right in the sight of God. God is tremendously in earnest. It will not do for you to prefer something else to God. You go into a store where it is the merchant's business to wait upon you, and you find him engaged in a trivial conversation with a friend. You wait and wait, and after a while that friend goes out and another one comes in and takes his place; and the merchant continues talking with him and pays no attention to you. At last you say, "If that man will not attend to his business and pay attention to me I will patronize some one else." And it will be a long time before you will go back to trade with him. O friend, God will continue pleading so long as there is the slightest possibility of moving your heart; but if you continue to put Him off, and put something else in His place this pleasure, that money, this pride, that self-indulgence the time will come when your heart cannot be moved, and God may have to give you up. Think about this and you will see it. If a man had robbed you of one hundred dollars and was able to repay it, but kept putting off the day of payment, saying, "I will restore this money some other time," every day and hour and minute that he refrained from paying you what was yours would show that he still had the dishonest spirit. You have robbed God: you have stolen from him your time, your property, your influence-it may be, your children and your friends. Ten, twenty, thirty, forty, fifty years have you stolen from God! And if to-night there be in you a disposition to delay the payment of your debt to God, that very disposition is an indication that your heart is not right in the sight of God.

There is no question about it, that a large measure of the sons of men that lose their souls do it by saying to God, "Not today," "Not to-night;" men that intend some time to be Christians, but never find the convenient season when they want to yield to God. If you lose your soul it will be in that way; if you lose your soul it will be in just that way, because you say here to-night to God's entreaty, "Not now!" "Not now!" and put him off to a convenient season that may never come for you. I beseech you, do not trifle with God. Yield to Him now while He is pleading with you. The procrastinating heart is not right in the sight of God. God stands to-night and tells you it is only necessary for you to do one thing. He says, "today if ye will hear My voice, harden not your hearts." "To this man will I look, even to him that is of an humble and contrite spirit, and that trembleth at My word." "A broken and a contrite heart, O God, Thou wilt not despise." Will you let your heart grow tender? Will you let God's influences move upon it? Will you let God's sunshine and God's rain mellow it? Will you let God's truth come into it? Will you let God's spirit take possession of it? Will you let God transform your heart to-night and make you what you ought to be?

You may remember the allegory of the council of the devils in hell, at a time when Satan heard that a revival had commenced in a certain community. According to the story, he called his counselors together and asked them for advice as to how this spiritual atmosphere might be changed. One said, "I could break up this revival. I would go and laugh at the people, and tell them they were a pack of fools; that there was no God, no devil, no heaven, and no hell. And I would say, ' Eat, drink, for tomorrow you die. ' " Satan said, "You need not go. You would not find any one that would believe you." Another, shrewder than the first, said, "Let me go. I would go to them and tell them that a portion of the Bible is true; that there is a God and a heaven, but no devil and no hell, and that no matter how they might live here they would go to heaven when they died." And Satan said, "You need not go. You might find some people that would try to believe you, but not many, especially at this time of spiritual awakening." "Let me go," said a third, the shrewdest and meanest of them all. "I will go and tell them that the Bible is all true; that there is a God and heaven, a devil and a hell, and that the people are making their choice in this life as to where they will spend the future ages. And then I will say, 'But you have plenty of time. Put this off. Wait until tomorrow.' And Satan said to him, "Go!" This is only a parable, but I think that it is true to-night. I believe that this emissary of Satan's has come into this audience, and has been going down these isles and into these seats, and saying to this man and this woman, and that young man and yonder maiden, "Put it off. Wait till tomorrow." You will heed this voice at your peril. Listen rather to the voice that says, "My son, give Me thine heart. ' today if ye will hear My voice, harden not your hearts." "Now is the accepted time; now is the day of salvation." Which will you hear? Which will you heed? Who is there present to-night that would like to have the heart made right in the sight of God? Who is there that would be glad to have the heart of stone exchanged for a heart of flesh; that will say, "Create within me a clean heart, O God, and renew a right spirit within me?" Unto you will God fulfill the promise made unto the Israelites: "And I will sprinkle clean water upon you, and ye shall be clean: from all your filthiness, and from all your idols, will I cleanse you. A new heart also will I give you, and a new spirit will I put within you: and I will take away the stony heart out of your flesh, and I will give you a heart of flesh. And I will put My Spirit within you, and cause you to walk in my statutes, and ye shall keep My judgments, and do them." Who will join in a prayer for this?

Let us say, "Purge me with hyssop, and I shall be clean; wash me, and I shall be whiter than snow ... Hide Thy face from my sins, and blot out all mine iniquities." "Cleanse Thou me from secret faults. Let the words of my mouth, and the meditation of my heart, be acceptable in Thy sight, O Lord, my strength and my Redeemer!"

Rev. W. L. Lemon
Chairman Devotional Committee

Rev. William Macafee
Pastor of Broad Street Methodist Church

Rev. Henry Stauffer
Secretary Executive Committee

The Choice of Life

"I call heaven and earth to witness against you this day, that I have set before thee life and death, the blessing and the curse: therefore choose life, that thou mayest live, thou and thy seed." - Deuteronomy 30:19.

Moses was a great man. He was a great general: he brought several millions of slaves out from the power of the proudest nation on earth, and led them to the borders of a land into which they entered victoriously. He was a great statesman; he was a great judge and a great ruler and a great lawgiver: the laws of Moses form today the basis of the jurisprudence in every civilized nation. And he was more than these he was a great philosopher, a great orator, and a great poet. But he was more than all these he was a great man. He so possessed the qualities of gentleness and bravery and meekness and resolution and self-sacrifice that he was worthy of the name that was given to him, of "Moses, the man of God." And when he was about to be separated from the people over whom he ruled and whom he so thoroughly loved, he reminded them of the principles the observance of which had brought to them success, and the failure to observe which would bring certain disaster; and in this remarkable address he used the words of the text: "I call heaven and earth to witness against you this day, that I have set before thee life and death, the blessing and the curse: therefore choose life, that thou mayest live, thou and thy

42

seed."

Man has been defined as a "rational animal," and whether or not that is a complete definition, this much is certain, that God has given us reason, and that He expects us to use it. Reasonableness and righteousness are the same thing. A man must be a moral idiot who does not see that a man is unreasonable when he is wrong, and that no one can be thoroughly reasonable except as he is thoroughly right. But I believe more than that: I think that a man cannot be right except as he is godly. Reasonableness and righteousness and godliness are identical. And I desire tonight to appeal, not so much to your emotions (although a man may wisely be moved by his noblest emotions) as to your reason and your conscience and your judgment, and ask you to choose life rather than death, and blessing rather than cursing, because it "is your reasonable service."

In the first place, I call upon you to give yourself to the service of God because this is the way to be manly. I am a Christian because I want to be a man. No one even knows what a man is intended to be except as God has told him. When I was a boy an elder brother asked me to write a composition on manhood. I took a sheet of foolscaps paper and wrote in large letters at the head of the sheet, "MANHOOD." And then I commenced: "Man is-" and then I stopped. I did not know what a man was. I put the manuscript away for some time, and after a few weeks I took it out again. I was not exceedingly well pleased with it, so I burned it up and started again with a fresh piece of paper. I wrote again in large letters, "MANHOOD." And I said, "Man is - " and then I stopped as before. I could not define a man, and you cannot define a man unless you have found out from the revelation of God in Christ Jesus just what a man is intended to be. You might better stand over a sculptor and instruct him how to perform his work-to make this line longer, to shorten this curve and extend the other one-when you did not know what was in his mind, and then expect him from his endeavor to produce a symmetrical result, than for a man to interfere in the slightest degree with the thought and will of God concerning him, and think that he could become a man. I never heard but one person give a real reason for not being a Christian. I have heard many excuses but only one reason. This man was prominent in the community where he lived, and for some time I had felt that I ought to speak to him about becoming a Christian; and yet I felt considerable embarrassment in addressing him upon this subject. But one day I met him and walked with him for a little distance on the street, and, after a moment's hesitation, I said to him, "My friend, why are you not a Christian?" And then it was his turn to be embarrassed. He paused and hesitated and stammered a little, and his feet pattered on the ground; and then he said, "Well, I will tell you honestly. It is because I am not man enough." That is the only real reason that I ever heard a man give for not being a Christian. To be lost is to be something less than a man; to be saved is to become a man in the largest sense. A Christian is a man - nothing more, nothing less. No one can be a Christian without being a man, and no one is a real man who is not a Christian. There are some men that expect some time certainly to become Christians, and yet they seem to think it is manly to put off the time of decision and keep the control of their own lives, promising to pay God what they owe Him at some future time. You would not think that it was a manly thing in business for a man to say, "I could pay you this debt, but instead of doing that I will give you my note for it." And then when the note was due to come and say, "I will settle this note by taking it up and giving you another in place of it." You would be afraid that the man was insolvent and that you would not get any of your money. I have even known men who cherished the contemptible idea that they would live selfish and godless lives until they came to die, and that then, on account of the great mercy of God, they would try to creep into His eternal kingdom. I think that is the meanest thought that ever stirred the human breast. I do not doubt that there are men to whom Christ might not have been adequately presented in their lives, but who may so see Him in their dying hour as to lead to the glad surrender of all they have unto Him. And I would that all Christians might have such a genuine experience of the transforming power of God's grace as did the penitent thief upon the cross. But I think that no man may go on in his sin, speculating, as it were, on the forbearance of God, putting off the time when he will surrender himself to the divine service, and then successfully try to enter heaven at the close of a wasted life.

I have heard of a hunter who carried with him a deer charm-a whistle which imitated the voice of the fawn-and one day when he blew upon it there came a beautiful doe and put her head out of the thicket and looked this way and that, wondering where the child was that was calling for its mother. She saw the hunter standing there and knew that he was her mortal enemy, seeking her life; and although she trembled with fear, she did not stir. And when the hunter saw that great exhibition of mother-love he could not bear to take advantage of it. So he put down his rifle, and, lifting up his hand, frightened the doe back into the thicket. But, O friends, what shall be said of the man who, because he thinks God is so compassionate and long-suffering, and has borne with him so long that He will bear with him still, will selfishly try to keep the control of his own life through his days upon earth, and then cast the dregs of his wasted life into the face of God with a pitiful cry for mercy, and thus endeavor to get into a place of peace after death? Does that meet your idea of manliness? My brother, never cherish a thought like that and lay any claim to being a man.

This first reason should be strong enough to move you toward the service of God, but there is a better reason than this: God's work needs you.

You may remember that when Moses was leading the children of Israel out of Egypt they had come to the borders of the desert and found there the brother-in-law of Moses, whose name was Hobab. Moses, as you may recall, had been married on the border of the desert to a daughter of Jethro, the Midianite. We read that Moses said to Hobab, "Come thou with us, and we will do thee good." And Hobab practically said, "Moses, I cannot go. I have my farm to look after and my family to care for, and you will have to excuse me." And then Moses said, "Hobab, you know all about the desert, and we do not. Come with us, and be eyes for us." And Hobab said, "If you really need me, I will go." And so he left his farm and went along, to be eyes for the people of God.

I came across this question in the Bible some time ago: "What wilt thou say when He shall punish thee?" I do not feel concerned about the answer. But I do feel concerned about the answer to this question: "What shall I say when I meet you again?" What shall I say concerning this month spent in your city, if I have not lived a pure, unselfish, godly life, and have not used all the influence that God has given me in order to help my fellows to come into fellowship with Him? If you have not been living a Christian life, what are you going to say when you meet your earthly associates again? What will you say when you meet that wife, upon whom you have bound a burden too heavy to bear, whose faith has been blighted or overthrown by your indifference to the things of eternal life? What will you say when you meet the children who never heard their father pray, and that, but for your influence, might be walking tonight in the paths of peace? O man, I appeal to you to come with us and be eyes for us, because God's work does need you; and that is another way of saying that the world needs you, and that the city needs you, and that the church needs you, and that your home needs you. There are men here tonight who have been casting cold water upon their wives' Christianity by the indifference of their lives. There are men here that by their spiritual indifference have been crushing in their little children every aspiration for a good and pure and honest life. There are men here who have been worse than the Chinese that dwarf their children's feet, for they have dwarfed their children's souls and kept them away from God. There are men here tonight that, if they would be Christians, might bring every member of their household into the church of Christ; and there are men here tonight that, if they do not become followers of Christ, will be responsible for scores of men and women that their influence might have brought to God. Does that move you? It moves me tremendously. I want to be able, when I stand before the throne of God, to say that I have done all I could for my wife to help her to be a good Christian, and for the little children that God has given me, whom I have tried to bring to God as His children, that they might be made into His image. And God knows I could not say that, and you know that you cannot say it concerning your dear ones, unless we have been earnest, positive, devoted Christian men. You have been harming your wife, you may have been cursing your children, you have probably been in this world as a hindrance rather than a help in its progress toward righteousness, if you have not been an outspoken, openly confessed child of God. There are not ten men in this hall tonight who do not realize that if they did all their duty to their fellow-men they would be all that they might be as earnest, confessed Christians, living in the spirit of Jesus Christ.

We have too long had the notion that Christ came to call people to come and be saved. He did, indeed, invite men to lay hold on eternal life, but the way in which He did it was by saying, "Come and be saviours." And the call that He brings to us tonight is for the sake of those about us, for the sake of our children and our children's children, for the sake of causing the kingdom of God to come upon earth, and His will to be done as it is done in heaven; that we should choose life rather than death, and blessing rather than cursing.

There are some men who try to excuse themselves from their duty by saying, "Well, I am not a member of the Church." Such a plea as that adds to your responsibility instead of removing it from you. If you are not a member of the Church there is just as much obligation resting upon you to save men as there is resting upon any church-member in this world. In fact, I think that the burden that you bear is a heavier one. We who are members of the Church have tried to do something, and you have not tried to do anything in the Christian service. It is just as much your duty to endeavor to lead men to God as it is the duty of any minister or any church-member. Some of us who are in the Church have been unworthy and have done our work but feebly, but many of us have tried to do something; and you have not only not tried to do anything, but have been willing to let your influence tell upon the other side. Your excuse is like that of the son who spent the morning in idleness while his brother worked, and then gave as a reason for not working in the afternoon, that he had not done his duty in the morning. It would simply be an added reason why he should work harder in the afternoon. And, my brother, if you have come to be forty years of age without giving yourself to God, that is ten times the reason why you should spend the rest of your life in the service of your Maker.

Some time ago I said to a business man, "Are you a Christian?" And he said, "No, sir, but I have made my influence all right." I said, "How did you do that?" He said, "I have seen each one of my six clerks, and have told them that if they felt like attending the meetings now in progress here I hoped they would do so. And I said, "If, when you are in the meeting, you feel that you ought to stand up and indicate your desire to be a Christian, I should advise you to do it. But if you do not take this step, remember that, although I am not a Christian, I made my influence with you right in this respect, and that I told you if you really felt like becoming a Christian I should advise you to make the decision." I said, "You remind me of a man who should be going along a highway and should see a woman in a burning house, and she should call to him and say, 'Help! help!' and beg him to put a ladder up against the house and save her life, and he should say, 'Madam, you will have to excuse me. I am sorry to see you in such a fix, and if you really feel like getting out I should advise you to do so. But the fact is I am not engaged in saving women from burning houses. I do not belong to the fire department; but I will go along the street, and if I see anybody who does I will tell him about you and he can come and help you down. But if you stay there and burn to death, let no one say that my influence had anything to do with it, for if you feel like getting out I should really advise you to make your escape.'"

I know of a physician who told a patient that he was about to die, and the sick man said, "Doctor, you have told me that I am going to die. Can you not tell me something that will prepare me to die?" And the doctor said, "I am not a minister. I will go out and see if I can get a minister who will come and talk to you." And I know of a brother who looked into the face of a dying brother, and the sick man said, "Joe, it is awful to die the way I am dying-without hope. In the name of God, cannot you do something to help me?" And Joe said, "I wish I could, but you know I am not a member of the church, and I hardly know what to say. I will go out and see if I can find a church-member who will come and talk with you and pray for you." I knew of a wealthy man who was suddenly summoned to the bedside of his boy, who had met with an accident; and the young man knew that he would have to die. This lad was the pride of his father's heart-an only son-and as the man stood there and looked into the face of his seventeen-year-old child, he said, "My son, I will do anything in this world that I can for you. I wish you would make some request of me. Ask anything on earth that your father can do for you, and he will be glad to do it." And the stricken youth turned his head feebly and said, "Father, will you please pray for my lost soul?" And that prayerless father turned away and went to the window and bit his lip until the blood came; and a few days after that, when he was coming away from the grave of his son, he said to the friend who was with him, "I would give all that I have in this world if I could call my boy back and offer a prayer to God in his behalf."

O men, you have been robbing your children, you have been robbing your employer or your employed-you have been robbing them of the influence you ought to have exterted to make them godlike; and right here in this hall tonight, as I call upon you, if you will serve God, to manifest it openly, your influence will have an effect on the man that sits on your right, or the man that touches your elbow on the left, or the man that sits behind you, or on him whose eyes are fixed upon you from yonder gallery. You cannot live unto yourself, and this very night your influence may tell on the lives of men to continue throughout the ages. "Choose life, choose life, that thou and thy seed may live."

And the third reason why you should give yourself to God tonight is because there is great blessing in His service. There is a "hundredfold in this present time" for the man who has forsaken anything for the kingdom of God's sake. This Moses was a wise man, and yet it is said of him that he would rather "suffer affliction with the people of God, than enjoy the pleasures of sin for a season." And I believe I would. I think I would rather have the worst that could come to a Christian man than the best that could come to a Christ-less one. I think I would rather be a pauper; I think I would rather be hungry and thirsty and cold and naked; I think I would rather see my friends die or desert me one by one; I think I would rather have my good, evil spoken of and my reputation blasted; I think I would rather have some deadly disease lay its hand upon me, having all the experiences of the wretched Job, if I were also able to say, as did Job, "I know that my Redeemer liveth, and that at the latter day He shall stand upon the earth;

and that although after they have destroyed my skin, and worms destroy this body, yet without my flesh shall I see God: Whom mine eyes shall yet behold for myself, and not another." I think I would rather have the worst that can befall man, and have the consciousness of the presence of God that is in my heart tonight, than to possess all wealth and worldly friendship and honor and power and have to be without the conscious presence of God. I would be a happier man - let me say it again: I think I would rather have the worst things that could come to a Christian than the best things that could come to a man without Christ.

One evening in Chicago, some years ago, I went into the Pacific Garden Mission. There was a congregation of three or four hundred men and women. I say men and women, but the men had lost every semblance of manhood, and you might not recognize the women save by the fragments of the dresses that they wore. It was a congregation of moral lepers who would not need to cry "Unclean" in order that most people might shun them if they saw them upon the street. Colonel Clark was speaking of the power of God to save sinners unto the utmost, and when he finished he said, "If any one here can testify concerning the mighty power of Christ I would be glad to hear from him." A man rose up on the right hand and came and leaned upon the platform. He might have been forty years old and he might not have been over twenty - you could not tell. He was the wreck of a man, and yet it seemed as if something of manhood was struggling to assert itself within him. It was a few minutes more before he could command his voice sufficiently to speak, and then he told a piteous story. He said that he had been one of the wickedest men in the city of Chicago, and that on the previous Thursday morning he had been turned out of the station-house, and the policeman had said to him, "Don't you come back here." He said, "I had sunk so low that they did not want me even in a prison, and I made up my mind to end my life. I did not have money enough to buy poison, I could not get any one to give me drink, and I was on my way to the river to drown myself when I came by this place. A man was standing in front of it, and he spoke to me very kindly and invited me to come in. I thought that it would only postpone my act for a little while, and I went in. I heard men whom I used to know living lives of sin say that they had been saved by the power of God, and when the invitation was given to those who desired to become Christians to lift up their hands, I stood up and said, 'I am a desperate man, but if you think I am worth praying for, you can pray for me.' The colonel asked me to come and kneel down where I am standing now, and I came and knelt down, and some kind men and women knelt and prayed for me, and I tried to pray myself. And when I rose up there was a spark of hope in my heart that has been growing brighter ever since. I came in here Friday night and I told something of this story, and I came again last night and spoke of it again, and I heard that some of you fellows that used to know me said that you thought I was getting paid for telling it. And to - night I want to tell you that you are right-I am getting paid for it. I wish you could have seen my boyhood's home. I lived in the best home that any boy ever had. I had a kind father who did all that he could to make me and keep me right; but I lied to him and I swindled him, and I did all that was vile and mean that a young man could do, until at last he said to me, 'My son, will you do two things for me? If you will, I will never ask anything from you again.' I told him that I would. And he said, 'In the first place, I want you to go away from home and never come back; and in the second place, I would like to have you change your name. I do not want you to take my good name down into the depths where I fear you are going.' And I told him that I would, and I left my home and came to Chicago; and I have not heard my own name for more than three years. And I went down, down, down, until I looked into hell. And I have a sister. My sister is so good and pure and sweet that my foul lips scarcely ought to mention the fact of her existence. And my mother-my mother died of a broken heart because I was so wicked. But Friday morning I sat down and wrote to my father, and I said, ' Father, I do not ask you for money, and I do not ask you to take me back, but I do want to tell you that I feel that I have sinned against you, and I want to confess my sin and ask you to forgive me.' I told him that I had confessed my sin to God, and that I believed He had forgiven me. And, boys, this morning I got these letters. And here's a letter from my beautiful, sweet sister. I should have thought she would have had to blot my foul image cut of her heart long ago, but instead of that she says that she has prayed for me three times every day, and that the best news she ever received in her life was the news that I am going to try to be good. And here's a letter from my father, and my father says that he will forgive all my sins against him and that he will forget the past, and that I cannot come back too quickly to please him. And, boys, tomorrow I am going home. I have had the first quiet night's rest that I have had in years; I have had the first moment's peace of conscience that I have ever known in all my life. O boys," he said, "I tell you I am getting paid for it, I am getting paid for it!"

And oh, my brother, you may not have sunk as low as had that man, but you know that just so far as you have tried to do the will of God have you found peace; and tonight the loving Heavenly Father sends to you this message: that you cannot come back too quickly to please Him.

The fourth reason why you should make this wise choice tonight is in order that you may have a good hope of everlasting life. It is a noble ambition, and I am not ashamed to say it-I want a good hope of everlasting life. I want something better than great wealth or business ability or bravery or power of intellect or culture or unbelief ever brought to men.

I want something better than great business ability brings to men. John Roach, the great ship-builder, was in many respects a noble man; he had built more ships than any other American, but he had built no ship that could carry him across the eternal sea, and when he came to the close of his life, the last week upon earth, he sent for a minister and said, "I want to be baptized and received into the Christian church before I die." I want something better than that.

I want something better than mere bravery ever brought to men. General Grant was not a coward, and yet you may remember that several months before he died his physicians thought that he was passing away, and Dr. Newman baptized him. And then afterward, to the surprise of all his attendants, he somewhat recovered his strength and lingered for several months. Bishop Newman told me that he said to him during that time, "I wish I could live at least a year in health and strength, that I might be a consistent member of the church of Christ."

I want something better than purely intellectual endowment or culture ever gave to man. Aaron Burr was one of the most intellectual Americans and one of the most debased. He is said to have been the most brilliant student that ever studied in the College of New Jersey at Princeton, but he lived a sinful, selfish life and died a miserable death. Lord Byron had the most brilliant brain of any man of his generation; it seemed to be able to shoot out sparks of fire without an effort; and yet this brilliant man, who was known throughout the world when he was thirty, was a decrepit, prematurely old man at thirty-six, and spent the last days of his life in writing words like these:

> "My days are in the yellow leaf,
> The fruit, the flower of life are gone;
> The worm, the canker, and the grief
> Are mine alone."

O men, I want something better than that. I would like to have a "leaf that shall not wither," and be able to "bring forth fruit in old age." I should like to be able to say, as did that hero of the early Christian era, "I have fought a good fight, I have finished my course, I have kept the faith; henceforth there is laid up for me a crown of righteousness, which the Lord, the righteous Judge, shall give me at that day."

I want something better than the best disbeliever in Jesus Christ ever possessed. God forbid that I should ever say an untrue or an unkind word about any of the sons of men-least of all that I should seem to tear aside with ruthless hand the veil that hides the secret place of sorrow! But the occurrence to which I am about to refer was not done in a corner, and I only bring to your mind what you all know when I mention the time when Colonel Ingersoll endeavored to fulfill the promise he made to his brother, who was also his boyhood's playmate, and pronounced his funeral address. It was in June, 1879. This brother had died in Washington, and Colonel Ingersoll stood by the coffin and tried to read his address. His voice became agitated, his form trembled, and his emotion overcame him. Finally he put down the paper, and, bowing himself upon the coffin, he gave vent to uncontrollable grief. When at last he was able to proceed he raised himself up, and among other words he said these: "Whether in mid-ocean or 'mid the breakers of the farther shore, a wreck must mark at last the end of each and all; and every life, no matter if its every hour be filled with love and every movement jeweled with a joy, will at the last become a tragedy as sad and dark and deep as can be woven of the warp and woof of mystery and death. …Life is a dark and barren vale between the cold and ice-clad peaks of two eternities. We strive in vain to look beyond the heights. We lift our wailing voices in the silence of the night, and hear no answer but the bitter echo of our cry." Could ever words more sadly hopeless have been uttered at a time like that? And then he added what to me were the most pathetic words of all - something about "hope trying to see a star, and listening for the rustle of angel's wings." Mrs. Browning most truly writes:

> "'There is no God,' the foolish saith,
> But none, 'There is no sorrow.'
> And nature oft in bitter need
> The cry of faith will borrow.
> Eyes which the preacher could not school,
> By wayside graves are raised;
> And lips cry, 'God be pitiful!'
> Which ne'er said, 'God be praised!'"

I think I should like greater comfort and a better hope than that.

Dwight Moody had a brother, and after his own conversion be earnestly pleaded with him, until the brother also yielded himself to Christ and became such an earnest worker that he was the means of leading a number of his friends at his home into the kingdom. And then this brother died and was buried. A few years ago, as I spent a day in Northfield and was driven through its beautiful streets by one of the old residents, I said, "I wish you would tell me something about Mr. Moody that may not be generally known." And as we passed the old white church he said, "I remember his brother's funeral." He said that there were a number of ministers in the pulpit, and that after they had finished the usual services and the coffin-lid was about to be put in its place, Mr. Moody arose, and, stepping forward from the seat where he had been sitting, with a shining face, he laid one hand upon the coffin, and then lifting the other he poured out such a stream of thanksgiving unto God for the life that was gone, and for the wonderful comfort and joy and hope that came to him in Jesus Christ, that it was said by this onlooker that it almost seemed as if the heavens were opened and they could see the angels of God ascending and descending upon the Son of man. At last he ceased, the coffin lid was placed in its position, and the body was carried out and laid in the grave. On one side of the sepulcher stood fifty young men, many of them led to Christ through the influence of this one who was gone, and they held in their hands beautiful white flowers, which they cast down upon the coffin in token of the glorious resurrection. And on the other side of the grave stood Mr. Moody; and he said that as he stood there and thought of how his brother, being dead, was yet speaking, he felt that if he were silent the very stones would cry out, and he cried with a loud voice, "Glory to God! Glory be to God! O death, where is thy sting? O grave, where is thy victory?"

O friends, Moses may have made some mistakes, but he made none when he said, "Their rock is not as our Rock, our enemies themselves being judges."

And tonight I am not ashamed of the gospel of Christ, which is the power of God unto salvation. When the time comes when the death angel knocks at my door and lays his resistless grasp upon my loved one, and I must go out and stand by the open sepulcher, while the dark clods come rattling down upon the coffin lid with their unutterable sound, and when I must turn and go back to the home that will be desolate so far as any human comfort is concerned, I want something more to cheer me than the thought of a wreck and tragedy and a "dark and barren vale between the cold and ice-clad peaks, and the bitter echo of my wailing cry." I want One to stand by me Who stood by those bereaved sisters of Bethany, and to hear a voice saying, "I am the resurrection, and the life. Thy brother shall rise again." And when the time comes for my own feet to tread the waters of that cold, dark, rapidly rolling river that we all must cross, I want to be able to go through the valley of the shadow, saying, "Thy rod and Thy staff they comfort me;" singing:

> *"My hope is built on nothing less*
> *Than Jesus' blood and righteousness.*
> *On Christ the solid rick I stand -*
> *All other ground is sinking sand."*

"How much did he leave?" was the question asked, as two friends turned aside from the grave of a wealthy man. "He left it all," was the reply. Did he not leave it all? I can see him as he goes down to the river's brink, his arms laden with riches, his head crowned with worldly honor, only to realize that he has saved his life and now must forever lose it.

On the other hand, there is no break to the Christian when parting from this world. He knows Whom he has believed, and he gazes into the life to come with the glorious anticipation of the fruition that will be granted unto him in Jesus Christ.

There is one more reason, and it is this: you must make some decision now. You may say, "I will not decide it now," but in one sense you must decide it now. Not to decide to be a Christian is to decide not to be a Christian, as for a man who is considering whether or not he shall be a soldier to say, "I will not decide the question now," is to decide, for that time at least, he will not be a soldier. Men, "I call heaven and earth to record this day against you, that I have set before you life and death, blessing and cursing: therefore choose life," because you must make some decision now. I believe you are in just the position of that rebel against Rome to whom was sent an ambassador to summon his surrender. And he said, "I will consider, and will give you my answer in the morning." And then the ambassador drew round about him on the ground a circle with his staff, and he said, "In the name of eternal Rome, if you do not immediately step outside of that circle, Rome will consider that your answer is 'No.'" O my brother, in the name of Eternal God," Whose I am, and Whom I serve," if you do not openly take your place on the side of Christ, God will consider that your answer is "No." I do not mean that you may not rise and walk down this aisle and along the pavement to your home without openly acknowledging God to be your God, but I mean, if you are willing to do it, that the very treading of your feet would echo back to God your practical refusal, "I won't!" "I won't!" "I won't!" There are tides in the affairs of men which, taken at the flood, lead on to glory; there are critical moments in your personal and domestic and social and business life; there are critical moments in your spiritual affairs, and such a moment has come to some men within these walls at this time.

I have read of a captain of a ship, who, with his wife, was on a vessel, wrecked not far from shore, but too far to reach it unaided. They found footing on a ledge of rock perhaps the size of the top of a small organ; but as the tide was coming in and the storm was increasing in its fury, they almost gave up hope of rescue, when, just in the moments of their despair, they were discovered from the shore. The people upon the shore knew just what to do, and they sent out rockets into the sea with cords attached to them, until at last one of the rockets fell beyond the rock upon which this imperiled couple stood, and the line fell where the captain could reach it. He knew what to do with it. He drew upon it until he had a stouter cord, and a stouter line, until at last he had in his possession a good strong rope. He took that rope and tied it about his wife under her arms; and then he called to her above the fury of the sea and reminded her of the mighty force of the undertow: how the water comes rushing shore ward and breaks upon the coast, and then pours back again into the sea with seemingly greater force. And he told her that she must spring into the water at the time of the incoming wave, and that he would give her the signal. He waited until he saw a larger billow than the others come toward them, a great mountain of water, foaming and tossing its crest, and seemingly about to break upon them; and then, just as it was breaking, he called to her above the fury of the sea, and said, "Now! Now!" The poor woman hesitated, she shrank back, she tried to cling to her husband, she tried to hold onto the rock; but she found that she was to be swept over, and so she let go and cast herself down into the sea, only in time to be caught by the fury of the receding wave, and the life was dashed out of her on the rock where her husband was standing. There was another rocket and another line, and the captain took this and bound it about himself. He could not tell his wife's fate as yet. And again he cast his eyes seaward, until he saw another great towering billow, and as it came upon him he cast himself with it toward the shore, and helping hands pulled upon the rope and brought him there in safety, where he found the dead body of his poor wife, who had been just one moment too late.

And tonight the Word of God, and the providence of God, and the Spirit of God, and the minister of God, are all joining in saying to the men who are gathered here, "Now! Now!" "Now is the accepted time; now is the day of salvation." And now again do I call heaven-yes, I call heaven: God, Father upon the throne; Christ-Christ of the pierced hands and feet, of the bleeding side and the breaking heart; Christ of Gethsemane and Calvary; Christ of the resurrection and of the hope set before us; Holy Spirit of God, tender, loving, persistent, pleading Spirit; angels of God; loved ones gone before father, mother, wife, child: look down tonight and help, if it be possible, these men to choose life rather than death, and blessing rather than cursing! And earth-yes, I call earth to witness: the men that sit with you in this great throng, the wife who weeps as she prays at home for a Christian husband, the children who wait for a praying, godly father, the men associated with you in business, the generations yet unborn-I call them all to witness your decision tonight, for life or death, for blessing or for cursing. Choose life! Choose life! By the crisis that God brings to you this moment, by your duty to yourself because it is manly, by your duty to God, by your duty to your fellow-men, by the issues of time, by the issues of eternity, by the possibilities of the kingdom of God, now and hereafter, do I plead with you to say, "As for me and my house, we will serve the Lord."

Self-Renunciation

"So likewise, whosoever he be of you that forsaketh not all that he hath, he cannot be My disciple." -Luke 14:33

If that were the only verse of the kind in the utterances of Christ I should not take it as a text this afternoon; but instead of its being some isolated passage it is the heart of all His teachings concerning discipleship. That word "likewise" is perhaps the first one that impresses us. Like what? Like the man that tried to build a house and did not have money enough to finish it; like the man that went out with ten thousand to make war against one who came against him with twenty thousand, and so was overcome. I studied over the question for a long time, why it was that a man could not be a disciple of Christ unless he were like that, and then I found the answer. It is because a man who undertakes to fight this battle in his own strength will surely be overcome. It is because a man who undertakes to build his character with any resources independently of God, will find that he has undertaken an impossible task, as much so as if he tried to build a twenty-thousand-dollar house for one thousand dollars. But when a man turns over all that he has unto God, then God puts all His resources at the man's disposal. When a true wife gives herself unto a true husband, then the true husband gives the wife all that he has; and when a man gives everything over to God, that he may do only the will of God, then God takes up his cause and the "battle is the Lord's." Then he finds that he can truly say, "Those that are with me are more than those that are against me."

Mark that word "cannot" in the text. Christ says he cannot be His disciple. He does not say that unless a man forsakes all that he has "he shall not be My disciple," He does not say "he must not be My disciple," as though He were making some arbitrary test, but He says, "he cannot be My disciple." It is as though he said that a weak man cannot lift a heavy weight, or that a blind man cannot see, or that a bird cannot fly without wings. It is the necessary condition of doing certain things. A dog is not a man, and a dog can never become a man; but if there were a possibility of the dog getting the nature of a man, having a mind to think like a man and a spirit that he might appreciate spiritual things like a man, it is not impossible that we might imagine such a transformation. But the animal may as well stay the animal and try to fulfill the functions of a human being as for a man to try be a disciple of Christ and keep the control of his own life at the same time. It is an impossible thing. Self-sacrifice is not a hard thing when you look at it from the completed side. The complete surrender of one's self to God is the only easy way by which any one can ever do the will of God. While the door looks strait and the way looks narrow - so narrow that a man cannot get through with anything by his side - it leadeth unto life, and happy are they that find it.

I have intimated that this passage is not an isolated one. You have heard quoted this morning and this afternoon other passages that have brought you the same message. There was that first thought of the morning: "I beseech you therefore, brethren, by the mercies of God, that ye present your bodies a living sacrifice." The idea of a sacrifice is that of something that has passed forever out from the offerer's control, just as truly dead as though the knife had been at the throat and the blood had flowed, just as truly dead as though the bound sacrifice had been laid upon the altar and the fire had entirely consumed it. Yet the thought in these words is that you are to live - not to be your own any more than though you were dead, but to offer unto God yourself, a living sacrifice, a complete sacrifice; to live and yet be able to say, "Not I, but Christ liveth in me." There are those other words of Paul's: "Ye are not your own, for ye are bought with a price: therefore glorify God in your body, and in your spirit, which are God's."

This is the same lesson that Christ taught in the parables of the pearl of great price and the hidden treasure. I have heard men speculating and arguing as to whether the pearl of great price was a reference to Jesus or to us-as to whether He was the desirable thing for which we had sold everything in order that we might possess Him, or whether we were the pearl for which He sold everything in order that He might possess us. I do not believe that this was only an illustration; it was the announcement of a principle - the fundamental principle of discipleship - for Jesus the Son of God and for the disciples of the Son of God. I do not believe that there is any principle that binds us that does not bind the Eternal God and His only begotten Son. I believe that it is the fundamental principle of the kingdom of God that a man shall ruthlessly sacrifice the lower for the sake of the higher-nay, that a man shall recklessly and completely sacrifice the higher for the sake of the highest, and never be satisfied until he has given up everything and has received the very best that God has to give. The devil is all the while trying to make us satisfied with a halfhearted consecration and with half the blessings of the kingdom of God. He always wants to make us satisfied with things good in themselves, but which are not the best things. You may get some good things with an incomplete sacrifice; you can only get the best things by selling all that you have. Was it not true of Jesus? Did He not sell all that He had in order that He might purchase us? Is it not necessary for us to have the spirit of Christ so long as there be in this world sorrow or sin? Is it not necessary for us to sell all that we have in order that we may possess Him? It does not take a very strong nor a very rich nor a very learned person to be a consecrated Christian, but it takes all there is of a man or a woman. When you make up your mind to be all for God you will find that God has eternally made up His mind to be all for you.

I believe this was the teaching of Jesus when He said, "If any man will come after Me, let him deny himself, and take up his cross daily, and follow Me." He had been conversing with his disciples concerning the decease He was to accomplish at Jerusalem, the topic, also, on the Mount of Transfiguration. He began to explain to them how He must suffer many things of the chief priests and elders, be crucified, and rise again the third day; and Peter took

Him, and began to rebuke Him, and said, "Lord, this shall never be so unto Thee." What did Jesus call him? He turned to Peter and said, "Get thee behind Me, Satan: for thou savorest not the things that be of God, but the things that be of men." Then He said to them all, "If any man will come after Me, let him deny himself, and take up his cross daily and follow Me." Between the suggestion of the condition of coming after Him and the word that says "let him follow Me," He puts two things: let him deny himself, and let him take up his cross daily. Those two things are very important. What is the way to follow Jesus? I have seen people who have sat down and measured the feet of Jesus, and then they have measured their own feet, and have taken bandages and even chisels and begun to work at their feet in order to make them the size of the feet of Jesus. I have seen people who have measured the stride of Jesus, and they have tried every time they took a step to step just so far and no farther. That is better than nothing, but it is not the best. The thing to do is to get inside of you the divine organism, so that your feet will grow to the same size, and so that when you step you will naturally have to take the same steps that Jesus took. That is the only way to follow Jesus: not by trying to imitate Him, but to be like Him, so that you cannot walk in any other way. How do we get to be like unto Jesus?-" Let him deny himself, and take up his cross." What is self-denial? We have used that term so much that we have blunted its meaning. What does it mean to deny a thing? It means to affirm that it is not so. A man comes to you and says, "How do you do, Mr. Jones!" You reply, "My name is not Jones, it is Smith." You have denied that your name is Jones and confessed that your name is Smith. The literal interpretation of the denial of self and the confession of Christ would be to say, "I am not myself, but I am Jesus Christ." This is to come to that place where you can say, as did the great apostle of the Reformation, "Martin Luther does not live here - Jesus Christ lives here," or until you can say, with a greater apostle than Luther, "I am crucified with Christ: nevertheless I live; and yet not I, but Christ liveth in me: and the life that I now live in the flesh I live by the faith of the Son of God, Who loved me, and gave Himself for me." Augustine had lived a profligate life, but after his conversion he kept away from his former associates. One day on the street he was seen by a woman with whom he had associated in his life of sin, and as he saw her he started to run. She ran after him and cried, "Augustine, why do you run? It is I!" And Augustine said, "I run because I am not I!" Blessed be God! there may be such a transformation where man may say, not only "I am not my own, but I am bought with a price," but where he may say, "I am not myself, but I am Jesus Christ." Do you say, "I can see that would be the secret of leading a holy life-just to be Jesus and have Jesus be in me?" What is the secret of getting there? It is in those next words, "Let him deny himself, and take up his cross"-"the cross of Christ," says Paul, "by which I am crucified to the world, and the world is crucified to me." Dead to the world and the world dead to you-does that have any meaning to you? Here was a man yesterday who was concerned about the affairs of State and the price of wheat and the fluctuations of the market; he was concerned about his family and his friends and his money; but today he cares about none of them, and tomorrow we will carry his body in front of the altar and then bear it out to lay it away in the ground. The things which used to interest him interest him no more. He is dead. I knew of a fireman who seemed to be lying asleep upon his couch, and the bells rang out an alarm, and his little daughter, surprised that he did not start at the very first sound, ran to him and cried, "Fire, papa! There is a fire!" But he waked not. He was dead. Formerly he would have sprung up at a moment's notice, ready for his duty, but now the things that used to move him had no power over him. John defines the world as the "lust of the flesh, and the lust of the eyes, and the pride of life;" appetite; choosing the apparent in place of the real good; selfishness; pride. Being dead to the world is being dead to all these, so that the things that used to draw upon you shall draw upon you no more, and the world shall be dead to you. I can see here today faces that I love, friends that are dear to me; and there are others in the world that are not gathered here whom I love. But if today the touch of death should come to them I would wrap them in shrouds and lay them in the cold ground; I would not keep them in my embrace. I would not want to have them with me. Death-how it changes what seem to be the loveliest things! How far would you go this afternoon that you might avoid the offensive sight and surroundings of a decaying carcass? How you would loathe it! And now to have the corruption of the world become so dead that you would loathe it - what an experience! You say, "It is easy enough to talk about these things, but I strive vainly and blindly to find the path. If I could find that narrow door I would enter; but I fail to find it." Ah, friend, take up your cross-the cross of Christ. It means something more than speaking in prayer-meeting. It means something more than doing that which is distasteful to you. The cross everywhere means death. Andrew Murray well says that there is only one place. where you can graft a branch upon a tree, and that is where the tree has been cut and the life is flowing forth. There is only one way in which you can graft it, and that is to cut the branch as the tree is cut, so that it will fit into the tree and the life may flow into the branch. Oh, let the Lord cut you as the Lord was cut, and let him make you so that you can be hanged upon that self-same cross until the life shall go out of you! If you will stretch yourself on the cross today the Lord Jesus will see that you are bound there until the life goes out, and if you will, as Isaac did, lay yourself a willing sacrifice upon the altar, the Lord God Himself will see that you are bound there until the self-will has been taken away. Will you not take the step? Are you not willing to stretch yourself upon that cross today, entering into fellowship with the Lord Jesus Christ?

Now I believe there is something more in this than can be expressed in words. Some one has said that what can be proved is not worth the proving, and while I do not believe that is entirely true else I should not be a preacher - it is almost true that the things best worth telling can never be told. And that is the trouble with our theological books: three thick volumes are written about a few verses from this wonderful Bible. Men have never been able to express God's thought as the soul can appreciate it when it is consecrated unto Him. There is something infinitely more in the death of Jesus Christ than that He was my substitute for sin, or that He simply brought some moral influence that might make me touched by the picture of His sufferings and make me want to live a righteous life. There is here identification with the Lord Jesus, union with Him, the reciprocal act on my part to that great act on His part when He delivered Himself up as a sacrifice for my sin. "Let

Him follow Me," He says Who was He? He was the Lord of glory, but He came to be a minister and a servant. All heaven contained His mansions, and yet He had nowhere to lay His head. The angels were His proud messengers, and yet His peasant fisherman friends on earth deserted Him. He valued reputation more than you and I could value it, and yet He was crucified between two thieves. He cared for the smile of God as you and I never cared for the smile of an earthly friend, yet it seemed to Him as though God had hid His face from Him. There was a time when he said, "Father, forgive them," "Father, into Thy hands I commit, My spirit." But there was a time when I believe He could not say, "Father." In that awful agony, and in the darkness of hell that seemed to hover over His soul, He cried out, "Eloi, Eloi, lama sabacthani - My God, My God, why hast Thou forsaken Me?" He denied Himself - "having loved His own, He loved them unto the end." He went down into the deep blackness of death. My sins nailed Him to the cross; my sins put Him into the grave; and He would have stayed there if my sins had not been put away; but when He tore the bars away and came out of that sepulcher it was I that rose.

I believe today that if you are willing to do toward Jesus that which He did toward you, to deny yourself that you may confess Him, that you may be identified with Him in His cross; your sin shall go out of you, and down through the sepulcher you may come up into His glorious resurrection and ascension, to sit with Him in the glory of the Father, at the right hand of God. "If ye then be risen with Christ, seek those things which are above, where Christ sitteth at the right hand of God."

I could speak on for a long time in this way, but I want to call your attention to some practical thoughts concerning the manner in which we may forsake everything for Jesus Christ. Miss Havergal has suggested that you write your name at the bottom of a blank page of paper, and then at the top write the words, "I have given to God," and let Him fill in the blank space between with anything that He wants written down. That is good, but there is something better. I would give to Him everything that I knew, and then, when I had done that, I would give Him everything that I did not know. I would do it unreservedly. I would have confidence to believe that the paths

65

of righteousness were the paths of peace. I would trust Him enough to go wherever He would want me to go. I would have no more care and no more will.

A little while ago I heard a preacher, speaking on the verse, "The Lord is my shepherd," say: "I shall not want. How can I want? I want what God wants, and I want nothing else; I am bound to have it. God cannot take my wife from me nor my children. I have given Him my wife and children." That day. as he came into the meeting, a telegram had been handed to him from his home a thousand miles away, which said, "Your little child is very sick and will probably die within a few hours." Beloved, give your dear ones to God. Turn them over to Him first, and be satisfied with Jesus. If you know your child. after the flesh, know him so henceforth no more. If you have known any man after the flesh, know him so henceforth no more.

"Charles," said a mother in England, something like fifty years ago, to her son some ten or twelve years old, "I have trained you in righteousness. Your father and I have set you right examples. We have taught you the gospel. We have shown you the way of peace. My son, if you do not live a godly life I will stand before God in the day of judgment and bear witness against you." It takes that kind of a mother to make a son like Charles Spurgeon, and no such mother ever lost her son. No one that ever gave anything to God in such a concern for God's honor and such a lack of selfish concern as that, but found it to be true that no one leaves anything for the kingdom of God's sake but that he receives a hundredfold in this life.

Then how are you going to give up your possessions to Jesus? Some one says we ought to follow the Old Testament plan. What was it? Some people say the Jews used to give one-tenth, some say they used to give three-tenths of all their income; some say they used to pay the three-tenths before they gave anything. The tithe was a sort of rental which they paid, and after that, if they wanted to make any free-will offering they could do it. They never talked about paying their pew-rents and making an offering in that way to God. Some one says, "I do not want to live that way. We are not under the law, but under grace. We are in a new dispensation, and I would like to live according to the New Testament plan." What is the New Testament plan? Paul says, "I call your attention to the grace of God that was given to the churches of Macedonia because they gave more than they were able." They even went without the necessities of life that they might distribute to the necessities of the poor; and then he uses that magnificent verse as Dr. Taylor says, "as if he were using a Nasmyth steam-hammer to crack a nut" - "For ye know the grace of our Lord Jesus Christ, Who, when He was rich, yet for our sakes became poor, that we through His poverty might become rich." What was the New Testament plan? They were taking up a collection in Jerusalem. Like some of our friends down South, they did not pass the basket, but they had a box where the people came up and put in their contribution. The disciples and Jesus were looking on, and one of the disciples said, "Master, see what a man did! He put in two hundred dollars! Lord, is it not grand that we have such noble-minded, liberal people among the Jews that are willing to give their money like that to God's service?" Jesus said, "Do you see that old woman? She put in more than all of them." "Why, no, Master," they said, "that is just a poor old washerwoman. She is not able to work all the time. We doubt whether she has any money at all." And Jesus said, "I tell you she gave more than they all, for these rich men have cast in out of their abundance, and this woman has cast in out of her poverty" -How much? One-tenth? Three-tenths? No. Two mites? No "all that she had." Forsake it all-that seems to be the New Testament plan.

Brethren, you have prayed for a day of Pentecost. We have almost seen it. in this city. But do you know what they did after the day of Pentecost? "By their fruits ye shall know them. "They turned over all their property to the trustees of the Church to use for the service of Almighty God. Now, if you would like to have a day of Pentecost just go at it. I do not mean that I would have you transfer all your property to the church trustees-I would want some of them converted first; but if there is one penny anywhere that you own, it is an accursed penny. If there is one dollar in the bank over which you have control any longer, it is an accursed bank account. If there is any real estate that is recorded in your name, and you do not hold it in trust for God, the curse of God is on it and on you. Every penny that you do not spend for Almighty God is one that will bring you into the eternal judgment.

How about giving your time to God? Does not God want us to wash dishes and to run stores and factories and farms? Must everybody be ministers? and must we always go to meeting and sit and sing ourselves away to everlasting bliss? No, no! I have seen homes transformed when the wife has become fully consecrated to God. I have seen business transformed, like that establishment that the brother spoke of this morning, where a man went out from a godless partner at what seemed to be like a great sacrifice, and God increased his wealth tenfold. O friend, God only wants to get what you have in order that He may give you what He has. There is such a thing as giving every minute of the time to God. "Whatsoever ye do, whether ye eat or drink, do all - do all - for the glory of God."

I have read a very touching incident concerning Madame Guyon, who lived at a very dark time in the world's history, and yet was one of those few saints that never bowed the knee to Baal. She touches today the springs of holy living, after the lapse of more than a century, in thousands and hundreds of thousands of lives. She had a husband who was a very prominent man; and on one occasion twenty-two claimants for an estate brought to him their intricate case and said they would agree to abide by his judgment. They did not dare to take it into court, it was so complicated. He took the papers under advisement, and while he was considering the case he died. They then brought the papers to his wife, and said to Madame Guyon that if she would undertake to settle that estate they would all abide by her decision. She was not a business woman; she had always said she did not have a head for business; she could not transact anything in the line of business affairs. But the thought came to her that this would give her an opportunity to be a worker with God, if she could prevent quarreling and disturbance and dissension. So she said that if they would agree formally to accept her decision she would settle the case. They did so, and she shut herself up with God for thirty days. She did not go out of her room except to go to her meals or to the house of God. After the thirty days she brought down an outline of what seemed to her just. She had solved every problem, she had made every complicated point clear, as no godless lawyer on earth could have done; and when she presented her decision to these claimants they not only each of them accepted her decision and said that it was perfectly just, but the entire twenty-two united in saying that they were perfectly satisfied with what she decided. I do not believe that God would give such a faculty to you unless He put you in just that place; but when everything is given into the hands of God He will manage the business, and God's business always succeeds. That household always run smoothly which God is managing.

How about the talents? Will you give them to God? The consecrating blood in the Old Testament used to fall on the tip of the right ear, that it might hear only what God had to say; it used to fall on the right hand, that that hand might do only what God wanted it to do; it used to fall on the great toe of the right foot, that the feet might go where God would have them go, and nowhere else. O blood of Christ, fall on ears and touch the hands and the feet of the people here this afternoon-ears to hear, hands to do, feet to gladly run, but never to run until God says, "Go!" You may remember that old tale about the caliph of Baghdad, against whom a rebel had set up his banners. The caliph had surrounded this rebel chieftain in the mountain fastnesses, until it seemed as though he could not escape, and then he sent a messenger and summoned him to surrender. Before the chieftain answered he stretched out his hand and made a motion to a man, and the man cast himself over the edge of a precipice and was killed. He beckoned to another soldier, and when the soldier came he handed him a dagger and said, "Take this and plunge it into your heart;" and the soldier took the dagger and plunged it into his heart, and fell down dead. "Now," said the chieftain, "go back to the caliph and tell him what you have seen. Tell him I have five hundred men like these, and that before tomorrow night I will have him chained among my dogs." And he did. O, for the men and women like that, for the people who have no wish to live, no will to be, only to wish what God wishes, to will what God wills, and to be satisfied with Jesus! Bring out your ambitions today; bring out your pleasures; bring out your business; lay them all on God's altar, and never take them off unless God bids you. Turn everything over. Let everything be new, nothing old. If it be an old thing, let it be newly given unto you and it will be a new thing to you. If your right hand offend you, cut it off, and cast it from you. It is profitable for you to enter into life maimed rather than, having two hands, to sink into the fire of hell. I have heard men disputing about the effect of the death of Christ upon God. Let us realize what its effect should be upon us. Let us say today, as Paul said, "He died for all, that they who live should henceforth live not unto themselves, but unto Him Who died for them, and rose again."

Death is the only way to resurrection. The only way to newness of life is to have the old buried. Will you give up your will to God? Are you ready to say it from your heart, "Now let me die?" Are you ready to reckon yourself dead unto sin but alive unto God through Jesus Christ our Lord? "For whosoever he be of you that forsake not all that he hath, he cannot be My disciple." Beloved, this is what it means to be a disciple of Jesus Christ. Are you a disciple? Do you want to be? Will you be?

It ought to be said in justice to Mr. Mills, that the two succeeding sermons are a portion of a series of eight on "The Kingdom of Heaven on Earth." In order to appreciate fully the hopeful tone and constructive character of the series it would be necessary to hear them all.

The Kingdom of Heaven on Earth

I will preach this morning the first of a series of eight sermons on, "The Kingdom of Heaven on Earth."

I would ask your most prayerful attention to the thoughts that are suggested in the prayer we have prayed so frequently, as recorded in the sixth chapter of Matthew, tenth verse: "May Thy kingdom come on earth as it is in heaven."

We have all said it hundreds of times. It has been repeated millions and millions of times; and of all the millions that have ever prayed it how many have ever really expected the answer? How many people have applied to it the principle that Jesus taught when he said, "Whatsoever things ye desire when ye pray, believe that ye have received them and ye shall have them?" The thing we pray for is that God's kingdom may come and that His will may be done on earth as it is in heaven.

Now, we know what the popular idea of heaven has been in the past. I doubt whether there is any popular idea of heaven now prevalent among the people of Columbus. I scarcely know two people that think the same thoughts concerning heaven. We used to have an idea of heaven as a city, a material sort of city, with battlements and gates and streets and mansions. In fact, not long ago I read a sermon in which the brother said that anybody who read the Bible and believed the Bible, knew where heaven was. He said it was "up," and that we might know it was "up," because we had the expression, "Coming down from heaven." No one could come down unless heaven was "up;" and that Jesus went "up," and we read of different ones being taken "up into heaven;" and that the words spoken by the angels who said to the disciples after the ascension, were, "Why stand ye gazing up into heaven?" But the brother did not seem to think that if heaven was up when he made the statement it would be down twelve hours later, and would be in all sorts of angles in the meantime. And I think most of us have come to be moved away from material ideas of heaven, until at last, probably all of us here would agree to define heaven as a perfect society of perfect individuals. No man can be in heaven alone, no matter how happy he may be in his individual consciousness. No man can form a heaven alone. Our conception of heaven must include perfect individuals in a perfect society.

We are told in the Bible that in heaven there will be no hunger and no thirst, no oppressive heat, no pain, no disease, no death, and no sorrow; no impurity and no selfishness. These are the things that will make heaven the perfect satisfaction for every reasonable desire; but the thing we are taught to pray is that this shall come on earth.

Now, I do not want to destroy anybody's hope in anything that is worth hoping for. I would not want to say that we shall not be translated to some place of perfect felicity, but I do want to say with tremendous emphasis, that any such conception of the work of Christ is but a partial comprehension of His mission, and is not a description of the great purpose of Christ, which did not primarily concern some far-off heaven. "God sent not His Son into the world to condemn the world, but that the world through Him might be saved." And there is a certain sense in which no man living on the earth can be fully saved until all those who live about him are also fully saved. No man can be perfect alone. No man can be saved alone, and there will never be heaven anywhere except where there is an association of men that are living in absolute unselfishness, and wherever that exists, the kingdom will have come as it has already come in heaven. I believe it is a place where our activities shall be devoted in a larger and more effective form to the transformation of this world. I do not believe that we will change our prayer, but that we will labor that God's kingdom may come on the earth, "As it is in heaven."

What did you mean when you prayed that prayer? Did you mean to pray that there may come a time on earth when there would be no hunger and no thirst and no oppressive heat, no trouble, no impurity and no selfishness? Was that what you were praying for? No. You prayed that God's kingdom might come on the earth as it is heaven. We have these words put on our lips as the direct language of the Master, "When ye pray, say, 'May Thy kingdom come # on earth as it is in heaven,'" and the devil never executed such a triumph of his art as when he turned the attention of the disciples of Christ away from the transformation of this world. To be a Christian is to be a laborer together with Him who was in Christ reconciling the world unto himself.

Now, tomorrow I shall speak more particularly about the teachings of the Old Testament on this subject; but whatever may be said of the New Testament this is certainly true; that the Old Testament deals with the affairs of this world, and is filled with some of the most glorious prophecies concerning the ultimate state of affairs on this planet. "As truly as I live," said God, as he spoke through the writer of the book of Numbers, "all the earth shall be filled with the Glory of the Lord." The Psalmist says, "All the ends of the world shall remember, and turn unto the Lord, and all the kindred's of the nations shall worship before Thee." We read that there shall come a time when "The earth shall be filled with the glory of the Lord as the waters over the sea." And we read in Jeremiah that "They shall teach no more, every man, his neighbor, and every man his brother, saying "know the Lord," for they shall all know me from the least of them unto the greatest of them, saith the Lord.

Daniel draws pictures of the final triumph of Christ, that might have been written in the Apocalypse with the pen of John. We read in Jeremiah that "The Lord shall be King over all the earth; in that day shall there be one Lord and his name one." Then we turn to the New Testament and if we read it correctly, we find that it deals with exactly the same subjects. The very first words that Jesus uttered in his mission were these: "The kingdom of heaven." "Repent, for the kingdom of heaven is at hand." The conception of the Jews, that it was to be a terrestrial kingdom, was a correct conception. Jesus did not come to destroy this conception of the Jews, but to spiritualize it. The idea was a right one, and just so far as the Christian church has departed from the thought that God's kingdom is coming upon the earth, and that the people of God are called to bring that kingdom upon the earth, just so far has she lost her power. It was her selfish satisfaction that destroyed the old Jewish nation.

I do not know of but one place in all the gospel where Jesus refers to heaven in any sense that might be rightly interpreted in the ordinary idea. His call was a call to man to come and help him in the establishment of peace upon the earth.

I am to speak more particularly about this on Thursday of this week. But it ought to have been enough, if there had been no other line ever written and no other word ever spoken than this, that Jesus said, "When you pray say, "Thy kingdom come on earth as it has come in heaven.' ". When you turn over to the teachings of the apostles you find that they emphasize the same thing. Their preaching was characterized, as Jesus' was, by the title of the "Gospel of the kingdom," and we do not know of any other instruction that was ever given to the twelve or the seventy or any of the disciples of Jesus, except that they were to say to men that the kingdom of God had drawn nigh. That was not a portion of their mission. That was all of their mission; and we find Paul and Peter and John fairly thrilling with the conception of the vision that Christ was coming to bring together in one all ends that are in heaven with all things that are in earth.

I am one of those who believe that this was the conception of the earliest church. I have no idea that the church for the most part, in the first century, had any other idea than that they were called to work for the triumph of Jesus in this world. I even believe that Paul, up to a certain period of his life expected to see the earth transformed and the kingdom of God fully established before he should be taken away. There is a variety of opinion as to how this hope was lost by the church, but some of our wisest and most devoted thinkers hold that it was because of the persecutions that came upon the early church. "Hope long deferred maketh the heart sick," and in order to reconcile some things that Jesus said, with what they believed, it may be that as they endured these things, they began to change their conceptions of the mission of Christ into the taking of some people and putting them into a far distant heaven instead of transforming this earth into heaven itself. And some of our most excellent commentators on the Revelation of John, believe that it was written for the purpose of correcting the faith of the church that was already changing. And it was spoken in a mystical language for fear of the Roman, to tell the Christians that God was not dead, but that he was working in the confusion and destruction and overturning of all the forces of man, and showed them all the things that must surely come to pass. And all through the book John says, "The time is at hand," and you have not begun to appreciate that book in its thrilling power until you can see that all these things have taken place. I do not mean to say that they are not taking place today and will not take place again in the future.

The eyes of the Apocalyptic seer saw the New Jerusalem, the City of God, descending out of heaven to abide upon the earth, and he gave to the people that great vision almost at the close of his wonderful book; and he tells us that he heard the voices crying out in heaven and singing, "The kingdoms of this world are become the kingdoms of our Lord and of his Christ and he shall reign forever and ever."

Now, I believe this great doctrine is the one which should mould our thought and practice today, and instead of its having in it any of the sins that may be rightly called heresy, everything that contradicts it is the most pernicious heresy in paralyzing the energy of the church of Jesus Christ.

I am not mourning because some old doctrines are losing their grip over the hearts of men. I can occasionally weep a little with those that weep on account of tender-heartedness, but I never weep on my own account; as I see the faith of men being strengthened and their conceptions being enlarged. I shall not mourn over the chrysalis of the insect as I see the glorious development of the beautiful winged creature of God. You and I are able by the grace of God, to be more spiritual than any of the people who have gone before us and I should hardly hold my faith in God unless I realized that. God is always marching on. "I have many things yet to say unto you," said the Master, to his disciples, "but you cannot bear them now. How be it when He the Spirit of Truth, is come He will guide you into all truth."

And while I believe every suggestion that is made here is in the spirit of the love and teaching of Jesus, yet I believe the best truths might not have been apparent before these glorious years of grace in which we are now living; and more marvelous revelations are yet to be apprehended, and mightier works are yet to be done. What did the Master mean when he said, "The works that I do shall ye do also; and greater works than these shall ye do, because I go unto My Father?" And while our great conventions are passing their resolutions, the Presbyterians, the Congregationalists, the Unitarians, and all the rest defining what they mean by the Christian religion, the day of the Lord is coming as a thief in the night and the hearts and minds of the people are being changed into the conception of Jesus Christ, in such a fashion that we will have to be one under the power of the overmastering inspiration of the thought of the Kingdom of God. (Applause). I would be false to my experience if I did not say that for myself, more than that hour when I was first willing to abandon my sins and yield my will unto the spirit of God and there came to me a consciousness of personal forgiveness of sin, more even than that most holy day, when it seemed to me that I went through the narrowest sort of a door into the largest sort of a life, has been to me this mighty, cleansing, uplifting, strengthening and inspiring conception of the Kingdom of God. I had been troubled for a good many years, but I know now what the trouble was. 1 was in that condition which McDonald so beautifully describes as the time when "The soul is at once the mother who bears and the child who is born." And the distress and tribulations of those years, and perplexities may have been necessarily incidental to the enlarging of the thought and yielding of the entire heart and soul and spirit unto this blessed message and mission of the Kingdom of love. But when at last after prolonged study of the scriptures and reading and rereading, and trying the effect of it upon pure and simple minds, at last when I came to the place where I could see just the one thing, the great gospel of the Kingdom of God, from Genesis to Revelation, I was so full of it that I remember as I started from home on the railway train to go to Chicago I telegraphed a friend of mine in a city along the way, a noble spirited man and an officer in the late war, and I said, "I wish you would meet me on the train and travel a little distance." And when I met him I said, "My friend, I am a new man. You sit still in that seat, and do not open your lips until I give you permission." And as the train sped on for about two hours, with the open Bible before us, I tried to pour into him the truths of God; and when I had finished he said, "I do not want to say a word now. I want to say to you only goodbye. I do not know where I am. I will write to you." He left the train at the next station and went to his home, and a week or ten days afterwards wrote me a letter that fairly gleamed with glory. He said, "Oh, my brother, what an inspiration! I remember how I felt when the call came for the preservation of the union, and I was glad to go and fight for something practical to bind together our nation. It was nothing compared with this. Here is something for which a man may think and live and die, and may give all his energy for the establishment of the Kingdom of God upon this earth." If you cannot be saved by this impulse, there is no impulse that can save you. If all the blackness of selfishness will not be purged out of you by the thought that one sin may keep back the Kingdom of God, and that one sacrifice may help to bring it in all its glory, you are a hopeless soul. Oh, friends, this is the inspiration. Brother ministers, this is the Gospel that the people must understand, that parents must teach their children, and when they realize their responsibility, go forth to the conquest of places and powers of sin.

This is an inspiration for the individual to come and be saved. I said to a brother, "How would you modify your preaching under this conception?" I said, "I think I would not say quite so much come to Jesus as come with Jesus." And I propose to make this same "come to Jesus" mean what we mean when we say, "come with Jesus," for the accomplishment of the work for which He lived and died, and rose and lives again. Can we not see that this is all that is needed for the perfection and the enthusing of the church with a mighty power for the conquest of this world? And, if the church of Christ had the conception of herself that Jesus had of himself, that she had come to give her life for the world, for the saving of the world, we would not hear men on the streets saying that we ministers "talk through our hats," whatever that means. I am not sure I would fully agree with the brother who said the church was a union of all who love in the service of all who suffer, unless like the old theologians we go a little further and say that a man could not love except he have the Spirit of Christ in him. But, do you not see that when the overmastering passion of the ministry and the church shall not simply be to defend its dogmas, but to establish the kingdom of love, that before we know it, we will all be so heartily engaged in work for the same thing, we will be practically one. Even now, when we are engaged in this limited fashion in a practical effort for the uplifting of men, here come men of perhaps twelve different denominations, -all Christians, and join their hands. For what? Not that we may lift up any of our peculiar standards of doctrine, but because we have a practical aim of trying to do something in a practical fashion. And I can conceive that as the Spirit of God goes on diffusing this great thought among men that we will have to be bound together. I can see a united Protestant Church, clothed with power and inspired in such fashion that men shall not think of what they think, but rather of what they do; and I can see the Protestant Church look into the face of her mother, and see the old Roman Church purified by this inspiration with all of its history of noble achievements, as well as its history of shame and sorrow, united with the child for this and this alone, that God's kingdom may come and his will be on earth as it is in heaven. Further than that: even to the mother of Rome, I can see the old Greek Church called out of its slovenly inactivity, by the great thought of establishing the kingdom of peace, one united church of Jesus Christ. Back farther than that: Turning to that one that was the mother of us all, crying to God's ancient people that they may come and see the Messiah, visible in what he does for men, until there shall be a mighty union of all the so -called Christians with all the Israelites; and I am willing they shall lead us if they will, as we call the heathen world into this glorious fellowship, until in the darkest corner of the earth the kingdom of peace shall be established. Come and let us make a heaven below, into which the heaven above shall flow until they shall both be one, bound together in the manifest spirit of Christ, the Son of God.

And I come to say more than that, that I believe that not only is this the inspiration that is availing now, and that will avail until the final triumph comes for the purifying and unifying and empowering of the church; but for the regeneration of society through the instrumentality of the church. It will get into the blood. I fairly thrill with it. I feel like shouting as I go about your streets. I can look high above oppression, above the most deadly dishonesty and above the most evil combination of men by unholy methods that they may work unholy results, and I can cry, "Glory to God." He will make the dishonesty and wickedness and weakness of men to praise Him in the glorious revelation of the triumph that shall come in the nations. What else does the world need? What else does the chair of political economy need? What do we need in the legislative hall? What do we need in the Judge's seat? What do we need on the throne and in the Presidential chair? What do we need where the busy wheels of the factory turn out their productions for the world's need? What on the farm? What in the church and what in the home? Just this: The conception that life is a mission. The way for men to live is the way Jesus lived. The way for business to be conducted is on the principles by which Jesus administered His life. The way to administer a nation is the way the King of Kings administered Himself, in giving Himself away for the lives of others. You may have heaven today if you will administer your home on the principles of the kingdom of God. You may have heaven in your factory and store and on your farm, if you will administer your business on the principles by which Jesus laid down His life for men. We will be able to give ourselves with such an impulse, with such a practical knowledge, with such defined and direct suggestions, and with such a resistless force, that the very nation itself will be heaven in the breadth of its ministry in the kingdom of love. Politics, business, wealth, home, city, nation; individuals leading the Church, and the Church leading the city and the nation. May it not be that just such a company as are gathered here this morning who shall give themselves to the answering of the prayer that you have heard thousands of times, and letting that kingdom come in you as it has come in heaven, and in this Board of Trade, and in all the trade and intercourse of our fellows, and in our politics; may it not be that this company here today might make of this capital city of Ohio, a city of God, a New Jerusalem come down from heaven, until your sister cities round about should catch the inspiration and we should see a purified Cleveland and a purified Cincinnati and purified cities in all the borders, the North the South, the East and the West, and until Chicago and other cities throughout the nation might catch the inspiration from this gathering today, and one nation with the spirit of Pentecost might lead every other nation of the world into a holy fellowship of serving the blessed Christ.

And now, in conclusion, my brother, what does it mean to you? Are you absolutely living in your personal life by the law of love? Just so far as you are not, just so far as you do not decide every question and do every deed in answer to the question that ruled the life of Jesus, just so far you are hindering instead of helping to establish the kingdom of God. Is your home fairly thrilling with the spirit that caused Jesus to leave His home? Is it a heaven for love? Is it administered for love, and are you using your home to bear away the wretchedness around you? Brother, sister, prodigal child, having wandered away from the Master's house, in your selfishness and sin, here is the thing that will save you. Give yourself up now to love and to live love and to answer the prayer that God's kingdom may come upon the Earth. Come into this great army for the conquest of peace. Come, and let it transform your life as it never existed before, until you shall become a bearer of the standard of the Prince of Peace. I bring to you a glorious invitation. Come, come and be saviours, come and help Jesus, working with the Spirit of God instead of against the Spirit of God; come with Jesus and come with us; not that we may do you good, but that you may be to us instead of eyes; that you may lead us and work with us. And as for myself, Oh Father, Oh, Saviour, Oh, people of God, Oh, citizens of this community, I call you to witness that the last thought that my brain can think and the last drop of blood that feeds my heart, I give, and I give with such a passion of joy that no words can express it, for the establishment of the kingdom of God upon this earth.

At the sign of triumph
Satan's hosts do flee,

On, then Christian soldiers,
On to victory.

Hell's foundations quiver,
At the shout of praise,
Brothers, lift your voices,
Loud your anthems raise.

Onward, then, ye people,
Join our happy throng,
Blend with ours your voices,
In the triumph song.

Glory, laud and honor,
Unto Christ the King,
Thus through endless ages,
Men and angels sing.

For that glorious certainty let us devoutly watch and pray and sacrifice and labor, with hopes as high as heaven, with love as deep as hell, with charity wide as the universe, with a passion great as the unselfishness of God, with the sacrifice like unto that of Calvary; remembering that the foe in strongly entrenched, and that without the shedding of blood there can be no remission; believing in God, and in the redemption of the world, in Christ and through Christ and for Christ, believing in the Holy Ghost, let us go forth "leading captivity captive," in this war of love; never resting until our ears shall hear and our voices shall join that triumphant song of the Apocalyptic vision, "the kingdoms of this world are become the kingdoms of our Lord and of His Christ and He shall reign forever and ever."

Young Men's Christian Association Building

Headquarters of the Mills Meeting

The Church and the Kingdom

I f I were choosing a text I think I should select the words of Paul in the first chapter of Ephesians, 22 and 23, where he says that "God hath put all things under His feet, and gave Him to be the head over all things to the Church, which is His body, the fulness of Him that filleth all in all." That is Paul's definition of the Church, "The Church which is Christ's body, the fulness of Him that filleth all in all."

Jesus said, as recorded in the twelfth verse of the fourteenth of John, "Verily, verily, I say unto you, he that believeth on me, the works that I do shall he do also, and greater works than these shall ye do; because I go unto My Father."

Day before yesterday I attempted to show that the Old Testament taught us that God intended the establishment of a terrestrial, spiritual, universal, everlasting kingdom upon the earth, through human agency. Yesterday I endeavored to show that Jesus meant that same thing, that He came to renew in the minds of the people the ancient ideal showing them at the same time the methods by which this prophecy was to be fulfilled. At the time of the coming of Jesus there had been no prophet for four hundred years and the hearts of the people had waxed gross and their ears dull of hearing, and although they still expected a universal kingdom, it was with a deadly misconception that it was to be established by violence instead of love. God would have made the Israelites a kingdom of priests, but they would not have it so and their only ambition was that they might have the power to exert as deadly oppression toward others as was shown by the Romans toward them.

Then came John with his message of judgment as a motive of repentance, and then came Jesus with the announcement of the establishment of a kingdom of love of which He was the King, which should become universal and whose principle should be love.

His message was the announcement of the transformation of this world by the methods of self-sacrifice until men should be at peace with one another, and the calling of them by His example to overcome evil with good. He had announced the constitution of the eternal kingdom. After the statement that from that time Jesus began to say, "The kingdom of heaven is at hand," follows the fifth, sixth and seventh chapters of Matthew, what is called the Sermon on the Mount, and what might be described as the constitution of the kingdom. After He had announced that His kingdom was here and was to be peaceably established, He went on to tell what the kingdom was and pronounced blessings upon the poor in spirit, the meek, the merciful, the persecuted for righteousness' sake, the pure in heart. He told the disciples that they should not resist evil, that they should give to those who asked of them and from the borrower should not turn away, that they should love their enemies, that they were to pronounce no judgment upon their fellow-men, that the critical spirit was to be entirely absent, and that if they sought first the kingdom of God all other things should be added unto them. Then He gathered as disciples those who were willing to leave all for the sake of being His followers; and then there came a time when the visible Christ was taken away and the invisible Christ was manifest in the socializing power of the Holy Spirit; that men might be taught how to live with one another as Jesus had lived toward all men, and that there might come to be this holy fellowship in the spirit of God for the accomplishment of the purpose of Jesus. The passage in Ephesians is one that describes the power of the life of Jesus Christ. Paul had been saying that Christ had come to bring together in one all things in heaven, and all things on earth, and there refers to the Church which is Christ's body, "The fulness of Him that filleth all in all."

It is striking that Jesus only used the term "Church" twice, and once in a very insignificant sense, where it had no meaning in this connection at all.

He used the word "kingdom" over one hundred times. What was the mission of Jesus? The mission of Jesus was not to found a Church. The Church was incidental, as a school is an incidental thing to the development of the child. The Church was one of the agencies that was to be used for the establishment of the kingdom of God, and we have made a terrible mistake, some of us, if we have thought that the gathering of a Church was the object and aim and end of the mission of Jesus. "God sent His Son into the world that the world through Him might be saved," and Jesus wanted the Church to feel His unifying spirit, in order that they might be one, for the purpose of having the world believe that God had sent Jesus. Jesus went away, but when He went away He said to His disciples, "As the Father hath sent Me into the world, even so have I sent you into the world." He said, "The works that I do shall ye do also, and greater works than these shall ye do, because I go unto My Father." The head went away and left the body to do the work. The Church has no existence apart from the thinking Christ, the living Christ. The Church has no call to exist except for the purpose for which Christ existed. We are sent into the world as Jesus was sent into the world, that the world through us might be saved. We are the body of Him who filleth all in all. Now, the mission of the Church has been described by Dr. George Gates, who says, that one may hold any one of three theories concerning it. In the first place he stated that we may believe that the world is to become the Church; that is, that all the world is to become converted and join the church and with that idea we would simply work for the bringing of people into the Church, until at last every person in the world should be a member of the Church, and then Christ's work would be accomplished. That is what might be called the High Church idea. The second idea, is that the Church is not to bring the world into it and not to save the world, but to save some people out of it. That from the corruption of the world a few people might be taken and translated into another world where they should be purified and be at peace. That view is held by a very small class of earnest Christians. The third view is what I believe to be the teaching of the Scriptures of the revelation of the Holy Spirit. This is that the Church is called to do the work of Jesus, and the work of Jesus is to set up and manifest this kingdom of love upon the earth. Jesus said, "As the Father hath sent Me, even so have

I sent you." The Church is the body of Jesus. The Church is no more the kingdom of God than Jesus was the kingdom of God. Just like Him it ought to be a picture of it, a microcosm, but like Him it should give its life for the world. It is not intended to exist for itself, but to give its life for the ransom of many, and pour out its blood for the sake of the transformation of the world. The need, in my opinion, of the Church is four things.

First. We need to have God's conception of the mission of Jesus. He was the Son of man who gave His flesh for the life of the world. I never said there was no heaven. What I did say, was that heaven was to come down to earth. I also said this, that while it might be exceedingly important to certain individuals to be taken to heaven to abide for a little time until earth had been transformed into a heaven, that this was only incidental to the work of Jesus, which was to bring together in one all things that are in heaven and in earth. Heaven is not to be our aim, as a place of inactivity. It is to be a continuation of divine service in the divine spirit of Christ. A man who selfishly seeks to go to heaven, is fit only for hell and has the spirit of Judas and not of Jesus, who left heaven that He might bring a lost world back to God. The main thought of the scripture is not of the saving of individuals out of the world, but the saving of the world. There is no such thing as saving an individual out of the world. The man that was saved out of the world would be a lost man and not a saved man. Let us fairly understand this thought. I do not mean when we say the mission of Christ was the saving of the world, that it necessarily meant the transforming of every individual into a righteous life. I do not know about that. I do mean that the object of God's sending His Son into the world was not to save individuals out of it, but to save the world. There never was a time when individuals might not be saved. There never was a time in the world's history when a penitent man could not walk with God. Abraham was called the "Friend of God," and Moses was called "A man of God," and David was called, "A man after God's own heart," and there never was a time when the true Light did not "Lighten every man that cometh into the world." And you have not read the first chapter of John correctly unless you saw that the first portion of it was a description of the light that was always in the world. Christ was in the world before the time of the incarnation. And then John says, "The Word was made flesh and dwelt among us." The word of God was always in the world, teaching the hearts and lives of individuals to lead them unto righteousness. But it was necessary that Jesus should come to redeem the world. Oh beloved, it is redeemed now. As Dr. Strong most beautifully says in his little classic book, "The New Era," The work of Jesus was not to get a few people out of the ruined and sinking wreck, but it was to save the wreck, to quiet its confusion and disorder and cause men to live with one another in peace." "God sent not His Son into the world to condemn the world, but that the world through Him might be saved." "The bread that I will give," said Jesus, "Is my flesh which I will give for the life of the world." "I came not to judge the world, but to save the world." He said to the disciples, "And I, if I be lifted up, will draw all men unto Me." Then listen to the words of John as he says, "He is the propitiation for our sins, and not for ours only, but the sins of the whole world," and "The kingdoms of this world are to become the kingdoms of our Lord." The apostle to the Gentiles writes to the Romans, "As I live, saith the Lord, every knee shall bow to Me and every tongue shall confess to God." He writes to the Colossians, that the Christ "Has made peace through the blood of His cross, by Him to reconcile all things unto Himself; by Him, I say, whether they be things in earth or things in heaven." To the Ephesians he writes, that "In the dispensation of the fulness of times he would gather together in one all things in Christ, both which are in heaven and which are in earth; even in Him, * * * and hath put all things under His feet, and gave Him to be the head over all things to the Church, which is His body, the fulness of Him that filleth all in all." He writes to the Philippians that "God also hath highly exalted Him, that, at the name of Jesus every knee should bow and every tongue confess that Jesus Christ is Lord, to the glory of God the Father, of all things in heaven and things in earth and things under the earth," and he says in the same epistle that Christ "Shall change our vile body, that it may be fashioned like unto His glorious body, according to the working whereby He is able even to subdue all things unto Himself."

He writes to the Corinthians: "Then cometh the end, when He shall have delivered up the kingdom to God, even the Father; when He shall have put down all rule and all authority and power: for He must reign until He hath put all enemies under His feet."

Beloved, is that the message of the Bible, that God sent His Son into the world that the world through Him might be saved? This is the gospel that is to redeem the world and not to curse the world; and the work of the Church is to take a redeemed world and make it a saved world. Evil is already defeated. The man who believes that the devil owns this world and controls it, and that he shall be triumphant, is a man who is worshiping the devil and is denying Christ. Some one says, "Well, if the kingdom of God is here in such fashion as that, why doesn't it more powerfully manifest itself?" And I can answer you as Dr. Gladden has so beautifully done in his little book, when he says, it is here just as Spring has come when magnolias, the apple blossoms and the violets have come. It is not all here, but some of it is here and there is more to follow, until the perfection of the glorious summer.

In the second place we need to have not only God's conception of the mission of Jesus, but also the conception that this mission is the work of the Church.

I want to read you a little extract from a lecture that Rev. Robert F. Horton delivered in London recently to laboring men, upon "The Kingdom of God." He said very much what I have said this morning, and then he concluded with these words:

"Let me leave you with some hope. I am full of hope in spite of the darkness which seems to prevail today. I am full of hope of what will result from the teaching I have uttered to -night, because I know it is the teaching of Christ, and I know also that men have not paid attention to it as it deserves. If the Church had studied and followed this teaching, and the world were in the condition it is today, should despair; I should say there is no hope in the gospel for this world at any rate. But if the Church has ignored the kingdom of God as Christ teaches it, if the Church has occupied itself mainly with securing a salvation for the other world without diligently following the commandments of the King in this world where the kingdom of God is coming, then do you not see what a hope breaks in upon us, that directly we begin to obey, directly we begin to see what our Lord and Saviour meant, the day of reformation will dawn, the future will take a new color, a new shaping, a more beautiful because a more holy and more Christlike form, and even you and I who have been assembled here to-night, may live to see the kingdom of God coming amongst us in power."

Oh beloved, I glory in the fact that these teachings seem to be new to us, although they are of the very heart and spirit of the Lord Jesus in all of His utterances. What are we here for? To do what Jesus did, and greater things. Are we doing what Jesus did? Let us go out and work a few miracles. Let us heal a few sick people, and raise some of the dead to life. Let us stretch out our hand and quiet the storm. We are not even doing what Jesus did. How can we expect to do greater things than He did? There are those who believe, and I think rightly too, that the whole paralysis of the mighty manifestations of spiritual power, which is the only power that is worthy of the name, is because the Church of Christ has not been living according to the teachings of Jesus, in attempting to establish the kingdom of heaven upon the earth.

There will be manifested unlimited power for the transformation of this world, if this is the consuming passion of our lives. When we think that the primary idea of Jesus and Paul and the other disciples was, not as has been supposed, simply to take people to heaven, but the transformation of this earth, then we will not stumble over the great fact of the final infusion of love into the world in such a way that it never would, and never could, be cast out again. And this is the enlarging and transforming principle that has been at work ever since, until we now seem to be approaching the ends of the ages in what some of us hope may be the consummation of the Gospel of Christ.

Is the world growing better? It would be like asking whether you are any larger today than you were when you were born. It has grown more rapidly than any human form has ever developed. You say, "How is it that you can tell us such things as this in one breath, of the greatest hopefulness, and then in the next can say words of the most stinging condemnation of the surrounding customs and practices of the world?" I can explain that.

Our customs ought to seem worse to us than more evil practices did to our ancestors. We have more light. And it is a sign of godliness and not of a hardened conscience that what did not trouble our ancestors is convicting us of sin in a sense of social shame. And the social unrest and the appreciation of our needs means that our appreciation of the true standards is growing faster than our character, and the old world is nearly ready to say, "God be merciful to me a sinner!" As Dr. Strong says, "You may say to the infidel, ' Do you believe in Christ?' And he says, 'No, I do not believe in any Christ. ' 'What do you believe in?' ' My creed is to do unto others as you would have others do unto you. ' ' That is Christ! The idea of a man telling you that he believes in the Golden Rule and does not believe in Jesus! He probably does not do what Jesus said any more than some church members I know, but his creed is right.

Do you think there is a man anywhere who can stand up and gain a hearing among any class of people who do not say that his creed is the creed of Jesus? He may not mention His name, but he will have to utter His teachings if he wins the people. That was not the creed of the world one hundred years ago; nor when I was a boy-and my hairs are not gray yet. The world never moved as it is moving now. We have to fairly leap to keep up with the world as it moves on with the spiritual electricity - even to see it as it goes.

Turn to the parable of the tares. God lets the wheat and the tares grow together until the harvest; but the harvest is not made the end of all things. The harvest on the farm is not the end of all things. It is the gathering of the wheat that you may get a larger harvest next year. This is what God gathers, in His harvest of the world, all His wealth is living Christianity scattered in all the earth that it may bring forth a greater harvest. And I do believe, before God, we are called to do greater works than Jesus could have done upon this earth. I think that men could do greater things in some years that have passed since Jesus lived in the flesh than Jesus could do when on earth, and I am confident that you and I are living in the great consummation when it is possible for us, by our thinking and sacrificing and by our loving and working to do such things. The world is so changed that it has become plastic and its heart has almost blossomed into an appreciation of the heart of Christ. You and I can do things today upon this earth that could not have been done by all the forces of the universe eighteen hundred years ago.

I believe with the best writers upon this theme, that the time will never come when the Church will become the State or the State will become the Church. I think some of us have made a mistake, on the other hand, that is more terrible than that as Freemantle says, when we have an idea that the Church is a society for worship or benevolence instead of a society for the transforming of this world. As has been said, there was a time when the Church in this country was the State, and the school, and included all benevolent institutions. I quote Dr. Gladden again, when he says that "Part of its work is done when the State assumes this work. But it is the business of the Church to see that the State conducts its affairs in a Christian fashion." It is the business of the Church to be the inspiration for truer character building in the school. It is its business to see that there is better care for the poor-to discover the sources of poverty and uproot them, and insist upon more enlightened care of the insane and all other unfortunates, to breathe purity into politics and unselfishness into industry and commerce, to suggest and lovingly compel the enactment of more Christian laws and contribute a holy courage for their enactment, to be concerned about the physical welfare of all cities and citizens, better pavement, cheaper heat, and light and transportation and communication, pure water and more of it; to regenerate the criminal and Christianize the prison, to promote the truest brotherly relationship of the employer and the employed, to be the spirit of Christ, to inspire the elector and the law-maker, the judge and the ruler, so that the kingdom of the reigning Christ may be more speedily manifested on earth.

And where the State will not do it, to "criticise by creation." If she will not properly care for the children and the afflicted and all dependent persons, let us do it as a Church. Let us continue where needed, to build our orphanages and hospitals and resorts for the aged and unfortunate. Let us endow our free dispensaries, and kindergartens, and day nurseries, and every institution that will make men holier and the earth happier. Let us find out what Christ taught about property and society and industry and every human relationship, and believe Him enough to practice what He taught, and summon others to do the same. Let us say to the State and the city and the factory and railroad and the trust, "You belong to Christ." Let our commission be limited only by the commission that God gave to Christ. Let us "Count nothing human, foreign to us." Let our work be worship and our daily living praise, until the "Earth shall be filled with the knowledge of the Lord as the waters cover the sea," and the city of the New Jerusalem shall be upon the earth and we shall sing the glorious anthems of the Spirit of Love, unto Him Who hath redeemed us from sin and washed us in His own blood.

The Church has been compared with a machine which has just steam enough to turn its own wheels, but not enough steam to make anything. What would you men think of a factory that had just steam enough to keep its own wheels going, but never manufactured anything?

We are like the boy that President Gates tells about who would take a run in order to leap across a ditch. He took the run and when coming just to the point of springing, he stopped and did not make the leap, but looked around and said, "What a great run that was I made." We seem to be just getting ready to do something, but almost wholly occupy ourselves with trying to save ourselves.

There is a poem which I think was written by Bishop Coxe, of New York. I am not sure about that, but it runs like this:

> *A parish priest of austerity*
> *Climbed up in a high church steeple*
> *To be nearer God, so that he might hand*
> *His word down to the people.*

> *And in sermon script he daily wrote*
> *What he thought sent down from heaven;*
> *And he dropped this down on the people's heads,*
> *Two times one day in seven.*

> *In his age, God said, "Come down and die,"*

And he called from out the steeple,
"Where art Thou, Lord?" and the Lord replied,
"Down here, among My people."

In the third place, we need the establishment of moral, spiritual and practical, rather than theological and ecclesiastical standards of fellowship in our churches. Now I am not making any reference here to "preaching doctrine." A man came to me one day and said, "You don't believe in preaching doctrine, do you?" I said, "Indeed I do." I am preaching doctrine now. But the theological opinions of men were never meant to be the test of fellowship among the followers of Christ. And I think it is a damnable thing, no matter how clear a man's views may be concerning what he thinks about the truths of God, to make these opinions a test of the fellowship or a definition of the aim of the Church of Christ. And our best historians in these days, with their wide opportunity of research, are telling us that this conception of doctrine, meaning by that the theological opinions of men, is purely a pagan, Greek conception. What was the doctrinal qualification for membership in the first band of disciples? Jesus said, "Follow me!" "And they left all and followed Him." What was the doctrinal qualification at Pentecost? Peter said, "Repent and be baptized." That is what he told them at that time. He did not ask anything about their opinions. Now, I believe in ancient creeds. I like to see old creeds, just as I like to see mummies, and things of that kind. (Laughter). They used to be alive. (Great laughter). But I think, when we take a mummy and try to live with it and treat it as though it had life in it, and could have children, it becomes a great monstrosity. Do not misunderstand me. I stand squarely with both feet on what Paul said concerning "sound doctrine." "Sound," that means healthy. "Doctrine," that means teaching. Healthy teaching! Healthy teaching! As one has recently said, healthy teaching makes healthy people. There is no healthy teaching that makes sick people, and there is no healthy teaching that does not fill people with the love of Jesus. Paul does not leave us in any question as to what he means by sound doctrine. Paul never refers to "doctrine" in the remotest sense, as speaking of the theological opinions of men. He does define what he means in his letter to Titus. It is temperance, sober-mindedness, faith, love, patience, reverence, love for husbands and children, chastity, industry, obedience and faithfulness of servants, denying ungodliness and worldly lusts, living soberly, righteously and godly in this present world.

In writing to Timothy, Paul says, "If any man teach a different doctrine, and consenteth not to sound words, even to the words of our Lord Jesus Christ, and to the doctrine which is according to godliness, he is proud, knowing nothing, but doting about questions and disputes of words, whence cometh envy, strife, railings, evil surmisings, wranglings of men corrupt in mind and destitute of the truth, supposing that godliness is the way of gain." The word "doting" is given in the margin of the Revised Version as "sick."

The very earliest Church manual we have (The Didache), in connection with the instructions to converts and the way by which they should be received into the Church, gives in contrast, "The Way of Life" and "The Way of Death."

THE WAY OF LIFE

1. Love to God.
2. Your neighbor as yourself.
3. The Golden Rule.
4. The Sermon on the Mount, commencing, "Resist not evil. "
5. Rules about alms-giving.
6. Gross sins forbidden.
7. Other sins forbidden.
8. Various precepts.

THE WAY OF DEATH

The way of death is this: First of all, it is full of evil, and full of curse, murders, adulteries, lusts, idolatries, magic arts, rapines, false witnessings, not pitying a poor man, not laboring for the afflicted, not knowing Him that made them, murders of children, destroyers of the handiwork of God, turning away from him that is in want, afflicting him that is distressed, advocates of the rich, lawless judges of the poor, utter sinners. Be delivered, children, from all these." To be a Christian is to renounce all that one has. The heart of the teaching of Jesus was, "Whosoever be he of you that forsaketh not all that he hath, he cannot be My disciple."

A few years ago I had an idea of the kind of a church I would like to have. I would require that the last penny and the last corner of the house and the business and the last everything be given to Jesus; and I told a brother who is a Christian minister about this and said, "Don't you think that is the kind of a Church we need? I think that is the sort of a Church we ought to have." And he said, "We have all that in our Church covenant now;" and then it occurred to me that we did have most of it in our covenants, but it didn't seem to produce the desired effect. And now I see that the only possible union of value will be the unity of a common purpose inspired by a common spirit.

I have no sort of a contract with my Brother Hillis here. We are doing this work because we want to do the same thing. If we didn't want to do the same thing, no amount of writing would bring us into one heart and one spirit. And what God is looking for is a union of people with a common spirit in a common purpose, that they may accomplish the same result.

In the last place, I believe God is calling His Church to a practical purification and enforcement of the teachings of Jesus.

Benjamin Franklin said that a single generation who practiced the teachings of Jesus would change the face of the earth.

There has been quite a discussion about experiments in Christianity. One man said, "We ought not to condemn it as a failure because it has not been tried." Some people think it was fully tried in the first three centuries. I hardly think that. I think we are ahead of the first three centuries. I think there are people here who would give all their gold and who would die for the name of Jesus. I am sure there are people here who would die for their theological opinions. (Laughter.)

I do not worship the Church as some do. I think we have a better Church today and are going to have a better Church tomorrow. I believe in the

Church. And while I believe that Christianity has been tried just as much as it ever can be tried by an individual alone, yet you cannot try Christianity fully in individual life, any more than Robinson Crusoe could have had a nation and an association with other nations, and national life, all alone on his desert island, before he found his man Friday. Christianity is a society, that is what it is meant to be. We have come to the end of an age and this is a critical time. This is not a "simple gospel." What we need is the adjustment of the principle of peace among men. As Christ said, "How is it that ye do not discern this time?" All lands explored. All tongues known. All religions revealed and compared. We are living in Christian lands on a social volcano that is already smoking for the earth-transforming eruption. Facility of intercourse among men. Development of science suggesting annihilation of time and space, when Peter's vision shall be fulfilled and the elements melt and pass away, and the present physical heavens and earth be destroyed with fervent heat, and men see eye to eye in the revelation of the glory of the King; in the union of the new heavens and the new spiritual earth wherein dwelleth righteousness.

> *"We are living, we are dwelling*
> *In a grand and awful time,*
> *In an age on ages telling;*
> *To be living is sublime."*

I see the moment has come when we usually close our services. I have not yet stated some of the most important things I wanted to say. (Cries of, "Go on! Go on!")

I believe that it is just as true as ever in the world's history that without the shedding of blood there is no remission. And as I say some of these things at the close of this morning, I want you to recall that I have said other things as well, and also to remember this; that as I speak about it, I speak as tenderly and as lovingly and patiently as a child might speak of an afflicted mother. I think a man who would say unkind things of his mother has reached the lowest depths; but if the mother was sick, there might be a loving gathering of friends and sons and daughters, that they might look plainly at the symptoms and see if they might not remove the sickness.

I am a child of the Church and love her, and I believe not only in the past, but in the future, and when we ask the question, "Is the Church ready to fulfill this conception?" I wish I could sink down through the floor rather than be forced to give an answer. "Well," some one says, "How about our year books and our great conventions and great missionary work?" There is much of value in some forms of our Church activity, but it would not make any difference how long or how large a rope was if it were made of sand. The thing that is needed just now is no sort of formal organic union among Christians. We need the mission and spirit and power of Christ. Some one says, "Look to our churches and colleges and hospitals." Some of them are built by money that is the price of blood and by methods that have been born in the darkest pits of hell. The most conspicuous Christian university of this continent, bidding fair to be the greatest Christian school of the world, was built by money drawn from various sources, but most of it money that was gained by the commission of almost every sort of crime that is possible to the hands and heart of man. The largest and most extensive industrial institute of modern times was built by money that was gained by such nefarious traffic in the necessities of life as fairly caused men to die of hunger on account of it! Beloved, does the Church represent Jesus? Does it misrepresent Him? Does it inadequately represent Him? And I answer, "all three."

The great Baptist convention, representing the entire country, comes together and sings the doxology, when it gets a few hundred thousand dollars from the cursed robber of his fellowmen.

I am told that the Methodist Church spent four days at its last quadrennial conference in discussing whether the ministers should occupy seats with the laymen or whether they ought have different places assigned to them in the hall; and they elect their highest officers, some of them, by methods that would disgrace the lowest politician in the country. (A Methodist pastor: "That's so; that's all true.")

The Southern Presbyterian Assembly spent days in awful agony and fever of anxiety for fear that the Endeavor Society would get a greater hold in the South; and that women would learn to speak in meeting. And the Northern Presbyterian Church has spent its time for the last ten years in its greatest conventions in a terrible wrestling (certainly not altogether in the spirit of Jesus), over the question whether two or three men are heretics or not. Now, if they were heretics, we ought to have had life enough in us to cast them out long ago, and if they were not heretics, then the disturbance is undoubtedly worse. What does represent the Church? Are these bodies representatives of the Church of Christ? Are they representatives of Jesus in these performances and lack of performance?

The most distinguished religious body in New York City, the Presbytery of New York, went in a procession, with the most noted minister of New York City at its head, that they might bow their knees before the greatest monumental robber of all the centuries, while they returned humble thanks to him for the gift of ten thousand dollars for city missions. Now his children have built a church, "To the glory of God and in memory of Jay Gould." I believe that the words of Dr. Herron are none too strong when he says that ministers of Christ who can see these things unmoved, and participate in some respects in using the spoils of the corruption, are no better than the priests who used to sail with the pirates in order that they might say mass for the repose of the souls of the dead robbers. I know of one church in New York City that voted by its official board to allow liquor to be sold in one of its buildings because the occupant offered it an increase of three thousand dollars a year in its rents. And I thank God, it lost its pastor by that operation, too. I know of another church in New York where the people actually voted to move away for no other reason than that the people around them were so wicked.

And the most conspicuous church in the United States has been recently soundly rebuked through the courts because it has some of the filthiest and vilest and most degraded and most disease-bringing tenement houses in the city of New York; and it takes the revenues it gets from these places, where they are murdering the people, body and soul, in order to establish missions in the name of Almighty God. How do we administer our churches when we can do that? I said yesterday a word about church trustees. How do we run our churches in regard to financial affairs? I was in a New England city a while ago, in a beautiful home, and the baby was playing with a doll that turned somersaults down an ironing board. She called it "McGinty." I said, "Where did you get it? I want to get one of those for my baby." And she said, "At almost any of the churches (with Laughter)." I said, "Churches! What do you mean?" They said a large proportion of the churches of that town were supported by the sale of "McGinty's." I believe in trustees; you know God made Philip and Stephen trustees of His early Church because they were filled with faith and the Holy Ghost. There is no church that is poor that has men like Philip and Stephen to manage its financial affairs, and no church is rich when it has to have godless men in power anywhere about it.

There are thirteen million young men in this country, and the Y. M. C. A. authorities tell us that only one million of them ever enter a church of Christ. There are two hundred and fifty thousand young men in our prisons and two hundred and thirty thousand women in houses of shame, five hundred thousand young men and young women in prisons and places of shame.

And what influence do we have in politics? We stand by, while godless and tyrannical laws are enacted and the power of the rich and the helplessness of the poor increase with every passing day, and the cursed demons of drink and licensed or tolerated lust, destroying many of the best. The temperance orators say, "Fifty thousand converted by this denomination, and sixty-five thousand drunkards' graves." Some one stands up and says, "What are you preaching that to a Christian audience for? We don't drink the liquor." No, we do not, but we are responsible for other people drinking it. (Applause). The security of the saloon and the distillery and the gambling house and the brothel is founded in the indifference and the selfishness and the cowardice of the people who profess to believe in Christ. (Great applause). I said the other day I feared there were members of churches in your city co - operating in this movement who gained revenue from open gambling houses and places of shame. I have not been able to make a complete investigation, but a little one only. I took four blocks and found twenty-two houses in which there was open gambling. You can almost fire a rifle into the first of them from the place where you are sitting. I want to tell you a joyful thing. I have investigated twenty-two owners of the property and I do not find one church member on the list. (Great applause).

I am going to tell you who does own some of this property. One of the men who owns one of these gambling houses is a trustee of one of the leading churches in this city. Four of them are owned by presidents of banks in this city; one of them is owned by an ex-sheriff; one of them is owned by the wife of an ex-judge and another is owned by an ex-judge himself. One of them is owned by the heirs of the estate of one of your prominent attorney generals. I have not been able to investigate all the rest, but while I am told that none of these others are members of the Church, they are, some of them, people that hold up their head and associate with you in your society as some of your most prominent citizens.

I have not spoken these things because I despise the Church, but because I love it. "Let my tongue cleave to the roof of my mouth if I prefer not Jerusalem above my chief joy." Not because I am a pessimist, but because I am an optimist; not because I am an infidel, but because I believe in God and His promises, and know the over-turning is bound to come, and that speedily; because I think I see the opportunity of the Church. Unless we, the ministers of Christ, are true to Him in our own self-renunciation and the fearless proclamation of the full teachings of Jesus, unless the Church shall cease to elevate the rich and fail to minister to the poor, unless like the Father, she shall cast down the proud and give grace to the humble; unless she shall cease gazing up into heaven and saying, "Lord, Lord," and failing to do the things which He says, then God will have new witnesses who will fulfill His will and lead the world into its rightful inheritance of peace. "And think not to say, ' We have Abraham to our Father,' for I say unto you that God is able even of these stones, to raise up children unto Abraham." "But beloved, I am persuaded better things of you and things that accompany salvation, though I thus speak."

I find in a magazine a most appropriate word for the closing thought: "When Napoleon was crossing the Alps, his army sometimes grew laggard in the way. He ordered the music to play. This was enough for most of those in the ranks. But some there were who still toiled on, spiritless and forlorn. These at last he put by themselves in one vast battalion. Still confident in the use of his singular expedient, he bade the bands play for them the home songs of France, that the thought of sunny scenes behind might kindle the men's enthusiasm. That succeeded very well with many of the sad platoons. Yet still there remained a class among the rest whose drooping was inveterate. Finally the great commander marshaled these into a troop by themselves once more. Suddenly he ordered the trumpets to sound the charge of battle. This was a thing no French soldier ever refused. Wild indeed was the fire which ran thro that hitherto dispirited host. They knew nothing of the way in which the instant engagement had been sprung upon them, nor just where lay the foe. What they did know was that the clang which was pealing through the mountain solitude's meant war.

I am sure there is a lesson in this. Most men need some inspiration in religious life to keep them up. Songs of home and songs of heaven will do much; but the day arrives to many when only summons, peremptory and sharp, will arouse them. The blast of a war-cry, the trumpet of the Church militant, alone can make the hearts kindle which before were low," and lead us to the final victory.

Christianity and Socialism

THIRD AVENUE METHODIST CHURCH

Where the Meetings in the North District were held

"The communion of the Holy Ghost be with you all." -II Corinthians, 21:14.

I think we shall all see the appropriateness of this text before the close of this meeting. There are just three views that are possible concerning the relationship of Socialism and Christianity. The first is that they differ and are entirely distinct from one another. The second is that they are naturally hostile in their aims and methods, and the third is that there is a relationship between them that would suggest co-operation and possible identification. The first view is held only by the ignorant, reactionary or pietistic Christian, or by the narrow, selfish, materialistic Socialist. There have indeed been some pure minds who have had a conception of Christianity as strictly individualistic, and who have looked at the aims and power of the spirit of Christ only in its relationship to individuals. Some of these would place the Christian religion as a high form of development in a progression of religions, but would say that it fails to provide for the proper association of men and is in time to be superseded or complemented by a larger religion that shall grow out of it, which shall provide for the association of men under all possible relationships. But almost all the Christians, who are now worthy of the name, have come to see that the aim of Christ is not simply to produce a pure individual in a personal sense, but to produce the right individual for the sake of a righteous society; and I am sure that by far the larger proportion of the true-hearted followers of the humble Nazarene would join me in saying that if I had to choose between being a Socialist in the spirit of Christ, but without His name, or being an unsocial Christian, I would be more loyal to Him in the former choice than in the latter. But we are living in a day when such choice is not a necessity for men, but where he who chooses to carry out the plans of Jesus cannot but be one of the elect, entering into the perplexities and bearing away the sins of society. Regarding the second theory, that Christianity and Socialism are essentially hostile, it might suffice to say that it would be easy to so define them as to make them seem essentially antagonistic. There is an old story about two divines who had bitter discussions concerning certain theological questions that ended in serious enmity, when finally one of them brought to the other a book and said: "As we cannot talk in free discussion without quarreling, I have brought you a book which exactly expresses my views, which I beseech you to read, and you will then know my opinions without any necessity for a break in our friendship." The other minister burst into a laugh and said: "Why, I wrote that book myself for the purpose of expressing the exact views with which I thought yours were in conflict." There is an old saying that "definition is the end of controversy," and it is certainly true that the best definitions of Christianity and Socialism, instead of causing them to seem hostile, one to the other, would reveal principles of unity that are necessary to both. This brings us to the third theory that they are naturally related, and in some respects identical in their aims and methods, and we might say, interdependent. The fact is that neither Christianity as at present conceived, nor Socialism as at present represented, will either of them attain the fulness of its mission, the one without the other, and it is possible to so define them as to make them seem identical. For instance: Proudhon, one of the authorities on Socialism, says that it is "every aspiration toward the improvement of society." Adolph Held defines as socialistic "every tendency which demands the subordination of the individual to the community;" and while we may not recognize this as a complete definition of Christianity, we certainly could see that it is one of its most prominent characteristics. The fact is that Socialism will have to be Christianized in order to have any possibility of success, and that, as I have already suggested, Christianity is social from the very necessity of the conquest of society which it contemplates. Both deal with the same problems; both anticipate the same results, when the perfect individual shall exist in the perfect society; but it is also true that both have extravagant and unrepresentative forms, and that both of them suffer from the misrepresentations of their so-called friends as much as from the falsifications and detraction's of their adversaries. Kirkup, in the Encyclopedia Britannica, says the aim of Socialism is to "terminate the divorce of the workers from the natural sources of subsistence and culture," by making land and capital "the property of society, to be managed by it for the general good." This would probably be recognized by most advanced Socialists only as a very limited definition; and it may here be said that there are as many sects in Socialism as there are in Christianity; and to say that a man is a Socialist is no more definite than to say that a man is a Christian when he may mean that he is a Roman or a Greek Catholic, or that he belongs to any one of the numerous divisions of Protestantism, or possibly only that he is not a Heathen or an Israelite. But the more

I give my mind to the best words that have been written on these great themes, and to the meditation upon them in the spirit of Christ, the more am I thoroughly convinced that there may be and must be a Socialism which shall be thoroughly and wholly Christian, and that without such a possibility there can be no hope for the final improvement or humanity. And while it is true that the larger Socialism includes the spiritual view of things, we may. for the purposes of this sermon, define Socialism at present, "as the hope and plan and effort for the administration of material things, with a just regard for the greatest good of the greatest number." And the fact is that now we are surrounded by many practical developments of modern life that are thoroughly Socialistic. The very fact of the existence of a government "of the people, by the people, and for the people," is a Socialistic achievement. The administration of such a monopoly as the post office, and in some countries and communities the control of the telegraph and telephone and railroads and water and light, as well as the establishment and support of public schools, are all indications of what is being accomplished in a Socialistic way, in the strictest as well as in the largest sense. There have been some cities, such, for instance, as Birmingham, in England, where, under the mayoralty of Joseph Chamberlain, the city indulged in a little speculation in land on its own account. The original procuring of this land by the city was for the purposes of public health and morality, and they took possession of a district of wretched buildings, occupied by still more wretched people, analogous to, but probably not so degraded as the lowest district that exists in the heart of this capital city. They tore down the old rookeries and erected appropriate and sanitary buildings in their places, with the result that this portion of the city was so transformed, that the Sinking Fund, caused by the surplus rents of the buildings erected by the city, has, I think, entirely paid the original cost; and there is now a probability of a revenue great enough to give to the citizens free water, free artificial light, and possibly, free transportation upon the city railroads, or a great enlargement of the public parks, or of the school system, or other institutions of general advantage. It should be distinctly understood that there is no reasonable Socialism that bears the

106

slightest resemblance to Anarchism. In fact the vital principles of the two are radically opposed-as the one is destructive and the other constructive. It should also be understood that Socialism, as held by its leading advocates, does not contemplate any sort of robbery of property, nor injustice; but that it has in mind only the establishment of the highest justice in the equal opportunity and the good of the multitude. It has grown into being as a natural re-action from the teachings of the Reformation, which emphasized only the value and rights of the individual. The ordinary Socialist does not depreciate the individualistic regime of the past, nor does he fail to see that it has accomplished, in many respects, the most beneficent results, but he holds that as serfdom was an improvement upon slavery, so individualism is an improvement upon serfdom, and he believes that Socialism is to be the final achievement and permanent condition of the human race on earth. He suggests motives in various ways, that, so far as he ignores the Christian spirit, seem to me entirely inadequate for the accomplishment of the results he has in mind. As for example, his hope for a general diffusion of the necessary unselfishness of humanity for the carrying out of his plan, is without foundation and is more mysterious in all its suggestions than many of the mystical theories of the Middle Ages. And while his hope for the general tempering of the spirit of men with altruism by the effect of agitation, and the influence of such reforms as may be accomplished in producing future reformations, has undoubtedly in it a suggestion of power, it is a power that must be supplied by itself and cannot very well be generated from without. Now, on the other hand, if we were to try to define Christianity, we would find a great deal more difficulty than in giving a satisfactory characterization of Socialism. Let it suffice to say that in the sense in which I shall use the term today, that I mean the transformation of the world is righteousness and love through sacrifice, as manifested and taught by Jesus the Son of God. The great theory which a Christian needs today is the realization that Jesus was the Son of God, and the Son of Man, and that we, too, being the sons of men, are called to realize that thereby we may enter into the full inheritance of the Sons of God; and for present purposes I should be willing to accept the definition of Professor Hennon in one of his classic works on the Higher Evangelism, where he says that "he is a Christian who organizes his life to save rather than to be saved from the evils that he sees devouring the world." The French Socialists of 1850 put a picture of Jesus on their walls with the subscription, "Jesus of Nazareth, the first representative of the people." Rudolph Todt says, "Whoever would understand the Social question, and contribute to its solution, must have on his right hand the works of political economy and on his left the works of scientific Socialism, and must have his New Testament open before him." Kirkup says, "The ethics of Socialism are closely akin to the ethics of Christianity, if not identical with them." F. W. Sprague says that "private capital, freedom of contract, and free competition, all move as satellites about self-interest." "Individualism is pure industrial anarchy, minus violence." "Socialism is a new science of political economy. Its object is to realize the ethics of the religion of Jesus Christ in the possession of economic goods. The capitalistic system, by its gross inequality in the distribution of wealth, has been the archenemy of this ethical principle. Socialism is an evolution. It is related to capitalism as the butterfly to the chrysalis, as Christianity to Judaism, or as democracy to monarchy. Both Judaism and monarchy have done good service, but they have had their day; the same is true of capitalism as an economy. Society will no longer tolerate its old dogmas respecting private property, freedom of contract and free competition; its conception of the State as a mere political institution, of labor as a mere commodity, its necessary conclusion that money is of more consequence than men, that might makes right, that men, being unequal, must take the consequences of their inequality, that some may justly live in idleness and luxury, while others toil and starve, that the social grist of vice, crime, want and misery, ground out by the economic laws of capitalism, is necessary and natural, and that the only way for the individual to save halftime is to thicken his competitive armor and secure a new advantage over his weaker brother. These dogmas, while they prepared the way for a better order, have at length become so offensive to the prevailing sense of right as to be no longer tolerable." To all of which I say, "Amen." Professor Commons, of Syracuse University, one of the ablest of our young political economists, said in my hearing: "I became an atheist when I studied theology, and I became a Christian when I studied sociology." It is probable that by this time you have begun to comprehend my thought and purpose in endeavoring to show you that Christianity and Socialism are not antagonistic in any real sense, but on the contrary are naturally related. Christianity without the conception of Socialism will fail in her mission, and Socialism without the inspiration and instruction and modification of Christianity will be but the most impracticable sort of a dream. We are not meant to lose and we never shall lose the magnificent inspiration of the Sixteenth century, that put the proper value upon the individual; and the whole problem of the Twentieth century and of the world's history, concerns not a submerging of the individual into characterless association with his fellows, but the voluntary socializing of the individual man by the possession of the spirit of the loving sacrifice of Christ. The spirit that says, "All mine is thine," is to be born only from a conception of good that is revealed on Calvary alone, and is to be perfected by the reception of such a Holy Spirit as was given the disciples of Jesus upon the day of Pentecost. It seemed to them upon that occasion, and for some time thereafter, that the possession of this spirit had relation to their communion in material things, as indicated by the words of the Sacred Book, which tell us: "That all that believed were together, and had all things common; and sold their possessions and goods, and parted them to all men, as every man had need." This was the original practical "communion of the Holy Ghost," and there are those who think that it was this practical voluntary fellowship in material things that caused the coining of this benediction which is still used in our form of worship in every Christian communion today. While this may not be true, it is certain that the glory of Christianity is this Holy Spirit, which leads to voluntarily sacrifice for those who have need, in a manner that is far removed from the spirit that would require an unwilling yielding of possessions into the hands of others. And it is also certain to every sane thinker that Socialism can never gain one substantial victory except through the reception by men, of this same Holy Spirit that was manifested on the cross and indicated in the unselfishness of the early Christians. The one great idea, the one clear experience, the one inspiriting and inspiring power, that will ever make Socialism more than an iridescent phantasm, will be this communion of the Holy Ghost. I would say this then: That the great contribution of Christianity for the transformation of society, beyond the highest form of any Christ-less Socialism, would be from three sources: FIRST: Christianity takes account of sin as manifested in human selfishness. There have been those who have criticised Socialism as immoral, but its calmest historian has well said that "it would be a more reasonable criticism to say that it inculcates an unselfishness unattainable by any probable development of human nature." Unless there may be some method by which all forms of selfishness may be eradicated from the individual, the final social triumph of men will be an impossibility. While in some respects it may be more satisfactory on principles of poetic justice to see the few governed by the many, rather than the many controlled by the few, it is clear to the best observers that the selfish rule of the unintelligent many would probably be a more terrible experience for humanity than the selfish government of the intelligent few, and would ultimately result in an oligarchy that would be the most tyrannical and despotic of history. Why should we get the idea that God would any more tolerate the oppression of the few by the multitude than the grinding of the multitude between the upper and nether millstones of the few? An employer of thousands of workmen wrote a letter to the New York Tribune, at the time of the great Brooklyn street car strike, under date of January 25, 1895, in which he closes a remarkable communication with these words: "Disguise it as we may, industrial society is divided into two vast armies hostile to one another-like armies, imputing to one another unfair and generally false motives-misinterpreting each other's acts, and trying to use their legislative power, by fair means and foul, to curb their opponents' power and to thwart their opponents' plans. Meanwhile, the people at large look on, more or less bewildered, trying, in a helpless, hapless way, to devise some legislative remedy, and at last losing their temper and coercing by strong measures the side which they conceive for the moment to be lacking in proper respect for their (the people's) convenience, and for the law, as it stands on the statute books." There is also a dim suspicion in the public mind that the very existence of the State is being jeopardized by the quarrel. Meanwhile the philosophers are assuring us that association is one of the highest attributes of the human society, and that the present struggle is only one phase of that "social evolution" through which man rises from the brutal state of individual selfishness to the higher and useful state of collective helpfulness and happiness. It does not follow that the philosopher is wrong because in the struggle so much selfishness is evoked, and because selfish individuals and selfish classes are exerting every nerve to avert the consummation. For, if philosophers read the Good Book a little more, they would find that it says exactly the same thing, only in different language, when it enunciates the law that "God maketh the wrath of man to praise Him, and the remainder of wrath He will restrain." It is quite evident that some restraint must be exerted. Upon whom? And by whom? Time will show. It will not necessarily be upon the poor, who, driven to despair, injudiciously throw stones and cut trolley-wires, but, possibly. on the presidents, who in the board-room, regardless of the convenience of the people, who have foolishly granted them valuable franchises, are almost controlled blind, with what the old theologians called "judicial blindness," to the ultimate consequence of the course they are pursuing, in exciting the passions to reckless fury, of a class which, by force of numbers, holds absolute political power, and will assuredly, sooner or later, use it. today it may be possible for men like the Brooklyn presidents and Mr. Pullman to calmly suppress all appeals and arguments by denying that there is any thing to arbitrate. There are, however, only two presidents to six thousand trolley-men, and one Pullman to ten thousand employees. Does there never cross the minds of the presidents and Pullmans the faintest shade of a suspicion that the day will come when the thousands will be their masters, and that these thousands will, in even fewer words, decline to arbitrate, but subject their former masters to a harsher treatment than they are themselves today receiving?" To give men political equality and industrial despotism is to store dynamite for an earth-transforming explosion. The only possible reconciliation will be the Christianizing of the individual, who shall gain a rational conception of the purposes and character of God, and shall give himself in glad submission to the purging of selfishness from humanity, by the practical yielding of himself to the spirit of the cross of Christ. SECOND: The primary need of men is spiritual rather than material. There are some radical Socialists who hold that all men's selfishness is caused by the fear of want, and who tell us that even Jay Gould trembled until the last moment of his life from a conviction that he was at last to be reduced to poverty, and that he continued his terrible cruelties to men, and hoarding of his illicit gains with the thought to protect himself against such a catastrophe. But clear illustrations will readily occur to all of us in which we could not conceive that a man's mind had been at all distressed from fear of possible poverty, and yet where he has shown himself to be possessed of the spirit of anarchy and hell. Nero could not have conceived of his coming to physical want, and yet he manifested such a spirit as has rarely been indicated outside of the confines of the lost world. And there is no theory that will be of value in considering the welfare of society that does not have for its motto that "man's life consisteth not in the abundance of the things that he possesseth," and does hot utter fearlessly the statement that "man shall not live by bread alone, but by every word that proceedeth out of the mouth of God." There are three bonds of union that may be suggested among men-physical, intellectual and spiritual. Regarding the first, we realize that the ties that bind men may be most easily broken. After the great Industrial Exposition of 1851 in England, the peace of forty years was broken, and Europe was filled with armies costing untold millions; and it would not need a philosopher to tell us that intellectual unity may be most selfish and disastrous; and while it is true that Christianity produces and stimulates the physical and intellectual development of mankind, it is also true that the regeneration of the individual or society can only be accomplished when it shall be "born from above," so that it may see the possibility of the reign of love, which is another name for the kingdom of God. We have been justly repelled by mechanical and fictitious theories concerning the salvation of the souls of men, but the great lesson that the Twentieth century must learn is that "it shall profit a man nothing if he shall gain the whole world and lose his own soul," and that there is nothing that a man can "give in exchange for his soul." Neither the individual nor society will be saved in any fashion except by the spiritualizing of conception and practice; and all the labor of man will be utterly thrown away that does not take into account as its chief endeavor, both in the material and intellectual world, as well as directly in the department of religion, the saving of the soul. If you could save the soul of the Turk, he would be the proprietor of one of the fairest and most fruitful lands on earth. If you could save the soul of the African, the Great Desert would indeed "be made to rejoice and blossom as the rose." If you could save the soul of the Irishman, and the soul of the Englishman, the distraction of years would cease and the tyranny of centuries would be a thing of the past. If you could save the soul of the statesman, the manufacturer, and the merchant and the operative and the clerk, of the farmer and the lawyer, all of the problems of modern life would be simpler than the Rule of Three. And if you could save the souls of the citizens of Columbus, you might have a community that would be worthy to be called a City of God, instead of having men in your places of authority who represent the worst elements existent in the community and who neither fear the righteous judgment of God nor the aroused conscience of law-abiding men. And every theory concerning the regeneration of society in the ministry to the poor, the elevation of the ignorant and Christianization of the powerful, will be utterly useless unless it includes the great invitation by which you shall say: "Come home to your Father's house." In the last place, Christianity emphasizes not only the ultimate perfection of society but the value of the individual and his relationship to God. I have already referred to this subject. But the Christian conception of the individual and his relationship to his fellows is the only one that can cause the righting of the wrongs of men and the producing of the reign of peace. It is only Christianity that teaches men to hallow the name of Father, and there is nothing that men need to realize more than that there can be no fatherless brotherhood. If Jesus is not divine the social problem is insoluble. If he is not thoroughly human there remains nothing for men but despair. The progress of revelation has been through the manifestation of the character of God through the revealing of God's relationship to man and man to God, under the present dispensation of the Holy Ghost which concerns man's fellowship with man. The first lesson was learned by the Israelites in their existence as a separate nation; the second lesson was taught us through the incarnation and Calvary; the third lesson by the Holy Ghost. If there be any meaning in Calvary and in Pentecost, it is the affirming that the only value that man possesses may be realized alone by the giving of himself away; and the inspiration of a right relationship with God, for personal purity, for unselfishness and for an adequate sacrifice for humanity, may come only from the communion of the Holy Ghost. With a spirit born on Calvary, nurtured by the Holy Ghost, perfected by the blood of the martyrs and the self-denial of all who have wrought in the spirit of Jesus, with the largest hope, with undying zeal, with crucifixial consecration, do I call you to give your lives to the uprooting of every social wrong, to the establishing of right relations between man and man, to the planting and harvesting of the good fruits of the kingdom of God. I have heard of a Heathen deity who refused to be saved unless all could be saved; and he might well have been named with the title of Immanuel. Jesus said: "My Father worketh hitherto, and I work." And our call is to be workers together with God, until the consummation of all into one body, Christ the Head, "till we all come in the unity of the faith and of the knowledge of the Son of God, unto a perfect man," and "the love of God, and the grace of our Lord Jesus Christ, and the communion of the Holy Ghost, shall be and abide with us all. Amen." And the Socialist and Christian may unite in a common creed in the beautiful words of the poet:

Love thyself last. Look near; behold thy duty
To those who walk beside thee down life's road;
Make glad their days by little acts of beauty,
And help them bear the burden of earth's load.

Love thyself last. Look far, and find the stranger
Who staggers' neath his sin and his despair;
Go lend a hand and lead him out of danger,

To heights where he may see the world is fair.

Love thyself last. The vastnesses above thee
Are filled with Spirit Forces, strong and pure.
And fervently, these faithful friends shall love thee,
Keep thou thy watch o'er others, and endure.

Love thyself last; and oh, such joy shall thrill thee
As never yet such selfish souls was given.
Whatever thy lot, a perfect peace will fill thee
And earth shall seem the anteroom of heaven.

Love thyself last; and thou shalt grow in spirit
To see, to hear, to know and understand.
The message of the stars, lo, thou shalt hear it,
And all God's joys shall be at thy command.

Love thyself last. The world shall be made better
By thee, if this brief motto forms thy creed.
Go follow it in spirit and in letter,
This is the Christ religion which men need.

-Ella Wheeler Wilcox

THIRD AVENUE METHODIST CHURCH

Where the Meetings in the North District were held

III

Proceedings of the Christian Convention

Held in Columbus, Ohio, Dec. 3 to 6, 1895

Morning sessions in the First Congregational Church; afternoon sessions in the Second Presbyterian Church.

Topic for Tuesday, Dec. 3 - "The Sins of the City."

The convention was opened with devotional exercises conducted by Rev. S. W. Seeman; the chairman of the convention, Rev. B. Fay Mills, then introduced the first speaker, Dr. C. O. Probst, Secretary of the State Board of Health, who spoke as follows on ***"Evils in Material Conditions."***

Evils in Material Conditions

Dr. C. O. Probst

There was a time in the history of the Church when one might have presumed that on such an occasion he would be expected to say that all material conditions are necessarily evil; that the flesh must be mortified, and the eyes turned from all but spiritual things. The broad and enlightened Church of today, and the selection of a worker in another field to address you, give assurance that the real thought in the minds of those who chose this topic for discussion was, the results-moral as well as physical-of evil material conditions.

Evil associations corrupt good manners, we are told, and experience proves this true. By "associations" is usually meant moral or spiritual relationships; but it may well include "material" surroundings; and in looking after man's spiritual welfare it should not be forgotten that physical or material conditions make for or against his spiritual advancement. When body and soul are sundered death comes, and in dealing with vital questions concerning living men let us not attempt to put asunder what God has joined together.

Man has largely lost the animal instinct which tends to self-preservation, and must depend on reason to guide him in his selection of food, raiment, and habitation, i. e., his material surroundings. But how often do we see men doing the most unreasonable things in regard to these essentials of life.

To consider food. -The majority of men do not know how or what to eat, and the women, many of them - pardon me for saying it-do not appreciate the vital necessity of having food properly prepared. Dyspepsia is one of the demons of American life, and is the penalty paid to bad cooking and hurried, intemperate eating.

A dyspeptic is unfitted for both the moral and physical duties of life. He is apt to make his home unpleasant, to fail in winning the confidence and sympathy of his children, and to be cross to his wife. The world is looked at through a bilious haze, and he would often rather be out of it than in it. It has seemed to me in some cases that it were better he were out of it.

Indigestion has another moral aspect. A craving for stimulants frequently goes with this affection. An appetite is whipped up with alcoholics, and they are again resorted to to allay the pain and distress arising from the imperfect digestion of food. Occasionally narcotics are used for the purpose, and the opium habit may be formed. DeQuincy, you will remember, was driven to opium by dyspepsia. And though his "Confessions" have taken a permanent place in literature, something better, he would doubtless have given us, under the stimulus of a healthy digestion.

But not only is man injured by badly selected and illy prepared food-he is in constant danger form its adulteration. This nefarious practice has grown to gigantic proportions. Nothing is held sacred by the adulterator; not even the wine used in the holy ceremonies of communion.

What is the moral condition of the man who intentionally introduces poisonous or injurious substances into food products to be sent broadcast throughout the land? Let us hope that those of you who are the moral guides of mankind will bring this sin home to these men.

You will say, "These are material conditions." Indeed; but we cannot ignore the stomach. Let us rather look with sacredness on this human laboratory where the coarser elements of food, in God's mysterious way, are endowed with life and feeling, and even influence the soul. For we cannot escape the fact that a man may be made worse, morally, by the food he eats.

Take alcohol, which is akin to food products, and which is, to a limited extent, a food. With this stimulant coursing through a man's brain with the circulating blood, how changed are his views of life and of his moral responsibilities. How rapidly he goes through the stages of first enduring, then pitying and then embracing vice. And undoubtedly there are other products of fermentation elaborated when digestion is badly impaired, which lower moral as well as physical tone.

Think of this, ye wives and mothers who minister to your husbands' and children's material wants. Do not despise the science of good cooking, for the happiness, and the moral welfare of your dear ones depend, to some degree, upon the material food you give them. Let us remember, too, that in supporting those who are in authority who are fighting for pure food, we are protecting even more than the pockets and health of the people; for pure food tends to pure morals.

Raiment, the second of the sanitary trinity mentioned, is not without influence on moral conditions. As a sanitist I have no right, perhaps, to consider clothing except as conducive to health, but I cannot forbear remarking upon some of the features of raiment which are not only prejudicial to health but to morals.

My lady in her decollete evening dress may be a "thing of beauty," but is apt to be not a "joy forever." A young couple of my acquaintance united in the holy bonds of matrimony. She was an interesting, beautiful woman, the picture of health, and he was in every way her equal. It was a pleasure to witness their growing happiness under the expanding influence of married love. A few short months of enjoyment and the wife was laid away in her burial garments: the result of imprudent dressing, or rather undressing. Let all things be done decently and in order, even dressing. I saw it recently announced that in Chicago-that city of sin-thirty young ladies, dressed in bloomer costume, would attend a certain church in a body. Alas: what must be said of "material conditions" when our churches resort to such a bid for attendance.

A highly sensational divorce suit in Columbus, which our papers have delighted in parading before their readers, grew out of familiarities, it is reported, only possible at bathing resorts. A ballet dancer being taken to task for the shortness of her skirts, by a reformer, who was also a society woman, retorted that the only difference between her dress and that of her monitor was that hers was cut short below while the society woman's was cut short above. But what shall we say of the modern bathing dress, cut short at both ends? Let us remember that the human form is divine, and treat it with due sacredness.

How often do we meet with the motto, "God bless our home;" and yet how often do we miss this blessing because our homes are not constructed or kept in conformity with His laws-light and air, nature's great vivifiers, are religiously excluded from many homes. Uncomfortable and unaired beds rob one of sleep and poison his respiratory system. Slovenly, untidy rooms lessen his sense of order, which a high moral nature should possess. A healthy, happy home, flooded with fresh air and sunlight, with a cheerful, contented wife, and a lot of rosy cheeked children, is a moral anchor which every man in this great struggle for existence needs to keep him fast to all that is best in life. These are material conditions in which there is no evil; a foretaste of the heavenly home where all is love and peace.

The physical evils resulting from bad material conditions are more obvious, and are deserving of the attention of all classes of men. The laws of health are as inexorable as the laws of morals, and no one can disobey them and escape punishment. Within my memory public meetings have been held by our churches to offer prayers to stop the pestilence of yellow fever; but the laws of the physical world, at least, cannot be set at naught by supplication. Fire will burn and destroy, although a martyr's faith may stop the pain.

God has given us in abundance pure water and pure air, the two great essentials of health, but man in his blind ignorance has gone on polluting and corrupting these; and hundreds of thousands yearly pay the penalty with sickness and death.

This city has recently been scourged with typhoid fever, due to the use of impure water,, and more than twenty homes have been made desolate during the past two months by the loss of loved ones from this disease. Many other cities suffered from the same cause, and this is, to some degree, a yearly occurrence.

Is it not an outrage against humanity and an offense against all decency that cities should be permitted to pour their filthy sewage into the streams and lakes which must furnish our drinking water? And in spite of all prayers the Lord will continue to scourge the people who sin thus against His laws.

One-seventh of all the human race in so-called civilized countries is dying or will die of that great white plague-consumption. Think of this awful slaughter, and then remember that it might be prevented! While the ingenuity of man has discovered the exciting cause to be a vegetable parasite - a germ - the ultimate cause is largely bad ventilation, the pollution of the atmosphere we breathe. In the home, at the office, in the workshop, in the schools, and even in our churches, heaven's pure air is denied us, and we suffer and die.

Do not forget that health is the natural condition of man; sickness is the punishment for disobedience of the laws that govern it. Not administered in anger; nor as an act of justice, but by an all-kind, all-loving Hand, which seeks thereby to guide us into ways of right living. We must know His will and do it; there is no other way to salvation, neither in the physical nor moral world.

You who are attempting to lift men's souls up into the pure light of heaven should lend a helping hand to those who are looking after their bodies. Evils in material conditions lead to spiritual evils. Pure water, pure air, pure food, are material foundations for a pure heart. And let us not forget that in sanitary matters (is it not also true of spiritual relations?) every man is his brother's keeper. My neglect may not only bring punishment upon myself but upon my neighbor. The slums of a great city are the hot-beds of disease wherein arise the pestilences which sweep over the land and spare not the homes in more fortunate surroundings. Let all men, therefore, recognize their moral responsibility for removing the evils of material conditions which bring not only sickness and death, but which imperil man's immortal spirit and bar his progress to that higher life which, believe we as we may, is the hope of all mankind.

First Congregational Church
74 East Broad Street

DISCUSSION

REV. S. W. SEEMAN: I would like to find out where we can get pure water and where the blame all lies.

DR. PROBST: That would require a very long explanation and I think most of the people of Columbus are aware that the blame lies with our city government in failing to carry out the wishes of the people. It has been known for many years that Columbus has had a bad water supply. More people die in Columbus from typhoid fever than in any other city in the State according to the population, and they attempted to force on us a water supply that was far worse than we now have. This has now been abandoned, and they are now planning to get the water from the Scioto river by damming it four or five miles above the city. This is the only available place that will supply a sufficient quantity. The people of America do not realize that the water which flows in our streams is not fit to drink. In the European countries they rarely drink "raw water" (and most of our water is "raw"). It should be purified.

REV. HENRY STAUFFER: Is boiling a safeguard, doctor?

DR. PROBST: Yes, sir.

MR. MILLS: I am sure there could be no more important subject, if "cleanliness is next to godliness," than to make not only the outside of us but also the inside of us clean.

* * *

The Rev. T. G. Dickinson, pastor of King Avenue Methodist Church, then addressed the Convention on "Educational Defects."

Educational Defects

Rev. T. G. Dickinson

Following is the address in part:
Our whole conception of life has grown more and more secular; this stands before us now, but to my mind it never was the design of the founders of our Republic, or the fathers of our institutions. But the religious element has been steadily pushed out of our institutions, and it disappeared from our educational work some years ago, and even when we held to the practice of reading a little Scripture in our schools, it was simply the clinging to a custom after the life and spirit had departed. Our schools have partaken of the purely secular character of all our institutions. A writer has said, "Our schools are analogous to our civil government-a secular government administered in Christian lands by Christian men will act on Christian principles, and so a school without a verse of the Bible, in a Christian city, and taught by Christian teachers, will be, in a true sense, a Christian school, full of Christian spirit." I believe this is true, and therefore I advocate, first of all, a school board composed exclusively of Christian men and women; not a board of sectarian mould, but positively Christian, full of that devoted business sense and loving zeal so pronounced in the "Man of Galilee."

A second defect in our educational work is the employment of irreligious teachers. "The school," says an author, "is the most sensitive point of a community after the family." If this be true, and I believe it is, does it not copy the tone and color of its governors and instructors? In Columbus we have many noble, Christian teachers, true Christians, but for these our schools would be a positive curse to our city and a menace to our government, and a bar to the progress of the Church. But there are teachers of my acquaintance who are not in sympathy with the spirit of religion; there are those who, as teachers of teachers, use the public office in denouncing the principles of the Christian religion as embodied in the life and character of Christ. Truth and personality are the two chief elements in teaching; if truth is imparted to the scholar through a strong Christian personality the scholar not only imbibes truth, but also the charms and strength of a Christian personality and then the school is Christian indeed and blesses the homes represented by the scholars.

We should pay more attention to music and should sing a loftier type of song. Our schools need a book that will teach in song what Rev. George D. Herron calls the "larger Christ, We should pay" the Christ of the school and the State, the Christ as He stands related to all the social, political and economical questions of our day. We need to sing a song that teaches a religion of man's humanity to man, a religion more near and real to human life; a song in which there is no dogmatic narrowness, but one whose mission is to make men; then there will be hope of making the religion of Jesus Christ flow through education and by this channel enter every other department in life in which go the pupils of the schools.

A fourth defect in our educational system is the absence of a text-book in Grammar and High School of Ethical Christianity. If character be the man, teach character. We suffer today, if ruled by men void of moral character. To correct this, teach a positive ethics, such as Bishop Martensen, D. S. Gregory, Adolph Wuttke, Hugh Price Hughes, or Bordan P. Bowne simplified to meet the necessity of all grades of scholars. "The State," says a writer, "is a divine organism, it is the offspring of God." Then the motive of the state should be to teach righteousness through her schools. This should be a ruling principle in our school system, not to teach a religious phraseology but stand for what Christ stood while He lived-stand for the principle that today the cross stands for.

A fifth defect is the absence of Christian biography. I would introduce a few "Beacon Lights" in history, the lives of such men and women as have been conspicuous in the formation of governments, the maintaining of statesmanship, advancing of business, creating the home and planting the Church of Christ, Such study is an inspiration to be and do that which is noble and right. As it is, a child, if asked to mention a few great men of Massachusetts, will mention Gen. Benjamin Butler and forget Bishop Phillips Brooks.

A special effort should be made to teach unselfishness. Nothing is so positively Christian as unselfishness, from which grows the spirit of altruism. A child is first taught to get ahead, be first, render no assistance to another - this becomes life's principle. Our marking system may be at fault in a measure. I have thought it might be modified and in higher schools dispensed with altogether.

God should be kept before the scholar, not as matter or force, but as a personality, a Father interested in all His children, and to whom His children are accountable. We need today the idea of God kept at the front of our thinking and acting. Teach this in childhood and a nation of atheists cannot be and our schools can never be styled "The godless public schools." The next paper was by Rev. F. E. Marsten, D. D., Pastor of Broad Street Presbyterian Church. He spoke, in part, as follows, on "Domestic Sins."

Domestic Sins

Rev. F. E. Marsten, D. D.

F irst, I will mention, the traps society sets for the feet of the young in the city.

The maintenance of the saloon, the gambling den, the brothel, is a sin against the home.

Let a man build a beautiful home and adorn it with all that wealth, art, and culture can suggest; if he lets the noxious gases of the sewer pour into it all the loveliness that mind has created cannot prevent the dance of disease, destruction and death within its walls.

We make our homes the centers of religion, morality, purity, and then turn into them the baleful influences that flow from these fountains of evil.

If the home itself becomes tainted and corrupt, whom have we to thank but ourselves and our indifference to terrible evils entrenched at our doors.

When I left the church last Sabbath night with its atmosphere of peace, purity, and piety, not far away I found a woman heart-broken and weeping, with her little child clinging to her at the very door of a saloon. She had gone to the sacred service. And while we were pleading for God, home, and religion, her husband had been deluded into this trap of death and hell. It is an awful sin that society, that the Christian Church, allows these menaces to peace and love to plant themselves at the very gates of home and pour their inky tides into its crystal stream.

Think, too, of the corrupt and corrupting literature we allow to flow with impunity, a continuous stream within its walls. Tales of salacious revel, crime, divorce, and all that wicked imaginations can devise, enter the home in papers and magazines and books. Who can estimate the influence of a bad book or a vile paragraph on the home life?

If there is one thing needed today in the defense of the home, it is a crusade of good people against the hellish abominations of our modern press. For I venture the assertion that no boy or girl can read our daily newspapers and remain pure in thought and desire for a single day.

But in the brief compass of this paper I must pass to the sins within the home.

I will discuss these from the standpoint of Christ and the idea the Bible furnishes of what the home ought to be.

The first sin in the home I will mention is untruthfulness.

This springs very largely from that spirit of selfishness which is the curse of the race. We are all poor, selfish creatures, and the trouble is so many are content to be nothing else. Spirits are not finely touched but to fine issues. God gave His children noble gifts for noble uses.

How often petty deceptions are practiced at home.

The father and mother are tainted by this sin and the children soon learn to understand it.

They teach one thing and practice another. A father gave his boy a very hard whipping because he told a lie. The boy was sulky and defiant. His sister asked him why he took the matter so to heart. The boy replied, "Father licked me for lying and he lies himself. I see no justice in that. I heard him tell mother yesterday that the white horse cost him a hundred and fifty dollars, and he expected to make a pretty speck on him; and today I heard him tell Mr. Williams that it cost him two hundred dollars and he could not afford to sell him for one cent short of two hundred dollars. If that's not lying, what is?"

When the adult members of households are not sincere and truthful, what may be expected of the children?

Petty deception in the home is a sin that builds the fiber of the world kingdom and not the kingdom of God, into the child heart.

And next in this category of domestic sins are sins of temper.

"I know that sister is a Christian," said a little boy, "because she isn't cross to me any more, as she used to be, and when I want her book she will give it to me with a sweet smile."

Often bad tempers have destroyed the structure of Christian character. One of the very best Christian women I know of in this city is almost heart-broken because she is the victim of a bad temper, whose volatileness was not controlled in the mobile days of youth.

How much havoc an irritable temper works in the home. Can a person be good and be so cross? - is the simple querie of childhood. People who are angelic and full of solar radiance outside are thunder clouds and devils when once the house door has shut behind them.

A very gifted school teacher once told me that she never had any inclination to lose her temper when engaged in her professional work, but when she reached home and the cloak of the world was thrown off she had been ashamed of her temper again and again.

If there is any place for a sweet, beautiful. loving temper, it is at home. The home needs all the solar radiance at our command. Let the Christ shine out there.

How beautiful that home that the sunshine of a loving soul makes bright.

There is a sin that eats like acid into the heart of childhood and bears poisonous fruit for many years.

It is censoriousness and bitter criticism before the children of the family. The extent to which this is indulged in is simply appalling. Thoughtlessly, I will hope in charity, reputations are blasted in this way and influence impaired or forever lost. The way men and sacred things are spoken of in many homes is enough to destroy the last spark of reverence left in the average American small boy or girl. If parents only co-operated, instead of working against, pastors and teachers, the task of the religious training of the young would not be half so difficult as it is.

I have known the work of a Sunday School teacher to be completely nullified by the flippant talk at the home table about her and her teaching.

"We live by admiration, hope, and love." If you destroy all there is to admire, and undermine hope, love will take wings and fly away.

The next sin I will call to your attention in this respect, is foolish and silly talking. For every idle word that men speak shall they give account at the day of judgment.

It is just here that the minds of children are poisoned and their ideas of life and character lowered. The influence of a half hour's vain conversation may not be effaced by twenty sermons heard afterwards.

A mother invited a clergyman to her home during the progress of these evangelistic services now being held in our city. She was a woman of many prayers. She had sown with tears the gospel seed in the hearts of her children.

To her horror the minister spent the time in giving the young man a vivid account of the last social event he had attended, with a description of the costumes of the pretty girls, and laying particular stress upon charms never unveiled in church at least, and also retailing the pleasure he had at a recent champagne supper with some of the good fellows of his church.

Do we wonder that religion is at a low ebb, or the home needs purification when such things are common occurrences?

Parents are in despair over the vile, vulgar, or uncomely speech of their children. Much of it is laid to the street and the public school. But how much more than they are willing to acknowledge is heard right at the home circle.

Calling in a beautiful home one day, the little daughter of the household was playing with her dolls in a corner of the parlor. Both mother and pastor started when the little girl screamed out to one of her dolls, "Susie, if you do not sit still, I'll break every bone in your body."

"Where on earth she could have heard that I do not know," said the mother, "for she never hears any such things at home. It must be at school. Those public schools are just dreadful for what they teach the little people of vulgarity."

The next day I chanced to be passing the spacious grounds of that elegant home. Just as I drew near the mother of the household, on whom I had called the previous day, opened a side door that looked out into the garden, called to the children who were playing in the distance, and she cried to them in a high treble, "If you do not come here this minute I'll break every bone in your body." Then she wondered where the dear little people could have gotten such expressions. It must have been in the public schools.

The children are imitators. Sharp as steel and quick as the lightning, they are catching impressions and transferring them to the plate of daily life. Our children, in manners and speech, are very largely what we make them.

If we sin against the best and holiest they will do the same. The irreverence of our republican children is a matter of widespread comment. Does it not spring from the habits and character of their elders? Familiarity breeds contempt, is the proverb.

It is a sin of the home that there is so little reverence expressed for one another.

The Christian should cultivate in the home a higher idea of the value and nobility of the soul God has placed in the temple of the body.

We sin against God and sin against each other when we undervalue what the Divine Architect has wrought in the human frame divine.

When from the halls of sleep we meet in the morning for the early meal of the day, in the spirit of Emerson's noble thought, we should greet each other as travelers that have come from a far country. There should be a certain stately dignity. Every chair should be a throne, and every man and woman a king and queen. Then will the children of the home be princes and princesses.

The next sin in the home is that of formal piety. When religion is an unreal affair, and confined only to forms and expression, what damage is done to the idea of the home.

God and heaven must be realities to the father and mother who would make an ideal home.

I know of no more deadening sin than to bring children up in a home where religion lives always at a poor dying rate.

The reason we need a religious awakening is, that so many who have a name to live are simply dead.

Why there is no more piety in the church is, that there is so little genuine religion at home.

The father, perchance, prays for Jesus to abide with them and then throws wide open the door to avarice, irritability and discord. He never expected Jesus to come, he did not really want Him to come. He would be very troublesome in some homes, as He would in so many commercial enterprises.

The weakening of the sense of responsibility for the religious life of the children and the dwarfing of influence may be reckoned as among the sins that can be properly termed domestic.

If parents realized the influence they ought to exert over the children, they would not leave their guidance so largely, as they do, to the molding influences outside of the home.

Men tell me they cannot talk with their boys and girls upon the subject of personal religion. They want the pastor and some one else to do it. Why is it?

Is it not because they lead such lives in the family that they are ashamed to? If the Church is to be better, and society is to be better, the fountain head of all, the home, must be first regenerated. Here is the source of real moral and religious purification. Parents must face their responsibilities.

Rev. F. E. Marsten, D. D.
Pastor of Broad Street Presbyterian Church

DISCUSSION

REV. S. W. SEEMAN: Another sin is the admission of impure literature and a failure to provide good literature in the home.

MR. MILLS: It is a hard thing to provide good literature for the children of the home. I know it is a tremendous study with us in our home with a library of, I suppose, three or four thousand volumes, to find the right things for the children to read that they want to read. We can not blame the children for not wanting to read things that interest some of us, and we certainly can not blame them for wanting to read things that do not interest us. The ordinary child's literature would certainly not elevate the ordinary minister very much, nor any other intelligent people. I wish there could be some means for disseminating information concerning good reading in our home for the children, and that there might be more people of the very highest character, from a literary standpoint, who would feel called of God to produce the right sort of literature for our children. It is a tremendous question.

MR. MILLS: I would be glad if you would hand in a list tomorrow of books that are valuable for children and that would be elevating.

In response to Mr. Mills's request, Prof. J. A. Shawan, Superintendent of the Public Schools of this city, prepared for publication a very complete list of books suitable for children and young people.

Broad Street Presbyterian Church
Where the meetings in the East District were held

* * *

Next, address by Frank C. Eaton on "Business Sins."

Business Sins

Frank C. Eaton

B usiness transgressions may perhaps be broadly classified as those committed against the great world of customers and those against the smaller world of employees. The former class includes such ancient dishonorable practices as false weight and short measure, misrepresentation and deception, selling an imitation for the genuine, selling a lower grade for as much or more than the higher, all forms of adulteration and impurities in manufacture, betrayal of confidence and extortionate charges. These and a multitude of kindred dishonesties have, in varying degree, cursed the realm of exchange ever since the time when prehistoric man first conceived the plan of barter.

There are many reasons for believing that these petty schemes of cheating - though far from being extinct at the present day-are far less prevalent now than in ancient or even in recent times. The general scale of intelligence has so risen as to greatly curtail the field for such practices. The buyer has learned the legal commonplace, he knows he must beware, and he is much less easy to hoodwink than formerly. There has taken place, undoubtedly, also a growth in the ethics of trade, and enlightened self-interest has gradually taught the lesson that in the long-run fair dealing is more profitable than trickery. As a general rule it may be said that in the business world today the keynote of honesty prevails.

Turning now to business sins as they affect the great army of the employed, we find the situation one of distinctly less encouragement and of greater difficulty. The increasing ferment among our wage-workers-now for some years so marked and often so alarming-seems to be due largely to our very prosperity. This is no less true because it has the aspect of a paradox. For so long as our social conditions remained comparatively simple, and so long as the inevitable social differences were due more to talent and education than to riches, there was no organized discontent among the people at large. But with the advent of our first millionaire, little more than half a century ago, a change of temper seemed to begin to take possession of the masses and to become more and more marked as the list of merchant princes continued rapidly to lengthen. The civil war, with its enormous expenditures, gave unprecedented opportunities of enrichment to a legion of contractors and speculators. If there be a modicum of truth in the estimate of many sober minds that one-half of the three thousand millions spent during that conflict was either squandered or stolen, it reveals the tainted source of scores of fortunes. And since the war how stupendous has been the exploiting of our national resources, and how colossal the aggregation of wealth, until today in this land of democratic institutions with a manhood suffrage practically universal-we behold that we have bred a race of uncrowned kings in numbers sufficient to stock all the thrones of Europe and still leave a residue ample to control the Federal Senate and forty-five Legislatures as well. We have railroad kings, pork kings, oil kings, coal kings, iron kings, sugar kings, lumber kings, landlord kings, Napoleons of finance, silver kings, gold kings, irreverently styled "gold bugs," and many such merry monarchs, besides.

Many of these potentates are literally monarchs of all they survey, and much more also; for they possess acres by the hundred thousand and mileage of trunk lines by the thousand. It happens, too, that these royal personages, like politicians, have a way of occasionally getting together, and then we have the right royal combination of the trust or the syndicate, capable, in emergencies of controlling both the executive and legislative functions of the State. While, therefore, it must be conceded that these powerful interests are likely to continue to flourish so long as we adhere to the doctrine of private property, they require eternal vigilance in public sentiment and public officials. A wise and rigid surveillance would seem to be the soundest policy for the State to pursue toward them.

Mr. Aked recently told us in epigrammatic phrase that no amount of money giving can atone for money stealing-a proposition which is quite incontestable, and yet one difficult to apply. In certain conspicuous cases it is not hard to decide whether a fortune has been justly or unjustly acquired. But in many other cases our casuistry would be quite inadequate to the task. What ethical principle can enable us to say in the case of a given president or general manager of a corporation how much annual profit belongs to the shareholders and how much to the employees? A complexity of considerations must be taken into account in every instance, which, if fully known, must modify many of our summary judgments. Too well we know there are many hard masters-men who follow the plain old rule of taking all they can with no regard for the welfare of those who serve them, and thus grossly abuse an authority which they ought to hold as preeminently sacred. Here, indeed, is the one great and crying evil of business. Unmitigated greed; the sordid passion for gain at any cost; the moral callousness which cares even less for the man who tends a machine than for the machine itself; indifference to accidents and sickness incurred in the discharge of duty-these are the immoral and anti-Christian cruelties of much of modern business. On the other hand, the employer animated by a humane and Christian spirit-and many such are to be found, thank God, throughout our land-is one who does concern himself not solely with prices and profits, but with the daily welfare of those who labor with and for him.

Still another cardinal sin of business, which is often allied to the one already discussed, is the insolent display of riches. Perhaps no alarming amount of this evil spirit is in evidence immediately about us, yet wealth brings ever this danger to its possessors. Humanity, prone to self-indulgence, wastes much of its time in idly dreaming of the pleasures possible with ten, twenty or fifty thousand a year, and nothing to do but spend it.

AFTERNOON

Next followed an address by Rev. William Macafee, Pastor of Broad Street Methodist Church, on "The Sins of the Church."

The Sins of the Church

Rev. Wm. Macafee

T
he subject this afternoon, as just stated, is "The Sins of the Church." I think I shall not depart from the spirit and purpose of the hour if I consider our theme elastic enough to include some of the faults and weaknesses of the Church, as well as her more positive sins.

To my mind many of the most grievous sins of the Church arise from a false a too narrow conception of her mission. Our leader in the present series of meetings has repeatedly emphasized the fact (and our own views coincide exactly with his in the matter) that the Church is not a "Saints' Rest," is not an asylum, is not an hospital, is not primarily a school, is not a place where a man's chief and only object is the salvation of his own soul even. A man's own soul he must save, to be sure, but we are beginning to learn that the only way by which a man can truly save his own soul and keep it saved, is by working for the souls and bodies of other men. The Church is meant to be, and the true Church is, above all things else, aggressive. It is a great army. It is an organization of workers, achievers, bringers of miracles to pass. It is an institution whose program is nothing less than the salvation of the world. morally and spiritually. More than that, we are beginning to learn that there are some conditions-physical, material, social conditions-where it is next to impossible for a man to be saved morally and spiritually; and the truth is forcing itself upon us that part of the Church's work is to help to beget such physical and social conditions that moral effort will not be a mere "beating of the air."

The fact is, we are coming to realize in this modern day that the Church is a vast organization for human uplifting and betterment, in the broadest and most universal sense, and that there is nothing, absolutely nothing, in the whole process of the elevation of the race that is alien to her program. We believe that whatever improvement, moral, social, political, any other sort, is to come to the race, is to come, and should come, through the all - pervasive influence of the Christian teaching and the Christian spirit; and if great reforms are wrought, and great advancement is made without aid from the Church, it is because the Church is not living up to her program. The Church is meant to bring about the answer to the Saviour's great prayer, "Thy kingdom come," and everything that tends to the in-bringing of that kingdom is a part of her work.

I think a failure to appreciate this, the largeness and comprehensiveness of the Church's mission, lies at the bottom of many of the most grievous sins she is chargeable with today. When men join the Church simply to save their own souls, without much concern as to what becomes of the souls or bodies of other men; when men join the Church to be administered to rather than to administer; when men join the Church looking wholly "To their own things," and not at all to "The things of others;" when men join the Church under the impression that they meet the whole demands of the case by going to service once on Sunday and paying a few dollars for the support of the ministry, while the great, needy, sinning, lost world is permitted to "wreck its own ride," so far as they are concerned-when men join the Church with no broader views and no higher motives than these, I have not the slightest hesitation in saying that they wholly, or at least greatly, misconceive the mission of that institution and the responsibilities of membership in that body.

Immediately connected with this-indeed, largely growing out of the misconception we have just spoken of, is another evil, and that is, inadequate methods for reaching and saving the very classes of society which most of all need reaching and saving. The situation is this: On the one hand a church of almost unlimited resources and ability; a church so strong socially, intellectually, financially, that she can do almost anything she means to do with all her heart. On the other hand, the masses estranged from us; comparatively few conversions; comparatively few of the unconverted coming where we can, by our ordinary methods, at all reach or influence them; social and physical conditions existing at the very centers of our best civilizations, that make moral salvation almost an impossibility. On the one hand, great, unspeakable need; on the other hand, magnificent resources, but somehow vastly ineffectual to reach the need they would minister to; a great gulf between the men and women who need salvation and the agency that has been set for their saving.

There is no disguising the facts. Some of the most thoughtful amongst us are beginning to feel that the vast resources of the Church as today organized and operated, are not doing all that can be done, and that ought to be done, for the salvation of men and of society. There is a conviction growing in the minds of many that the Church, as now operated, is spending far too much time, labor, money, energy, in the work of edifying and entertaining Christians, who ought themselves to be flaming apostles of Christ's truth, and far too little in distinctively aggressive effort in the line of "Seeking and saving that which is lost."

I know, of course, what may be said on the other side of this question I know how large and manifold the Church's work is. I know that a part of her mission, to the end of time, must be instruction, edification, building up of character. I know that the Church is meant to be the great moral teacher of the world; that, in all that concerns public or private life, she is to be a "Terror to evil-doers and a praise to them that do well." I know that she is this hour, and at all times, teaching truths that are leavening society far beyond the pale of her own membership. But, notwithstanding all that, I think that no candid, earnest person, who has given thought to the facts, can fail to perceive that one of the chief evils of the Church today is absorption in self, and methods of work and forms of organization that are not as efficient as they ought to be in reaching those classes of society which most of all need saving.

Another sin of the Church is that sort of excessive denominational zeal that gives absolutely no consideration to the interests of others in seeking to promote its own interests. Now, let us be understood. I do not believe in organic union of the sects-at present. I do not believe it is possible. If it were possible, I do not believe it would be wise. I believe we can worship God better, and do our work better, under those several forms to which education, custom and temperament have adapted us, than we could under any one new form that can be devised. There is a measure of denominational zeal that is wise, necessary, in no sense reprehensible. But when that spirit is carried to excess, I have not the slightest hesitation in saying that it constitutes one of the supreme weaknesses of Protestant Christianity.

Think of the facts for a moment, as we find them today. Six Protestant churches in a little village of a few hundred inhabitants, where one or two could do all the work; every one of them struggling for mere existence; not one of them capable of anything like true, aggressive work; not one of them operated in such a way as to command the respect of the community, or exercise such an influence over it as a true Church should exercise. Two churches of the same faith on the same street, not half a square apart, standing there in rivalry with each other, for no other reason than that their members do not. happen to be of the same political faith. A spirit and a policy that lead people, when planting new churches, to give no more consideration to the interests of other churches that may be around them, or on the ground before them, than if these other churches were absolute enemies of the great general cause! And yet we profess to be marching under the banners of the One great "Captain of our salvation!" That, if you please, is one of the crying, damning sins of Protestant Christianity today. What a waste of energy and of resource it all involves! What a difference there would be in the power of the Church to cope with the evils of the time, if we could just come to look upon each other as brethren, and exhibit some sort of fraternal consideration for each other in our denominational movements and activities!

I know how many feel on this subject. I know that many think the matter is simply inevitable and irremediable. I doubt not that there are some-some perhaps here present today-who think that it is the very extreme of impracticalness to so much as mention such a subject in a convention like this. But that is precisely what we are not willing to admit, and indeed do not believe. We believe there is nothing wrong in this world but can be righted. We believe it is not impractical or useless to speak out against any sin, even that which has its foundation in the most ancient prejudices of men. We are coming to see that there is a great weakness here, a vast waste of energy and resource. We are coming to feel it, I think, as never before. There is a pressure bearing on us from the outside, from the pervasive skepticism of the times, that ought to make us consider. There are coming into our churches, and now in our churches, men of broad views, of business sense, of catholic sympathies, who will simply refuse to sustain, by their means, any policy that does not keep somewhat in view the interests of the great common cause as well as the interests of the particular denomination. And I believe that we are coming to a time of such mutual understanding, respect, good will, that the forces of Christianity will be marshaled in less antagonism to each other, and with more respect to the common weal of the Israel of God, than they have been at any time in the past.

There are, of course, many other very palpable "Sins of the church." If I had time I would like to speak of the sin of admitting social distinctions in the Church, of the great and ever-present sin of worldliness in its various aspects of greed, frivolity, etc., of the sin of dogmatism and illiberality, of that sort of ecclesiastical politics that is scarcely less scandalous in some of its methods than are those methods which have so often made secular politics "A shaking of the head" amongst us. It is not possible, in the time allotted to me, to do more than briefly touch upon a few of the many things in our church life, which need purging or reconstruction. I have chosen to speak of such things as I have, because I believe they are amongst the strategic and fundamental weaknesses of the Church today, and because, as I think, we too easily conclude that they are irremediable.

DISCUSSION

DR. J. C. JACKSON, JR: I think one of the evils of the church. that the speaker referred to indirectly, in the way of denominationalism, grows out of the want of toleration. The Roman Catholic Church as a unit forbids its people to think independently. Protestantism lets all men think and then prosecutes them if they do not all think alike; and every man has to have a new church to suit his idea. It seems to me that it would be well for the Presbyterians to quit prosecuting the higher critics and for the Methodists to quit prosecuting and persecuting those who might be guilty of some violation, and likewise all along the denominational line, and turn our attention to other matters and let every man think as he pleases.

* * *

Rev. Howard H. Russell, Superintendent of the Ohio Anti-Saloon League, delivered the following address on 'Political Sins."

Political Sins

Rev. Howard H. Russell

"Twice within ten years the people of Ohio have seen their representatives freely purchased; the Legislature has been brazenly debauched; the people have been betrayed for a price; law and decency have been shamelessly violated and wickedly outraged; seats in the United States Senate have been knocked down to the highest bidder, and through the unlawful, profuse, and corrupt use of money, Henry B. Payne, of Cleveland, Ohio, and Calvin S. Brice, of Wall street, New York City, have secured honors (?) to which they were not entitled. In the case of Henry B. Payne a plea in abatement may be entered. He was not a party to the purchase, but the evils resulting from the debasement of the sworn representative of a free people were equally as great and appalling.

"In the case of Calvin S. Brice there are no mitigating circumstances. His agents proceeded, under his personal direction, to the most deliberate defiance of the will of a free people, and the most audacious, bold and devilish methods human ingenuity ever devised to acquire an office without the honor. These acts, as consummated, are plague spots of infamy upon the tarnished name of a great commonwealth."

These are the deliberate statements made in the preface of the book issued the present year, entitled, "Bosses and Boodle in Ohio Politics." Its author is a former member of our General Assembly, who is of the same political party as the two senators named, and the details of the bribery are fully narrated in the chapters of the book. Neither Senator Payne nor Senator Brice has taken

148

the trouble to deny the charge and no suit for libel has been entered. That Ohio citizens believe them true, was hinted at when a member of the last Assembly, a candidate for re-election this fall, an unworthy preacher of the gospel, was easily entrapped into a written offer to sell his vote to Mr. Brice. It was further indicated by the emphatic defeat of Mr. Brice's Legislative ticket in the recent election. A member of the last General Assembly who sought a renomination called upon a citizen of his county and sought to allay this citizen's opposition. "Why do you oppose me?" he said. "Is it possible," said the citizen, "that you do not know why a great many people are opposing you?" "No," said the ex-member, "I do not." "They believe," said the citizen, "that your Legislative career has been a very remunerative one." Bribery by gold is not uncommon in Ohio. I am informed that in several counties, marked close, or doubtful, upon political tables, there are lists of voters tabulated and checked over every year who will vote as they are paid to vote, and money has often tipped the political scale. It was a hopeful indication in one such county this year that the two county executive committees of the dominant parties agreed in writing to prevent all corruption of this kind, and offered a joint reward for information that would lead to conviction of bribery. Purchase by gold is not the only form of bribery. There is also

BRIBERY BY OFFICE

No one can question that there is many an office-holder in Ohio today who, before his election, entered into a contract, expressed or implied, that he would hold harmless certain law-breakers, who, in return, pledged their support at primary and polls and aided in placing him in the post of official power. His official action is prostituted, of course, and his future political ambition is subject to the approval or disapproval by these bad men, of his treatment of them during his present term. This bribery by office is manifest when a prosecuting attorney in Cincinnati nolles the cases against law-breaking saloonists when ample evidence is forthcoming. We need not go away from Columbus for illustration. I state only the most notorious facts when I say that gambling and bawdy houses are allowed freely to run; that boys under age are allowed to frequent the saloons, that the Sunday laws are openly broken, and that the restrictive ordinances relating to liquor sellers are allowed to go unheeded. I could not charge that our mayor is bribed with gold to give the city over to the law-defiers. But when these facts stand charged, as they have repeatedly been, and no effort is made by the mayor's police force to check this general law-breaking, it becomes patent to all that Mayor Allen is either most pusillanimously incompetent; or, he is bribed to become the corrupt partner and abettor of gamblers and law-breaking saloonists by the office which he dishonors. A third species of bribery is

POLITICAL PARTISANSHIP

What will be the effect of law enactment and law enforcement upon our party? This is the question ultra partisans in official position are constantly asking and too many partisan voters are echoing the cry. It does not concern the partisan whether the issue be right or wrong, but whether "The party can make or lose votes by the action in question. This ultra partisanship is found in all the political parties, without a single exception. At the last session of the Legislature many members of both political parties in House and Senate, speaking of the Haskell local option bill, said: "It is a good bill. Personally, I should favor it; the principle is right; the plan you propose for the treatment of the liquor evil is a good one. It leaves the question to the people of each locality. It keeps up agitation by the recurring vote. It closes saloons where law can be enforced, and not where the condition of public sentiment will make the law a dead letter. It takes the whole question of prohibition out of the domain of partisan politics. BUT-I fear it will be politically unwise. It will be ' bad politics ' to pass the law." In the effort to prevent the enactment of a most just and wholesome law in the interest of morality because of partisan apprehension, officers of State and party henchmen mingled their cries of alarm with the howls of the liquor lobby. Party organizations and discipline and loyalty are necessary to good government. But there should be a limit beyond which conscience, for the sake of good government, ought not to allow Is to go. My party must not put me in a straight jacket and require me to vote for a dishonest nominee or one who has defamed the State or municipality by his official vote or action in the past. "The duty of loyalty to a party depends upon the loyalty of that party to duty."

I have briefly touched upon some of the political sins of commission. Grievous as they are, the most flagrant I know of is one of omission. It is

THE INACTION OF CHRISTIAN CITIZENS

I call this the most flagrant because it indicates inexcusable ignorance or heartless indifference upon the part of the most enlightened and influential portion of our citizenship. The field secretaries of our Anti-Saloon League have been asking for a showing of hands by the voters present at their meetings in the churches as to their attendance at the last primary election or caucus of the party in which they hold their respective membership. Upon the average, not more than fifteen per cent. of the voters present respond affirmatively.

It would seem like the most elementary statement to say that our laws are not made here at the capitol. They are here merely finished off. They are rough cast at the primaries or caucuses of the various political parties. They are in fact moulded in the pre-primary. We get back at last to the house that Jack built. This is the capitol of Ohio, where sits the dignified senator, who was elected by delegates at the senatorial convention, who were selected by a senatorial committee, which was appointed by the delegates to a county convention, who were elected at a ward primary and had been previously selected at a ward pre-primary. How will the dignified senator vote on the Haskell bill, or any other righteous law? That depends upon the kind of men who made up the slate at the pre-primary. And so it inevitably follows by rules as fixed and certain as the evolution of the fruit from the germ, that boodling will go on at the capitol and laws will be unenforced by the mayor until Christian men, ministers, deacons, elders, and the files of Christian citizens assume the functions of loyal citizenship which they have been

151

heretofore, in large measure, recreantly and treasonably turning over to the irresponsible and law-defying elements in the State.

The work of the Ohio Anti-Saloon League is an earnest, business like and very aggressive effort to put the principles of Christian citizenship into operation. The nomination and election of a majority of the Ohio Legislature, committed in advance to county local option, would be the election of a Legislature likely to enact good laws generally. The election of municipal and county officers throughout Ohio who will enforce the liquor laws will be the election of men of such probity as that all the laws will be enforced. All the issues of purer politics are involved in the campaign. "What ought to be done, must be done in the only manner in which it can be done." After a thirty month's campaign we have reached a point where we can say that a majority of the members of both houses in the coming General Assembly have pledged their vote for the special legislation desired at the present time. It remains to be seen whether these promises will or will not be redeemed. The gauntlet must be run of the political temptations to corruption mentioned in the first part of this paper. There will be gold to bribe; there will be partisanship to bribe, and there will be ambition for office to bribe these men. Let us pray for them. Better still, let us make it plain to them that the Christian citizenship is now aroused to action and to the fulfillment of political duty permanently. The member of the House in the last Assembly, from a Southern Ohio county, refused to vote for the Haskell bill. He said concerning the men who were petitioning him to vote for the bill: "I asked these men to turn out to the primary and help nominate me, and they refused. I know who my friends were at the primary," and he voted NO. This year we went into that county and persuaded the church people to go to the primary elections, many of them for the first time in their lives, and the result was the nomination and election of a strong anti-saloon man who will faithfully represent his county this time, and will vote aye when his name is called on the Haskell bill. I shall never forget the sneer on John Locke's face in the last Assembly as he turned to his fellow members and said: "If you want to dig your political grave, just vote for this prohibition bill." On the 23rd of last May I sat in the City Hall in Springfield and heard him placed in nomination before the convention for the State Senate. He had already, since the last Assembly, been twice a candidate for a judgeship and had failed. There probably never was such an average of good citizenship gathered at a senatorial convention in the Eleventh District. A majority of that convention were Haskell bill men, anti-saloon men, anti-John Locke men, because of his opposition to our measure in the last Assembly. They were there because the church members of Springfield and Urbana and other parts of the district had performed their duties as citizens and had attended the primary, and elected the slate therefore arranged. And when the roll was called on the first ballot at the convention, and the anti-saloon candidate, William M. Jones of the Methodist Church in London, was nominated, we found out in that section of the State, as we have learned in many other localities, "who dug his political grave" by his vote on the Haskell bill.

How shall we cleanse the corruption in political life? By bringing the Spirit of Christ, and Christian fidelity to duty, into the active field of politics, and there is no other way to bring it to pass under our system of government, except for the Christian citizens of the State to rule in the party management of the various political parties. They must attend the party conventions; they must be enrolled on the party committees; they must give of their time and their talents, not spasmodically, but regularly, if our liberties are to be preserved.

In a Christian convention the question was discussed-"What shall we do with the full - blooded Indian?" A wise Quaker said, "I will tell thee what to do with the full -blooded Indian. Send a full-blooded Christian after him." Is it too much to hope that the sin of omission in our political life is now to be repented of; and in the name of the victims of misrule, in the name of our firesides, in the name of Christ, the well rounded full-blooded Christian citizenship shall bring to pass the domination of Christian conscience, whose right it is to rule in the politics of the State.

DISCUSSION

MR. THOMPSON: I want to say that some good citizens have gone to the primaries and found themselves pretty lonesome. When they got there everything had been arranged for before hand. The speaker spoke about the pre-primaries. How many pre-primaries must there be? The fellows that run this thing have nothing else to do while we are busy' men. They spend all day Sundays cooking the thing up and we haven't time to do that. I believe that we ought to go to the primaries, but we find ourselves "not in it" as the saying is.

DR. GLADDEN: I have a confession to make. I tried in the early part of my residence in Columbus to do my duty in attending the primaries, and I went not only to the primaries, but I went to the pre-primaries and undertook to get a good ticket nominated in my ward which would be a ticket that good citizens could vote for, and the next. day I found to my dismay, through the newspapers, that I had aided in putting upon that ticket a notorious gambler of this city. (Great laughter). There ought to be a pre-primary.

Rev. Howard II. Russell,
Superintendent of the Ohio Anti- Saloon League,
Chairman of the Printing and Advertising Committee

* * *

Address by Rev. A. A. E. Taylor, D. D., pastor of Westminster Presbyterian Church, on "Sins of Society."

Sins of Society

Rev. A. A. E. Taylor, D. D

T he root of all society sin is leaving God out and largely leaving brother man out, in pursuit of self-indulgence; and that, indulgence of the lower self. It is the spirit and determination that ruthlessly sacrifices the soul in its development and salvation, to secure the highest possibilities of this world; living intensely and wholly for the present; "Let us eat and drink for tomorrow we die." The fertile root is self-physical; with its pride, pleasure-loving abandonment to world-worship and thirst for world approval and applause. It is vanity, appetite, greed for the good things of this life; an intense, consuming, fleshly egotism.

These internal roots develop many poisonous branches. Let us write down some of them. One great temptation of society is love of ease and of luxury. This is manifested in lavish expenditures for dwellings, dress, furniture, equipages, service of personal attendants, delicate and dainty food and drink. The home of wealth is a castle of gold and silver, of precious stones, silks, satin's, velvet's, laces, tapestry, paintings, statues, and every luxury that wealth can import from the ends of the earth. It is a museum of all mechanical devices that human genius can imagine, bought with the blood of some brother's toil. All this is made to minister primarily to the pride of the heart, the coddling of the body, and the intoxication of the sense. "Soul, thou hast much goods laid up for many years; eat, drink and be merry." The mere possession of these things is not wrong in itself. Yet they prove a fascinating seduction to the soul. And while the needy are crying for bread and raiment and all things necessary to make life comfortable; while ignorance and depravity prevail, and while the poor have not the gospel preached to them, the heaping of these treasures in useless bulk for self, is likely to make God ask some day wherefore were they thus buried away in a treasure-house of selfish cupidity. Then think of the reactionary influence of such possessions upon the character of their owner; the lowering of the ideal of manhood and womanhood, and the surrender of life to indolence, the parent of vice. Attendant upon the possession of these things is that love of display, that is pride on exhibition, that tempts covetousness in others and wakens in them feelings of envy, jealousy, anger, desire. Were these things reserved for one's own eyes they might absorb the soul and narrow it down to sense, but they would not tempt others to love of the world and to the loss of their souls.

There is further, devotion of society to excessive amusement; pleasure seeking. To be lovers of pleasure is to be not lovers of God. Society is consumed by an insatiable craving, gnawing thirst for amusement, entertainment, pastime. Diversion in some form is its pressing thought. How shall we pass the day, the night, in pleasure-finding? This is often the supreme impulse. And it is the sensuous outgrowth of that idleness and laxity of being that often attends social position. It is followed by reckless carelessness and misuse of God's. precious gift of time; and time is life. Hours and days spent in dressing and dallying; in frivolity and play; in formal card-exchanging; flitting hither and thither without moral purpose; vain conversation, vain because it teaches nothing and acquires nothing. This waste of priceless moments is flinging life to the dogs; casting the pearls of opportunity to the swine of personal gratification. Also there follows forgetfulness of what others may justly demand of our lives. Society too often blots out the second great commandment of the Law. For no man or woman was created to live for self, and we owe our lives to our fellow-men. The loss of the deep sense of the responsibilities of human relations is ever most debasing and destructive to true manhood and womanhood. "Am I my brother's keeper?" is a divine question that seems never to have reached the ears of many society people or of society in its selfish and self-exalting moods and avaricious love of accumulation and of expenditure upon its appetites.

We may also mention the burning social ambitions and rivalries, with the jealousies and hate enkindled thereby. Mothers sometimes want their daughters to receive attentions of popular and wealthy men, whether they be morally pure or foul with pollution. Often everything is sacrificed to position and to gain a place in high society. The highest frown down upon the higher; and the higher snub and sneer at the high. And hearts are burning with the fires that destroy peace and make life too miserable to be endured.

There is again that wretched and abominable slavery to fashion, which is but the expression of the absolute bending of the knee of men and women to the tyranny of the world and its ways, that is bearing thousands away from God and heaven. Fashion in dress; in manners; in modes of living; in license to evil; attended by rivalries of pride and competition for display; by the servile fear of man that binds hard and hateful chains about those who yield to its demands. Fashion is the parent of vice in many forms of indulgence. We follow on like lambs to the slaughter; we sin because others do the same, and justify ourselves for that reason. A decent respect is due to our fellow-men and their opinions, but we should never fear to do right because it is unfashionable. Thus one tendency of society is to loss of conscience and loss of heart. The sacrifice of personal independence by asking, "What will the world say?" is petrification of the moral nature. An estimable lady said to me yesterday, "I am pained to see so few of what are called ' Society people' at these meetings." Worldly society dares not face the plain condemnation of its vices by Christ's simple gospel and by the requirement to deny self, take up the cross and follow Him. Our Lord sighed as He saw the rich young ruler turn away when probed by the crucial test of giving his goods to feed the poor. That was a society young man. Society has tendencies in it toward hard-heartedness for both men and women. We hear so much of the servant question in society talk. It is, in the main, severe, harsh, cruel criticism of the poor and slavish brethren and sisters, shut into the kitchen, the garret, and the stable-loft, at three dollars a week. It is pitiful to think how the face of the poor is ground by the relentless exaction's of society through its votaries, good-hearted and kind though they be by nature. Thus one fearful sin of society is the hideous example of selfishness and regardlessness for others set before the Lord's poor and humble, whose loss of opportunities alone prevent their being masters and mistresses.

I heard recently this remark from a woman of highest position: "How hard many fashionable women are upon their hired help. I should think it would make their servants bitter and revengeful (A voice from the audience said: 'It does')." Society is indeed sowing the wind whereof the harvest is the whirlwind. I recently saw a splendid equipage, with its outriders and rattling harness, drive up to a door, while at a short distance stood several workmen on the street, cursing the flunkeys and the rich owner of the carriage. I tell you, seriously, friends, the red flag of anarchy we have most to fear is not that one borne at the head of defiant processions of workingmen, but the red flag floating from these needless and criminal displays of wealth and luxury, taunting and embittering those who toil in the dirt at a dollar a day.

Another vice of society is its modern tendency to the separation of the sexes. The women gather in their feminine entertainments and receptions and the men collect in the club house, the pool room, the hotel rotunda, each finding their own entertainment. Many of the popular habits and modes of society are educating the sexes into loss of sympathy and into drifting apart in their loves and lives, bringing blasting blight into their homes.

If we now turn to enumeration of some of the practical outgrowths of these branches, how shall we recount them for number? Card playing pushed to extremes; whist clubs of the gentler sex, meeting morning, afternoon, or evening; progressive euchre, playing for favors or prizes - which being bought with money only, are but money in another form-thus playing with the fire of gambling and kindling thirst for unlawful gain and winning without work. Loss of precious time and opportunity of self improvement and of doing good to others; the breeding of envy, jealousy, cupidity, anger, hate. A prominent lady of this city said to me: "I have known of many strong, some of them lifetime, friendships ruptured at the card parties."

Thronged assemblies, "functions" with wine freely flowing amidst hilarious excitement and seeds of ruin sown, with luxurious dress-display, flashing jewelry and frivolity; turning night into day and the next day into night; "Ball-room morals" become a scornful and sarcastic by-word of the world itself. I give no false alarm when I aver that society is drifting into intemperance rapidly, recklessly; toying with wine and strong drink, the brandy or whiskey bottle passed around to flavor the lemonade with the poison that blights thousands of lives, young and old; strong drink at the table also, and in the gilded saloon. Out of all this grow fearful laxity of morals, sensual indulgence; temptation to virtue; feeding the consuming fever of passion; cultivation of lust in the lustful sex; and discoloring of purity and blighting with ruin fair daughters of the best streets. Hence, separation of husbands and wives; children worse than orphaned; divorce cases, with their unmentionable rottenness exposed in the police or other courts; elegant homes wrecked; some of them arrested in their very erection by divorce litigation; and mutual recrimination rendering future punishment almost needless. Then there is the feeding of the vilest passions in other forms; in sensual paintings and fleshly pictures; patronizing of lascivious displays, their vileness scarcely half concealed, on the stage; living pictures of disgusting and sickening exposure, which no youth of either sex can gaze upon and remain pure and clean in heart. These wretched and soul-destroying amusements are supported only by public patronage, which is the purchase of tickets. The divine law of love brother as self, or freely put, "Put yourself in his place," broken at every indulgence. "Modern novel reading," said a solicitous mother one day, "is one of the most destructive sins of society. Not merely waste of hours and impressions of the romantic and unreal in life and unhealthy excitement of the imagination; but its terribly debauching effects. For the ideal plot of the popular novel too often is a married person falling in love with some other person than one's wedded companion, with the usual consequences." I have seen a tender mother place in her budding daughter's hand a modern novel the climax of which is the willful sacrifice of her virtue to her lover to keep from losing him. The heroines of many of them are ruined women and rakes, and society is feeding the thirsty minds of her sons and daughters and seducing their souls upon such hellish poison and laughing at it as if it were some fashionable joke. Let mothers go to their sons' rooms and take down the licentious pictures of actresses from the walls and hunt up the cigarette photos and French novels in their table drawers. The impurity of the stage is invading our homes through these various channels. The other day 1 purchased a copy of a cheap, popular and elegant magazine of widest circulation and felt impelled to tear out four pages of illustrations before caring to take it into my home. And yet society is gravely defending the propriety of cultivating the nude in art and calling opposition prudery, while the young are feasting their eyes upon glaring temptation and excitements of ungodly passion. All these symptoms are simply illustrations of the dreadful and damning drift of society away from purity and religion; from God and heaven. It is not liquid damnation, but printed damnation, that our generation and our homes have most to fear. God help us that we have to unfold such a tale of horrors and draw back from such moral precipices.

And what is the effect of all these things from first to last but soul neglect, opposition to religion, positive unbelief, desertion of God and lives wholly surrendered to pleasure, without fear of the future and a reckoning with God?

DISCUSSION

REV. N. C. PATTERSON: We had an example of expensive luxury a few years ago in New York City where a lady gave a reception to her poodle. It cost $500. REV. BYRON E. LONG: It seems to me that one of the sad features of this matter is not only indulged by all classes in our common every day life, but it is carried into the realm of death, and even at our funerals the "noses are kept to the grindstone," and I wish it might be true that the good Christian people who bury their dead and who have means to lavish, would at least, in that event and at that time, curb their passion for display, so that the poorer of this city and all other cities might at that time, at any rate, do for their dead what they can do, and not be ashamed of it. Rev. James Haig, Superintendent of Union Mission Association, was here introduced and spoke on the subject,

In Darkest Columbus

Rev. James Haig

D r. Gladden has spoken the thought in my mind since listening to the papers here this afternoon, and I wondered why I was assigned this subject of "Darkest Columbus," seeing that I have never run for office. My name was never mentioned in that connection, and I have no social distinction or honor whatever, and therefore am wholly unprepared to speak on "Darkest Columbus." And more than that, I have been so busy working among the poor and distressed that I have not had time to prepare a paper, and I suppose I owe you an apology. But I do want to speak out of the depths of my heart of some of the things that are about us everywhere, that so many seem to fail to see and realize; and I may best call your attention to these things by giving you pictures of what exists, rather than to give figures.

The darkest place in Columbus may be bounded by Main street and Donaldson; by Washington avenue and Third; by Gay and the depot; by Front and Fourth. There are other dark places, but these are the darkest. In these places there are not less than three hundred, and possibly five hundred, women who give their whole time and thought and power to degrading and destroying and damning society.

A brother: How many men?

Mr. Haig: I have a letter in my pocket from a society of ladies asking the same question. I do not know, sir; and I do not care to approximate it.

I want to draw a picture of what is going on all the time in these sections as the work of these women, and there is hardly a building in Columbus that has at any time been inhabited by these citizens, about which I do not know some such incident as I shall bring to your attention. A beautiful carriage, and in it a man, a servant and some beautiful flowers, drew up to one of these places. I stopped at the carriage and looked into the face of a man I knew well, and he blushed and stammered some kind of an apology, for we had been personal friends. A few months after that I was sent for. I went down to the city prison and found him behind the bars; and he said he had been arrested by his firm, for he was a traveling man and drew a salary of $2,500 per year. He had appropriated a certain amount of the firm's money and they had stopped him. A few months after this there came to me a little box, and in it I found a letter. The wife of that man had enclosed some silverware which she said was all that was left that was salable and she wanted to know if I would not sell it for her, and forward her the money, that she might keep her five little ones from starvation.

In passing a certain building on High street one night, I heard groans and hastened immediately to know the cause; and there, lying at the foot of the stairs, I found a woman bruised and bleeding. When we cared for her and learned her story, it was this: Her husband, a worthless fellow, had stolen the money she had earned by washing, and which she had in the house to pay rent, and he had gone to spend the night in one of these blocks. In her desperation she had followed him, for she knew if her rent was not paid, it meant that she would be put out of the house; and he had brutally kicked her down the stairs.

I went to a place on Main street, a place where colored women stay, and I found there a gray-haired man, nicely dressed, whose Christian wife is every Sunday in one of the churches of this city.

And now of the poverty of Columbus and the amount of it. Our papers the other evening recorded that one in seven of the population of Columbus had been helped by the City Poor Department alone. At the Industrial Relief headquarters, during the past six months, 2,600 persons have been helped by giving them work and the necessaries of life. We have in this city about fifty societies that, in one form or another, dispense charity. Add this to the work of the city, and then we can make a calculation of the number of people who must ask charity of some society.

I will speak a little more in detail. The Lord touched the hearts of the good people here in Columbus, and we were able to give dinner to about six hundred of our families on Thanksgiving day. The next morning we invited in a dozen or more poor women and told them to do up the work; and we divided among them what we had left. Among those that came there were two girls about twelve and fifteen years of age, I should think. After they had worked about two hours the twelve-year old girl fainted and the doctor came and said, This child is over-worked and under-fed, that is all. And my missionary told me that on Wednesday (the girl worked in a tobacco factory for one dollar a week) the girl had worked all day with nothing to eat, had gone home Wednesday night and, there being nothing in the house to eat, had gone to bed without supper. She came to our place on Thursday, got her dinner, came to work on Friday morning and fainted away. I tell you this because I have not yet found a place for that girl.

A few weeks ago I saw a father proud of his boy in his first suit of clothes, take him into a saloon, lift him up on the bar and tell him to call all the people in the room to see his new suit of clothes. They gathered about, called for the liquor and clinked their glasses and drank together.

The other night I went into one of the saloons of this city and was passing out invitations to our mission meeting. It was a gambling place and one of the young men followed me outside of the door and said, "Mister, I want to speak to you. My father, ever since I can remember, has taught me only to do wrong. He was a gambler and a drunkard, and led me in that way. I think there is a better life for me, but I don't know how to get it. I wish you would tell me some way by which I can get into a better life than this." And I talked with the young lad there and wanted to touch his heart, so I spoke about his mother, and thought that would surely touch his heart, and I could get access to him. His eyes blazed; he clenched his fist, swore an awful oath and cursed his mother, and said she never taught him anything except to carry beer and steal.

I went into a certain home and asked for two bright little boys for our

Sunday school, and the mother said, "No, sir; you can't have them." I said, "Why can't I have them?" She said, "You know their father." I did know their father. He went around with circuses and beat people, and she said, "I am going to make greater men out of them than their father." And when I got after them with the law they left the city; and I suppose she is still drilling them to be thieves and vagabonds.

I have known mothers to bring their own daughters into the mission hall, seeking there or on the street to find lewd company for them. And not more than five weeks ago, a girl hardly sixteen years of age, came to me for protection from her mother, who was bound to sell her virtue to any man who would buy for ten cents.

Gambling in our city everywhere is wide open. You can hardly go into a saloon anywhere in the low dives and darkest parts of Columbus where you do not find them gambling openly, bidding everybody who will to come and participate. I see the police officers go in and watch the game and come out again. The other day there came to my house a young man, pale, trembling and excited. He said, "Mr. Haig, what am I going to do? I had been collecting for my firm through the week, and Saturday night I went out with the boys and didn't mean to get into trouble. I am not a bad man. I got to gambling and lost what little money I had, and I had the firm's money, and I thought I would win back some, and I put that up and lost, and kept on losing until I had lost every dollar of the firm's money. And then I had a watch, and pawned that and came back, hoping to win back some of my money, but," he said, "I lost that and came home to my wife and children; and tomorrow I must settle with the firm. I must go to jail." And he wept like a child; got down on his knees and begged that I might help in some way.

There is sin abounding about us everywhere. I hope there may something somehow grow out of these meetings that will so touch the hearts of the people as to make it impossible for men to be bound in sin as they are bound everywhere this day.

DISCUSSION

DR. GLADDEN: I want to say with reference to this information which has just been given by one who knows what he is talking about, that the Director of Public Safety of this city is accustomed to say, whenever he is brought to account for negligence, that he does not think there is any gambling going on in the city at all. A gentleman of his own party who asked him about the matter, told me that he was neglecting to enforce the laws, and told me that the director said to him, "I do not think there is any gambling going on in the city. Oh, of course, there will be secret games that you cannot find, but there isn't any open and public gambling in this city." I do not think there is any other citizen half way intelligent in this community who has any such opinion.

* * *

Topic for Wednesday, Dec. 4-"The Redemption of the City."

"Shout! for the Lord hath given you the city."

MORNING

The devotional meeting was conducted by the Rev. Henry Stauffer. Hon. O. T. Corson, State Commissioner of Public Schools, delivered the first discourse of the day, on "The Moral Influence of the Public School."

The Moral Influence of the Public School

Hon. O. T. Corson

M y friends, I believe you will all agree with me in the statement that the two most important factors in all civilization are religion and education. In order that the higher type of manhood may be developed it is necessary that these two forces should move on hand in hand, each one complementing the work of the other. Religion without education is almost certain to develop a dark, narrow manhood, and ignorant, dark superstition. While on the other hand, education without the influence of religion is quite certain to produce a race of skeptics and atheists. Our forefathers recognized the truth and importance of this developmental process which must underlie all government of the people, and they not only founded churches in which their pious hearts should find rest, and in which they could thank God for His goodness in the past, but at the same time they founded that other institution which has had very much to do with the Church; and has today.

We all love the very name of liberty. We have all doubtless read and re-read, perhaps a great number of times, that old, old story of the Revolution, in which we find recorded the deeds of those brave warriors who sacrificed their lives that you and I might today enjoy our liberty. We have gone back, doubtless, in our imagination, to Bunker Hill and to Saratoga Plains and glanced at the places made sacred by the blood of these valiant warriors. We have been filled with enthusiasm as we have read of the valor of that little band of Puritans who left their homes and country for the sake of the human race, and we have felt that they were on the side of right. That has been more than a hundred years ago, and all who had any connection with that great drama have passed away; yet their influence is felt. But to my mind, as I travel over Ohio, and listen to the ringing of these public school bells, I cannot help thinking of that grand old bell in Independence Hall, which more than a century ago rang out liberty to mankind. I am very firm in my mind that our forefathers were right when, in that immortal declaration of the ordinance of 1787, they recorded these immortal words, that "religion, education and morality being necessary to good government, education and schools must forever be encouraged," and I am quite certain in my conviction that just so long as the public schools of this nation are permitted to do the work they should, without anything to interfere with them to any serious extent, and no one to criticise, which no one does who knows anything about them, just so long is our community and our nation safe.

I stand here today at the invitation of this committee to discuss the public school, and I take pleasure in discussing that question of the influence of the public schools, and I want to say to you, my friends, that the public schools of today are in the direction of success and on the right side of every moral question. (Applause). I know that the public school is often criticised, and I know that it is very often undeserved; but I have nothing to say about such criticisms; and I don't stand here to say that the public schools are perfect, by any means; but I want to repeat, and with emphasis, that on questions of morality the public schools are on the right side; its principles are right. There are persons opposed to public schools because they are free, and you are brought into contact with every one they are common, and so they oppose them. Such opposition ought never to be permitted lodgement on American soil. There are others who seek to criticise their management; these criticisms usually come from those who don't know anything about them. I believe the public schools of today are the great levelers of the public in this country. Some one has said, "The public school is the only place in the world where jeans and broadcloth are brought together side by side, and I find that it is usual for the jeans to get ahead."

I have said that the public school is all right, and I stand by this statement, yet I know that it is far from being perfect. In the first place the teachers stand for the best morals in this country. These teachers, and I stand here representing these teachers this morning, it is true, and to a certain extent am one of them, and I think you will grant me the privilege of making this statement - these teachers nearly all are connected with some Christian work-the Sunday school or prayer meeting, some of the things most sacred to men and women in every community, and are interested in the things which influence for good, and the highest morality. I presume it is true that occasionally, not often, a teacher is immoral; but, my friends, those teachers do not stand as representatives, by any means. They are the exception, and I don't believe you will find higher Christian character than you will find among the teachers of our public schools today, in this city and State. (Applause).

I am willing to admit, and that with regret, that in some localities the Bible has been taken from our public schools; but that is not the rule; and if the Bible be removed from the public schools in some localities the Book is still on the teacher's desk, and its influence is felt through the Christian teacher, and it is powerful; and so I don't think that we need be discouraged if the Bible has been removed from the schools as part of the exercises.

In the next place, I believe you will all agree with me that the discipline of our public schools is of the best, and has had much to do with its moral influence and growth. I believe the discipline of the average public school today is far higher than that of the average home in this State or city. This statement may seem hard; but if such outbreaks occurred in the public schools-such lack cf control of the boys and girls-as occur in some homes, it would occasion such a sensation that the newspapers would issue several editions, they would have a larger issue than the papers issued by the ladies-the woman's edition. I have had parents come into my office as school superintendent, bringing their son, six years old, and say to me, in his presence, too, "I hope you can control him; we can't." I have generally tried to do what they expect; and such parents, I have invariably found, are the first ones to complain of the discipline of our public schools. We occasionally hear, too, that the strict discipline and overcrowding of our public schools is ruining the health of our pupils. Oh, what nonsense that is, as a rule. It is possible that occasionally a child of extremely nervous organization might, through the pure ignorance of the teacher, who has not been informed by the parent of the condition of the child, has been physically injured; but for every time that you will show me a child injured - ruined in health or morals in the public schools of this city or State, I will show you twenty ruined by being permitted to run out to theaters, parties and balls, remaining until one and two o'clock in the morning, two or three times a week, when they ought to be home in bed. I believe that we do not want to visit the sins of the whole community upon the public school system as long as the homes are what they are.

In the next place I want to refer to one special line of work-work being done on systematic Christian lines on the part of the teachers of our public schools; and that is scientific temperance teaching. I believe that the schools of Ohio today carry out through their teachers this great work systematically. It is doing more to uplift the home and stamp out this curse of intemperance than all political parties organized or that ever will be organized. Perhaps you may say that this work is not bearing fruit; but we do not know what it is doing. Here is one instance that I have met with in which the teacher of the public school should have the credit: One day a man came to me whom I had known all my life, a hard-working man, and he said to me, "You know I used to drink." I said, "Yes, sir;" and he said, "I have quit." I said, "I am glad to hear that." He said, "Let me tell you why I quit. You know I have heard a great many sermons on temperance, but they never touched me. I had the idea of personal liberty-that I could do as I pleased in regard to this question of drink. You know I have been talked to a great deal by the temperance women of this town regarding this question of drink, but it made no difference to me. It had no effect upon me whatever. I have two boys-one in the public school of this town"-not this city, but the town I have referred to - "and the other day we were out walking together and I met a man whom I knew, and he invited me into his house, telling me he had some wine he wanted me to taste. He poured out a glass for myself and one for each of my boys, and I was about to drink my glass when my boy, seven years of age, a pupil in one of the public schools, said, ' If I were you, I wouldn't drink that; my teacher tells me it is wrong to do it. ' I had resisted all the influence brought to bear upon me before that, but when my little boy, who received his education in the public school, spoke in that way, I determined to quit, and I did; and I made up my mind that I would never touch it again." I believe the public schools are not only reaching the boys and girls in their lives, but through the Christian teaching and moral principles of the teachers, these good influences are reaching the parents themselves.

I believe the principal criticism of the public school comes from those who have never taught, or who quit teaching ten or fifteen years ago, and think all teaching-all art of teaching-quit when they did.

As I said a moment ago, I believe this country is getting better every day. I have no doubt of it. We would not infer this from a perusal of the daily papers, where the bad things are chronicled, and crime is fully set forth; but suppose some one were to set down all the good done through the country, or in this city this week-every good thought, act and deed; we know there would be no printing press in the country to print it all. I believe the world is tending toward a higher civilization, and in that higher civilization there will undoubtedly be many permanent factors, and chief among them, if not most prominent, these three: The Church, the home, and the public school. It is useless to discuss which of these three is the greatest; neither one is greatest; each is great just in proportion as it is willing to give liberally of its good, and do its duty, and combine against the crime and vice of the country in the future, as it has done in the past. (Applause).

Rev. J. C. Jackson, Jr., pastor of Third Avenue Methodist Church, delivered the following address on "The Elevation of the family."

The Elevation of the Family

Rev. J. C. Jackson, Jr., D. D

T he family is the oldest, holiest, greatest, institution on earth. God created it before the Church or State. It is the germ of both these institutions. They exist in it in embryo. The family is the unit of society. The first man and the first woman were made husband and wife by their Creator, and their home was Eden. Our fancy invests that ideal home with every virtue and grace which could adorn an angel's life, before the traditional fall. Let the picture serve its purpose.

The mission of the gospel is to restore that lost paradise to every married pair. Society will be, on the whole, what its families are in the aggregate. If we save the home, we shall save the State. The Church must save the home. It must do this by sanctifying marriage. It must re-emphasize the sacredness of holy wedlock. It must insist on the indissolubleness of the marriage bond. It must enjoin carefulness and prayerfulness in entering upon this sacred relation, and must hold that that relation shall remain intact, after it is once entered, except for the violation which Jesus named. Increasing divorce means the increasing disintegration of society.

How, then, shall we elevate the family to the Eden ideal? How shall we make it the synonym of all that is holy and happy? I suspect that the purpose of the committee was, that the writer on this topic should limit himself in the main, to the proposition of elevating the slum family. The sub-stratum, the submerged tenth, or fifth, or third, as the case may be, seems to stand most in need of being toned up. Doubtless this is true, and also most difficult to do. But it may not come amiss to enunciate along with it, some general principles, also, which can be applied to the whole range of the social gamut.

The Church must save the home by making every home a Church. Paul in his salutation to Philemon says, "And to the Church in thy house." What a pregnant thought! A Church all one's own, with the father and mother for its ministers; the children and entire family as its members: truly a "household of faith."

When the awakened Philippians jailer asked in his distress, "What shall I do to be saved?" Paul and Silas answered, "Believe on the Lord Jesus, and thou shalt be saved-thou and thy house." That is the gospel recipe for elevating the family-religion. When the household is saved to Christ, it is also saved to society, and society itself will be saved through such saved families.

Christianity began and spread in this way, and conquered the Roman world by its household religion. We read in the epistles of religious gatherings held regularly under the roof of one, Nymphas, in Laodicea, while Priscilla and Aquila, in both Rome and Ephesus, opened their homes or workshops for divine worship. We have an account of Gaius, in Corinth, doing the same thing, whom Paul calls "The host of the whole Church."

These were families converted into Christians out of the raw material of heathenism. We know the uplift it inevitably imparted to them. How beautiful it makes them appear in contrast to the unsaved million. Their homes became abodes of hospitality and comfort, wherein love and kindness reigned supreme.

It is by Christianizing the family that it is to be refined, purified, and elevated. The land of religious homes will be a land of intelligence, a land of freedom, and a land of peace. An eminent writer says, that it was by kindling the altar fires in every home of Scotland that Knox saved his country from tyranny. Is not that beautiful scene of the typical Scottish family, in "The Cotter's Saturday Night," when the old Scotch father takes down the family Bible, reads a chapter to his household, and then all together kneel while he leads them at the throne of grace is it not that scene which lends the chief charm to Burns' inimitable poem?

173

Oh, for a land of such homes; The transforming power of the gospel will produce them. But how shall we bring it in contact with those abodes of men which are hovels instead of homes? Jesus gave to John the Baptist, as one of the evidences of His Messiahship, that the poor had the gospel preached to them. But the poorest of the poor do not, as a rule, attend our churches in any large numbers, and open-air preaching is impracticable. Romanism secures the attendance of the poor as well as the rich, through its power in the use of the sacraments. Social distinctions are thus obliterated in their services of the sanctuary. This is the ideal at which Protestantism should aim. It is not wise to erect churches for the poor alone. This creates a spirit of caste, and is contrary to the gospel. But how shall we induce the poor to come where the gospel is preached? Two difficulties confront us; First, they are proud as well as poor, and shrink from presenting themselves in a fashionably dressed congregation. Secondly, very few of our wealthy churches have grace enough to welcome them, even should they come, in their ordinary condition. Nor is this strange: Malodorous from the use of beer and tobacco, their presence is not pleasant.

These are the extreme, slum cases. But even the better poor are not always desired. Never shall I forget the expression of regret in both face and voice, from one who was a member of a very select little congregation, worshiping in a large church, when the plainer preaching of a new minister filled up the long vacant pews with a crowd of the common people. With undisguised sadness a cultured, wealthy young lady exclaimed, "Oh! our pretty little audience is gone."

The warning of St. James, concerning the "poor man in vile raiment," coming into your assembly, and being received in a different way from "the man in goodly apparel, with a gold ring," needs to be read frequently as a lesson to the average congregation. The gospel must first be taken to these people, to prepare them to come and receive it in the churches. This is the work of the Church. Godly, consecrated women of wealth and culture must, in the spirit of Christ, go to the abodes of poverty and filth, and lead their inmates to salvation. The slums must be civilized as well as Christianized. They must be taught to wash up themselves and their children, and scrub up the floors, and to air their houses, and arrange that their children shall sleep in separate beds, as well as rooms, where this is practicable. If they can afford but one room, it should be partitioned off at least with curtains, that there may be privacy. Health, as well as morals, requires such separations. Without modesty religion is impossible. The slums need the gospel of soap and water to wash away the filth of their bodies, as well as

"The fountain filled with blood Drawn from Immanuel's veins"

to cleanse their souls. Count Rumford says, "Piety never dwelt long with filth." Our oft-quoted maxim of "Cleanliness being next to godliness," indicates the order of procedure.

A family thus cleansed and clothed rises at once in its own self-respect, and it is not then difficult to persuade them to church attendance. The church which thus interests itself in the physical salvation of the degraded, will welcome these redeemed ones to a place in its pews. This method is perfectly practicable. It has been done in numerous instances, within my knowledge, and is being followed extensively in all of our large cities.

A family thus regenerated is ready to receive more advanced instruction. Its children can be put into the public schools, themselves one of the most elevating and regenerating of all agencies.

With the reign of decency, order can be introduced into their homes. The mother can be taught how to prepare a wholesome and palatable meal. Digestion has much to do with disposition. The law of kindness can likewise be made to prevail. The courtesy of lovers should exist between fathers and mothers. Gentleness in correction and forbearance with childish follies, will "turn the hearts of the children unto their parents." Sad will it be for that mother who, by her constant nagging at her children's noise, drives them from her home into the street. She who makes home the dearest place on earth to her children and keeps herself young enough to be interested as a companion in their amusements, will have them rise up to call her blessed.

Hundreds are the cases where a pleasant home would also save the husband and the father from the saloon. Strange as it may seem, many a man goes to the drink-shop for peace, because of an untamed tongue at home. Rousseau said, "Men will always be what women make them." This is as true in higher circles, and even in high life, as in the poorest families. But it is harder to secure order and harmony in the cramped-up cabin than in the spacious mansion. It is not impossible in the former, and it is absolutely necessary to the promotion of the family in either. As a rule, the fault in family discords is with the husband, rather than with the wife, but we are speaking today of the home as woman's throne, and therefore dwell on that side of the line.

Two soldiers were talking together, when one of them asked, "Bill, how did you come to enlist?" "Oh, I was single and fond of war," was the reply. "What led you to enlist, Tom?" "Well, I was married and fond of peace," was the answer. I have known numerous instances where a worthy bread-winner was changed into a vagabond by a virago wife. This is a cause of poverty, as well as a condition.

The testimony of Joseph Corbett, a Birmingham operative, before a Parliamentary committee some years ago, may be read as present-day evidence applying to thousands of like cases in all of our cities. The law of love and kindness in the hearts of parents to each other and to their children, will make the plainest home an Eden; and that law is the spirit of the gospel.

Someone has said that there ought to be two bears in every home, namely, bear and forbear. Unfortunately, they are too often not the domesticated kind, but are grizzlies, with numerous cubs. Even our lax courts dismiss many divorce suits for resting on ground too trivial to tolerate.

Cleanliness and kindness must be attended with intelligence. The mind must be fed and clothed, as well as the body. Good literature in the home is indispensable to its elevation. I rejoice to be able to say that the reign of flashy, trashy novels and sensational papers is on the decrease. I was assured yesterday by the largest newsdealer in Columbus that he now sells but twenty-five or thirty copies of the Police Gazette to where he formerly had a call for from two to three hundred. He says the same thing is true of all such papers, and dime novels. His explanation was, that our new, bright, beautifully illustrated ten-cent magazines are supplanting this vile and worthless literature. This statement brought joy to my heart, and an increased respect for humanity. The regenerating power of the Church, the refining influence of good literature, and the education of the common schools, must result in the elevation of the family and society.

The limits of my paper forbid entering the extended problem of tenement houses, sanitation, and other features of sociological discussion, all of which bear directly on the moral life of the home.

Rev. J. C. Jackson, Jr., D. D.,
Pastor of Third Avenue Methodist Church

* * *

Rev. W. H. Fishburn, D. D., pastor of Second Presbyterian Church, delivered the following address on "The Christianization of Business."

The Christianization of Business

Rev. W. H. Fishburn, D. D

The subject given to me is the "Christianization of Business." The title contains a semi-logical fallacy. It assumes the possibility of doing something that can't be done. It takes it for granted that business, as business, can be Christianized. It can't. Humanity is a chain of welded links; when you carry one link you carry the whole chain; when you throw down one link, you throw down the whole chain.

Business is not a thing by itself; business is a part of our world; you can't Christianize business without Christianizing the world. It is logical nonsense to talk about doing it.

There has been much effort, and splendid effort, to save the world by sections. We have the anti-saloon section, and the anti-gambling section, and the anti-cruelty-to-animals section, and the anti-impurity section-each trying to drive some doting old wrong out of the earth-and I applaud them all and give all of them my hand-but I remember that the success of each section depends upon the success of all, and not the success of all upon each.

You can't go out to the middle of our city reservoir and purify one hundred gallons of the water and keep that one hundred gallons pure while the rest remains muddy. To purify any part of the water, you must purify it all.

What do we mean by the Christianization of business? That means the uplifting of business to that exalted plane where Christ can approve it; that means the purifying of all commerce, the cleansing of it, until Christ can lay His white hand upon it and say, "This is right."

How is it to be brought about, the Christianization of business? In one way only-by the Christianization of the business man. Get the man right and the man will make the business right. How shall we Christianize the man? I answer, by Christianizing the Christianizer of the man. If all Christians were Christians we need not discuss this question. The thing would be done.

I think all are agreed that business needs something to come to its help. I wonder whether there is a sane business man on our globe who does not wish in the soul of him that existing business methods might be changed. Is there a merchant anywhere who does not long for emancipation from the trickery, the falsehood, the scheming, the dishonesty that obtain amongst trading people?

It is a creed with uncounted thousands that dishonesty in business dealing is necessary-that a man with an enlightened and Christianized conscience has no business with business-that wheels would not turn, that factories would not hum, that machinery would not throb, that no swift trains would roar across the continents, and no fleets would steam upon the seas, if Christ were at the head of the world of commerce. To vast multitudes of solid, substantial business men, Christianity looks like an impossible dream, good enough as a theory, but not to be thought of as a stern, hard fact. To them the whole system is a flimsy bauble, a trinket to please their wives and daughters, but too utopian and vapory to bear the tug and thrust of a business man's life.

The business men of any community are the men of energy, of worth, of enterprise. They are men who spend their lives in the midst of facts. They are suspicious of theories and distrustful of psychological speculations. They are repelled by that imbecile thing that has been called "Christianity" which projects beyond the stars all of its rapturous visions of a celestial city, and menaces the godless with a distant hades through which, in shadows and perennial sorrows the manes of the departed must forever wander.

There is a region of song and sunshine; there is a realm of remorse and darkness; all of that is true; but hard driven men want something that will sustain them in this present life, some anchor that will not drag. They want no weak and vacillating thing, they want some strong thing, a tower, a fort, a rock-something that will stand fast against storms. They do not know it, but they want Christianity-and it must be real Christianity.

There has been much done for the helping of the world that was very useless. Theories and hypotheses for the uplifting of men-God knows we are getting theories and hypotheses galore!

How shall we uplift the world? Look at the theories:

The theoretical theologian is getting his theoretical theology right. It is very important that he should get it right, for how can this world ever be saved without theoretical theology? It is hoped he will soon get it right. He has been working with infinite patience for nearly nineteen hundred years, and still toils on, no nearer the end than when he began. He is straightening out the tangles in justification and sanctification; he is adjusting the scheme of the divine hypostasis down to the third degree; he is splitting the hair that insists on getting between infralapsarianism and supralapsarianism and then splitting the split; he dreams a wild dream of teleology and of a possible apocatastasis; when he wants to have a nightmare he raises the grisly spectre of anthropomorphism and has it; he is braining with his pen the monist and pantheist; making fine dust of the deist and the theosophist, and shaking the life out of the higher critics as he bumps their devoted heads on his threshing-floor. Ought not that to bring about the Christianization of business? The business man ought to get straight out of self-defense.

Look at the scientist. He is helping in the same way as the theoretical theologian. He has got into trouble just now with the Garden of Eden and the zoological garden, as somebody has put it. He don't know from which man came, but he strongly suspects it was from the zoological garden. He is thrilling us with his ponderous talk about atavism, and vestigial recollection, and parthenogenesis, and karyokinesis, and the segmentation of the ovum, and evolution. You can't trip him up on evolution. He knows what that is. Ask him: "Evolution is a change from an indefinite incoherent homogeneity to a definite coherent heterogeneity through continuous differentiation's and integration's." That is something everybody ought to know. And yet the business man goes on wrestling with his problems in spite of it.

The mental philosopher is busy too. He is showing us how much Epicurus improved on the hedonistic theories of Aristippus, and how Hobbes made an advance on Epicurus; how Locke was mixed on the question of determinism; how Hume and Bentham and John Stuart Mill required a Herbert Spencer to clarify their thought, which he has done in seven volumes of solid mud.

Isn't that pointing men up? Why don't business get right?

Does it make you think of Mrs. McFayden's criticism of Maister Auchtermuchty's sermon in the Bonnie Brier Bush: "It's rich feedin' na doot, but sair mixt an' no vera tasty."

I think it is a sore pity some of the theologians and some of the scientists cannot get together and do what Eugene Field's gingham dog and calico cat did to each other; they ate each other all up, you know, and there was nothing left of either of them.

The world is never going to be saved by theories. There have been an hundred-and-forty-and-four-thousand theories, but still this old world's sorrows are not assuaged and no stop has been put to her sobbing. If theories have proven inadequate is it not time we try something else? And what shall we try? Shall we not try the great, living, palpitating, practical thing called Christianity?

The Christianity that Christ gave to men has never, on a large scale, been tried. The theoretical sham has been tried and has lamentably failed; now shall we not try the practical thing? I do not speak of trying practical Christianity as if we were going to make an experiment, for I am assured in advance what the outcome will be.

Christianity in its babyhood shook the world; infamies that were grown gray with time's centuries went down at the touch of its hand; it gave the last push to staggering iniquities and they fell to rise no more; kings and princes felt the power of its arm; empires were consumed by its advancing whirlwind. Why do we not see such things now? Where is the nation that regards the saying of Jesus as the final word? Where is the society of men that listens with dumb lips and reverent hearts when Jesus speaks? Nowhere! Individuals listen; societies fling back an answer. Why? Because we have substituted a theory for a life, a doctrine about a Person for the

Person Himself.

Jesus is not gone out of the world. He is in it as truly as He was in it during the days of His incarnation.

There is a beautiful legend in the Greek Church that when Jesus ascended and the cloud received Him out of men's sight, he floated away and came back to earth again in a different form, and that He still walks about clothed in flesh and visiting the haunts of men. It is a beautiful legend and it enshrines a splendid truth. Jesus is still here. I have seen Him and you have seen Him. We see Him every time we see a man, a true man.

A Christian is not a man who subscribes the Apostles' and the Nicene and the Athanasian creed; he is not a man with the robust faith to believe that Noah had Polar bears and panthers and boa-constrictors in the ark-a man may do all that, and believe all that, and live like a devil. A Christian is a man who has looked at Jesus, who has fallen in love with Him, has taken Him into His life, who believes He is the best, and is trying, by God's help, to be such a man as Jesus was. A Christian is that and he is nothing else besides. There can be no broader definition of what constitutes a true Christian, and there must be no narrower one. Christianity of that type will commend itself to the business man, because he is a practical man, and wants a practical thing. It is that that every preacher who is moving and quickening men is preaching today.

I thank God that real Christianity is coming back to earth, and now I believe the earth will be redeemed, and that business will be saved from wreck and ruin. The business men are waiting for this Christianity that is old but has now become new.

Well, why don't we preach this practical Christianity? Our ministers go to the schools to get their heads rammed full of theories for the saving of the world. They spend eight or ten years loading their guns, and never fire them. Some can't fire them because the powder is damp from lying still too long-deliquesced, as the chemists would say - in some cases the guns are rusty; in some cases the bore is too small to let out the ball, and if they should fire them the guns would burst, and the man would burst, too; in some cases they don't fire them because they have no fire, and in some cases if they should fire them the congregation would fire the man.

Perhaps it is this last that we are most afraid of. And is it not because of our cowardice that the world looks upon us with disregard? We have a message that sticks in our throats. We see wrongs done, but the people have stuffed our mouths with gold and we keep still about it lest the gold should be withdrawn. John Baptist was not afraid to denounce a king; Jesus was not afraid to stand in the very shadow of the cross and to pour out words that scorched and burned and withered every evil thing that lay in His pathway. The earliest preachers of righteousness did not tremble when they told the truth. I confess that I, personally, have not done my duty. I can rebuke that poor fellow with the hard, brown hands when he goes wrong; I can go to the inan in the shabby coat, to the woman with the faded green shawl, and tell them of their sins, but am I man enough to denounce to their beards financial princes and commercial kings when they go wrong?

"Through tattered clothes small vices do appear.
Robes and furred gowns hide all. Plate sin with gold,
And the strong lance of justice hurtless breaks.
Arm it in rags, a pygmy's straw does pierce it."

- William Shakespeare

There are not many John Baptists just now in the pulpits and that is the reason there are so many Herod's outside the pulpits, that is the reason more wrongs don't get right. No, men in the birthday of Christianity were not afraid to speak out; they were there to speak out. They counted not their lives dear unto themselves. They stood for the helping of the world, no matter what happened to them.

The cradle of the infant Christian Church was a tempest, and her earliest lullabies were storms. That same old berceuse has sounded around her through all the centuries, and she has not been afraid when God shook her music out of the black sky, his fingers playing on the quivering harp-strings of fire which became vocal with the anthem of the thunder.

The Church that will command the respect of the business man and of every thinking man must know no high and no low, must treat all classes alike; she must be a sheltering mother who will fold to her breast and hide under her aegis the poor, the ragged and the vile as well as the rich, the noble and the ermine-clad, a sheltering mother who, with her left will keep them from the windy storm and the tempest, but who, in her right hand, will hold the hissing lightning to strike every man and every institution that would do one of her little ones harm.

Business men as a class are not worse than any other class as a class. They are men like other men, as easily reached as other men when we offer them realities, as quickly repelled as any other when we taunt them with effete speculations.

There are Christian business men, God be thanked, and the good is spreading. Some one has said, "When God made this world, He took precious care to so constitute it that it would pay to do right." There are business men who are living the religion of Jesus in their busy lives, and they are among our most prosperous and successful men. They have demonstrated that a man can be a Christian right here where the conflict grows daily hotter and hotter, that they can live as Jesus would have them live and go at the same time to eminence in the commercial world. If I believed Christianity took away the possibility of commercial progress, of enterprise, of on-swinging betterment for earth, I should walk ever after with bowed head. But when I see Christianity tried in the markets and succeeding where hard men clash with hard men, then my faith in it is fortified, and I can say to you and to all who will hear, the day is arrived when we may lift up our heads and hope, for the time of our redemption draweth nigh.

Rev. W. H. Fishburn, D. D.
Pastor of Second Presbyterian Church

AFTERNOON

The first address of the afternoon was delivered by Rev. J. C. Watt, D. D., pastor of First Presbyterian Church, on "The Purification of the Church."

The Purification of the Church

Rev. J. C. Watt, D. D

B y what means is the Church to be purified? You remember the words of the Saviour when He prayed for His disciples-for His Church: "Sanctify them through Thy truth: Thy Word is truth!" Also in his epistle to the Ephesians, the apostle said: "Even as Christ also loved the Church, and gave Himself for it, that He might sanctify and cleanse it with the washing of water by the Word, that He might present it to Himself a glorious Church, not having spot, or wrinkle, or any such thing; but that it should be holy and without blemish."

This language implies that the Church was originally impure; and that the object of Christ was to cleanse her; and for this end He used the Word, as a purifying agent, washing her by means of it. And this work of purification is still going on, through the Word-the spiritual baptism of the Word-the teaching of Christian truth. And how effectual the Word is, when accompanied by the power of the spirit! It is quick and powerful in its influence, and produces changes of view and life. It awakens prayer, and elicits cheerful and efficient service for Christ. In the blessed Word there is everything to enrich the sanctified imagination, to enlighten the understanding, to counsel the judgment, to purify the conscience, and to exalt the affections; and thus, it exerts a holy, transforming influence on the soul. It shows us what we must forsake, what habits to abandon, what society to relinquish, and also the necessity of turning from all evil, by genuine repentance, and hearty faith in Christ. Is it not so, my friends? Do we not all feel better and purer by the Word of God which has been preached to us in the past few days? Have we not received enlarged views of the gospel and of duty? Have we not received a spiritual vigor which better prepares us for the duties and engagements to which we are called of God? Yes, there is a divine energy in the Word, which searches the conscience, and purifies the soul-a power which changes into its own nature all that comes in contact with it.

My friends, a Church so purified-purified in the heart and life, and filled with the spirit of cheerful service, is ready, and not till then, to go into the world, to redeem the world.

But there is another thought, which I think is equally important, though we may not find it so definitely expressed. It is this: One of the most effectual ways of purifying the Church is to set her to work to fulfill her mission. Jesus said: "If any man will do the will of God, he shall know of the teaching." And I think it is equally true, that if any man will do the will of Christ he will become Christ-like-pure. There is a reflex influence exerted upon the agent in every good work of benevolence and mercy. It is an unwavering principle in the economy of the religious and moral world, that he that watereth shall be watered also himself. And not only so, but he shall receive in an infinitely greater degree than he gives.

There is nothing I know of that will destroy that selfishness, of which we have heard so much in the last few days, and which is so odious to God and so contrary to the spirit of Christ, as loving service rendered to our fellow-men. Such service breaks the bonds of selfishness and allows the enslaved heart to soar aloft, and obtain enlarged views of duty, and fills it with that broad sympathy which is so wonderfully exhibited in the life of Christ. Whenever the Church really imitates Christ as He went about doing good, she will be enabled to rise above all her shortcomings, and thrust herself out into the world, a light to lighten it, and salt to savor it.

By doing the will of Christ, the Church will develop spiritual strength which will enable it to lift the world up to Christ.

Now, what of the range of these operations? If the Church would be pure, and become a purifying power in the world, it must come in contact with the world in every proper relation of life. And yet she must keep herself separate from the world. It should enter into business, and politics, and social and domestic life, and sanctify them and make them pure and sacred. I believe the Church is able to do this-or would be able if she were filled with the spirit of Christ.

Can anything less than the Christ spirit in the Church make progress toward this end in an intensely busy and active world? Let the Church be pure even as Christ is pure-let her be filled with the spirit of her Lord, and she will no longer be indifferent to the movements of the world, but with divine vigilance will adjust herself to every need, to every changed condition of the world.

You remember the words of the Saviour as He communed with His Heavenly Father: "As Thou hast sent me into the world, even so have I sent them into the world." And so He continues sending His Church into the world to continue His work. And the living present demands all our energy in this work. I am in no sense a pessimist. I do not believe that the Church is going headlong to the devil.

There are other means of purification which might be mentioned, such as the means of grace given unto the Church, among which, prayer is prominent. But I believe the two already noticed-the Word and service are sufficiently comprehensive to embrace them all. The Word awakens in the heart the spirit of prayer, and the baptism of the Holy Spirit, so essential for Christ's service, is given in answer to prayer. And I believe that active, loving service for humanity and the world, will purify the Church of every sin that now destroys, in any degree, her power and influence in the world.

DISCUSSION

REV. MR. MORTON, Dayton: I want to say that I believe that good practical leaders is one of the great needs of the church. I believe that our people are willing to come forward, and I believe they are willing to take hold of any enterprise that is practical that we lay before them. That I think we as ministers of the Gospel, as leaders of the church ought to do.

REV. J. O. PIERCE: The church is the bride; I don't like to hear the church whipped as we have heard it here for several days. Oh, it is the bride of Christ, and if you preach His love from a loving heart the church will do its duty.

Rev. B. Fay Mills then introduced the next speaker by saying, "I don't think it is necessary that I should introduce the next speaker, who is so well and favorably known here and abroad, and whom I have to thank for many courtesies received during my stay here, and to whom it is a pleasure to listen."

Rev. Washington Gladden, D. D., LL. D., pastor of First Congregational Church, read a paper on "The Regeneration of Politics."

The Regeneration of Politics

Rev. Washington Gladden, D. D

S ome one said to me last Sunday, as he passed by the pulpit after the service, with this leaflet in his hand: "You've got the toughest question of all." Well, I rather like tough questions. And I am sure, since the foundation of this universe is the eternal reason, that there can be no important questions to which reasonable answers cannot be given. And I believe that it is quite possible to regenerate and Christianize the politics of the city and the State and the nation.

It will never be done, however, until some important changes are made in the ideas of most of us respecting this whole subject of politics. Men are transformed, Paul says, by the renewing of their minds. The trouble with many men is that their ruling idea about life is a wrong idea. All their notions about the good of life are false notions. They must get right ideas before there can be any radical change in their lives. And it is just so with our politics. The ideas of men and women in all our communities about all this business are, for the most part, utterly and horribly wrong. The ideas of the people of our churches of the great majority of them-concerning politics are about as false and mischievous as they could possibly be. I am using strong language, but it is carefully considered, and I believe that it is absolutely true. The bottom trouble with all our politics is in the false conception of political duty and obligation which infests the minds of the great majority of the members of our churches. What is that idea? Why it is, for substance, just this: That politics is essentially and wholly a secular interest; that it belongs to a department of life wholly distinctive from religion; that it is a worldly affair, altogether; that religion is contaminated by every contact with it.

There are those who go so far as to say that no Christian can take any part in political affairs without being false to his Master; because Christ said, "My kingdom is not of this world." But many of those who do not adopt this extreme view, still maintain that the whole realm of politics is essentially unholy and one must enter it at the call of duty as one enters an infected house, holding his breath, and hurrying away, the moment his ballot is deposited. And it is not merely because of the existing abuses and corruptions that political life is so regarded; it is because it belongs with what is known in the common phrase as "the world." We are bidden not to love the world nor the things that are in the world: politics are part of the world; therefore the devoted Christian will have just as little to do with them as possible.

I suppose that this conception of the essential unholiness of political affairs has been strengthened by the separation, in our country, of the Church from the State. The idea has prevailed that this separation involves contrast. But this is not quite true.

Of course, as things now are, the State must be kept separate from all organized ecclesiasticisms, for their name in this country is legion; each claims to be the true Church, and the State cannot be umpire: it must let them all alone. Moreover, if there were but one Church, it would not be right for the State, so long as it uses any form of compulsion, to exert that compulsion in behalf of the Church; nor could the Church, without forfeiting its charter from Christ, accept any such support. The Church, as such, can know no law but love. are one.

Nevertheless, the fundamental purpose of the Church and that of the State Both are established for the glory of God and the good of men. Both are instruments for the promotion on this earth of the kingdom of God. The one is precisely as divine, precisely as sacred as the other. In ancient Israel kings and priests were both anointed of God. Was the one office any more sacred than the other? In our Christian democracy we are all, by divine appointment, kings and priests to God; priests to mediate and to minister; kings to rule: is not the one function as sacred, as divine, as the other?

The powers that be are ordained of God. Those who possess the actual sovereignty have received it directly from God, whose righteous will is the source of all just law and all wholesome government; and they are directly responsible to Him for the use of it. Who are the powers that be in this country? Who are the sovereigns here? The voters. Every male citizen, native or naturalized, over twenty-one years of age, shares in this sovereignty. Every such man is ordained of God to take part in ruling this land. It makes no difference whether he wishes to assume the responsibility or not; it is put upon him and he cannot shirk it. To refuse to assume it is to rebel against God.

Our political duties are, then, in their essential nature, sacred obligations. They constitute an integral part of the charge that God has given us to keep. We, the people, are the powers that be, whom he has ordained to work together with Him in building up His kingdom here. The ballot is one of the talents chief among them-which God has entrusted us to use for Him. I do not believe that any serious-minded man, who believes in God, can possibly find any other explanation of his political obligations.

If these things are so, how great and terrible is the mistake of those whose habit it is to think of political duties as though they were essentially unholy, as though it were a kind of profanation of religion to bring it into contact with them; as though a Christian's piety must needs suffer detriment, and his spiritual life be impaired, if he permitted himself to become deeply interested in the political affairs of the city or the nation. Until this idea is effectually banished from the minds of the people who sit in our pews; until they are able to comprehend that the pulpit is not secularized by an earnest discussion of the duties which we owe to God as citizens; until Christians are made to see that a primary meeting requires, for the proper performance of its duties, just as much consecration as a prayer meeting, and the marking of a ballot just as thoughtful a self-devotion as the partaking of the bread and wine of the Lord's Supper, we shall never see the thorough regeneration of our politics.

"But you will admit," someone is saying, "that the actual politics of our day are very unsacred; that the influences which are apt to prevail in them are vicious and corrupting; that any man who associated much with those who make a business of politics would be likely to suffer moral injury." Admit it? It is the substance of my indictment; it is the very gravamen of the charge that I make against the Christian people of this country. It is so because they have made it so, by their false distinction between things sacred and secular; by their relegation of politics to the category of things worldly and profane and irreligious. That realm, they have practically said, belongs to the worldly-minded; they must be permitted to rule there: the people of God are not responsible for that, except as they may bring some pressure to bear upon its affairs now and then, from the outside, to restrain out-breaking iniquities. So Christian people, as such, have permitted the machinery of politics to fall, not wholly, but pretty largely, into the hands of those who fear not God, neither regard man. And those into whose hands it has fallen are warranted, by the philosophy of the Christians themselves, in considering it a wholly unsacred business; a business in which secular, that is to say, selfish, motives must be paramount, and in treating it so.

Accordingly we have had, as the corner-stone of much of our political philosophy, the assumption that men in politics will act corruptly and selfishly. Our political machinery is largely adjusted to this expectation; we provide all sorts of checks and balances; we try to neutralize one man's selfishness by that of another whose interests are antagonistic; we set one thief to watch another. It seems to be supposed that out of this clash and collision of opposing selfishness we can evolve order and security and peace. It is a fond delusion. We have never got such a result, and we never shall. Yet our political system-makers can hardly be blamed for building on this foundation; have we not furnished it to them? It is we, the people of the churches, who must first comprehend the truth that this is God's world, the whole of it; and that there is not one thing that a man has a right to do which he is not bound to bring under the control of a truly religious motive.

The regeneration of politics will come, therefore, as the result of a new conception of the sacredness of this whole department of our life. We have got to reach a point of view at which selfish and corrupt scheming for place and power in the State shall seem just as horrible as if it were in the Church. What would you think, how would you feel, if candidates for your pulpits were in the habit of pulling wires, and making corrupt bargains with your deacons and elders, and offering all sorts of selfish inducements to the church members, and bribing the committees to get themselves elected, and were in the habit of using their offices for their own enrichment and aggrandizement? What would you think, how would you feel, if the same methods which are now almost. universally employed in getting political office were employed in securing preferment in the Church of Jesus Christ? You will never feel or think rightly about political affairs until you regard such practices in that realm with exactly the same horror as would fill your soul if you saw them introduced into the Church. The fact that you would be shocked to see in the Church what you contemplate with but little concern in the State, illustrates the need of a radical reconstruction of all our thinking upon this important subject.

It might be useful to consider this question under another form of statement-namely, the possibility of Christianizing politics. We sometimes use this phrase what do we mean by it? I should say that politics would be Christianized as soon as we arrive at the general and practical recognition of the fact that no man is fit to hold an office who is not governed by Christian principles. I maintain that we shall never have good government in this country until this is the recognized standard. No man, I say, is fit to hold any public office who does not accept and obey the Christian law. I do not ask that he shall profess any creed whatsoever, nor that he shall belong to any church, nor that he shall attend any prayer meeting, or teach in any Sunday school. We have plenty of men in politics who do all these things diligently, and who are yet as far from obeying the Christian law as if they were Buddhists or Mohammedans. The Christian law of politics is simply this: "By love serve one another." The Christian law forbids any man to take an office or use an office for self-aggrandizement, but requires every man who holds an office to consider it as an opportunity of service. The conception of office as spoils or booty is as distinctly anti - Christian as the worship of idols. I wish to say, with the utmost deliberation, that any man who has any just conception of what the Christian law requires of him, as a citizen, could no more seek or use a political office for purely selfish purposes, than he could prostrate himself before an image of Buddha, or throw his infant into the jaws of a crocodile.

It seems obvious that our politics are not yet fully Christianized. And yet the underlying idea of a democratic system is that the office-holder is the servant and representative of the people; that he is chosen and inducted into office to promote the public welfare, and not to promote his own interests. Let us get clear ideas about this, for here is the center of the whole question. What is the fundamental principle of a democracy: is it mutual plunder or mutual service? It is the one or the other, and I think that it must be mutual service. I do not believe that any permanent association of human beings can exist on any other basis. There are people in office, I am sure, who accept the doctrine that democracy means mutual service, and that office is the opportunity of service, and who try to regulate their official life by this rule. And a strong proof that this is the only right rule is the fact that those whose purposes are most selfish never fail to assert that their aims are unselfish. The platforms of the parties ring their changes on the benevolent designs of the parties. It is assumed that the party leaders are animated by this purpose. If any man says that there is much hypocrisy in this, I will not dispute him; but this hypocrisy is the homage which the vice of self-seeking pays to the virtue of self-consecration. When any machine politician sneers at the idea of conducting politics on Christian principles, we have only to reply to him. "You yourself professed before election, to conduct politics on Christian principles, and would not dare to make any other profession. Would you venture to go before the people with the statement that you were in politics for what you could make out of it for yourself; that you proposed to consult your own interests primarily and the interests of the people secondarily? You know that you would not dare to do any such thing. Even you professed before election to be guided by Christian principles-to be an unselfish servant of your fellow-men. If you say, after election, that in making this profession you were an abominable hypocrite we shall be obliged to take you at your word. But what you profess is right, as you know perfectly well; and all that is meant by Christianizing politics is simply getting all the people in office to be what you, when you are seeking office, falsely pretend to be." "Dearly beloved brethren," Dr. Johnson was wont to say, "Let us clear our minds of cant." There is no class of persons who need this exhortation more than the people in practical politics.

Now I, for one, believe that it is quite possible to be what the office-seeker professes to be. I believe that it is not absurd to expect men in office, as in every other department of life, to be consecrated men; to follow, in the service of the State, Him who came not to be ministered unto, but to minister. I believe, as I have said, that there are men now in office who honestly try to govern themselves by this law. And I am perfectly certain that our government will never be purified until this principle becomes central and regnant in all political life. All other remedies for corruption and misrule are superficial: this is the only one that goes to the root of the difficulty.

If all the people in office were governed by this law, how quickly the evils that now threaten the peace-yea, the very life of the nation, would disappear! And how shall we contrive to get such men into the offices?

I have thought much on this question, and I see no clear prospect of securing this unless we, the voters, ourselves are people of this kind. Are not the officials, as a rule, pretty fair representatives of the people who elect them? Are not the voters, as a class, about as selfish as the office-holders? Does not the average business man may say openly that he is too busy making money to attend to his political responsibilities? He is ordained by God to rule this nation; that is the most solemn charge that is given him to keep; but he refuses to accept it; he says that politics must be left to those who make a business of it. Is not the selfishness of the intelligent and industrious citizens who prefer money and a comfortable time to duty and the service of the State, the root out of which all political disorders grow? And does not the work of Christianizing politics need, therefore, to begin with the people who sit every Sunday in the pews of our churches? The time is come in the purification of politics when judgment must begin at the house of God.

I do not know any good reason why a Christian man should not govern himself by Christian principles in all his relations to the political life of the city or the nation. It seems to me that he ought to see that perhaps the very loudest call to deny himself and take up his cross is that which comes to him in the opportunities of service to the city or the commonwealth. If all political service is essentially a divine vocation this is very likely to be true. I doubt whether there can be any holier enterprise, any more genuine missionary work than this. It involves sacrifice, of course. All heroic Christian work involves sacrifice. It may require him to take burdensome offices, and to associate with disagreeable people, and to neglect his business, and to forego many gains and pleasures. Nay, it will require all this. But the good soldier of Jesus Christ must expect to endure hardship. And never, until the conception gets firm hold of the minds of Christians that it is by just such services and sacrifices that the kingdom of God must come, shall we see the work of Christianizing the nation going prosperously forward.

Let me not seem to end this discussion with a questioning note. The one thing of which I am more sure than anything else is the fact that this very conception is beginning to get such a hold of the minds of Christians as it never had before in all history.

The very strife and turbulence of this time are the groaning's of the creation that waits for the glory about to be revealed.

"The world sits at the feet of Christ,
Unknowing, blind and unconsoled;
It yet shall touch His garment's fold,
And feel the heavenly Alchemist
Transform its very dust to gold."

-John Greenleaf Whittier

Rev. Washington Gladden, D. D.
Pastor of First Congregational Church

* * *

DISCUSSION

REV. MR. WILBER (Mt. Vernon): All I have to say regarding this very able paper I will say in the words of another, and they are ditto. ditto, ditto, ditto.

Rev. Alexander Milne, pastor of Plymouth Congregational Church, delivered the following address on "The Salvation of Society."

The Salvation of Society

Rev. Alexander Milne

That society needs deliverance from wrong and sinful conditions you were doubtless all ready to confess after Dr. Taylor's address yesterday afternoon. The purposelessness of much social life is demoralizing. The vulgarity and vanity manifested in the efforts to outdo one another in display, the newspaper accounts of social functions with their descriptions, not only of decorations, but of the dresses worn by the women, are painfully evident. Men were formerly spared such humiliation - a thing to be devoutly thankful for, but recently I have noticed in the daily papers brief, but significant items, naming men in this city who are noted as fine dressers. I am not at all vindictive or bloodthirsty, but such a mention would almost justify a man in threshing the reporter and threatening the editor with dire consequences.

Passing over the grosser evils of society, the extravagance which, in the face of hard times and suffering people, thousands of dollars for an evening's entertainment, the dissipation, the carousals, the darker sins not always kept under cover, let us consider the utter brainlessness of that section of the population which arrogates to itself the title, "Society"- with a capital "S."

I heard a young woman, bright and keen in intellect, with wide knowledge and high moral earnestness, speaking disparagingly of the young men she met in society. She defended dancing, because it was almost the only thing these young men could do. It was useless to try to hold a rational conversation with them, for they had nothing of any importance they could talk intelligently on.

That a Christian social life is possible, Christ's life and example justifies us in saying. The Son of Man came eating and drinking, so that His enemies spoke of Him as gluttonous and a winebibber.

If present society is so bad that it cannot be born again, then Christians must abandon it and build another. This, however, will not be necessary in most cases. If Christian people would set themselves against all foolishness and senseless customs, all low standards, all immoral and unmoral rules and practices, if they refused to countenance and fellowship so as to honor evil in any form, a vast transformation would speedily be wrought. We must begin where we are. There is a loud call for Christian missionaries to society. The discouraging feature of the present situation is the fact that Christian people, members of Christian churches, countenance and support these things. They are mixed up with the vanities and vulgarities and extravagances of society.

Let me indicate briefly, in conclusion, some of the characteristics of a Christian social life. It will always emphasize character. Character will be the one thing to be honored above everything else. The dishonest man will not be able to buy his way into it. The man whose character is the noblest, though poor, will receive the greatest admiration. The verdict of society will be one of the forces that make for righteousness.

Again, it will insist upon a true culture. It will not be satisfied with that superficial thing now known as culture, consisting principally of bows and gloves, and evening calls and cards, and dresses and swallow-tail coats. It will demand a deep culture of the mind, and especially of the heart. It will recognize that the motive of the heart is better than the motive of the hand. It will form select circles, select simply because one's social relations cannot be unlimited, in which there can be some rational conversation. The group to be found around the uncouth, barefoot and bareheaded figure of Socrates was the finest society of Athens. A cultivated society is a society in which people have brains and use them.

In such a society there will be a recognition and a cultivation of individuals. True individuality will be encouraged. At present society represses individuality. All must dress alike and act alike. Everything tends to become conventional. Society is hedged about by the statutes and ordinances of that despotic creature, Mrs. Grundy. A breach of etiquette is worse than a transgression of moral law. This stifles true individuality. A Christian society will be freer. There are, of course, laws which can never be abrogated. There are customs and courtesies which are simply happy and beautiful ways of doing things. These are limitations to true individuality only as the rails limit the locomotive.

In a Christian social life the spirit of Christ will be the motive power and the guiding principle. It will be guided by those whose hearts have been touched by the spirit of God, who have given themselves to Christ.

DISCUSSION

MR. C. S. HUBBARD: I think that if the Christian women would quit wearing so many birds on their hats it would be a good thing. Thousands of birds are killed every year to furnish vain women with these adornments. Let them have all the ribbons and flowers they want, but quit wearing birds. I never knew why women wore them, for they are not pretty on the hats; and one day I asked a lady why, and she said, only homely women wore them; then the people looked at the birds instead of the homely women.

The next address was by Rev. Rollin H. Walker, formerly of the Epworth League House, Boston, Mass on "The Cleansing of the Slums."

The Cleansing of the Slums

Rev. Rollin H. Walker

T here is a natural distrust of young enthusiasm, especially when it concerns so great and complicated a question as the cleansing of the slums. I beg, however, not to be classed as merely a youthful dreamer over our present unfortunate social conditions. I have lived three years in a University Settlement in the center of the Italian and Jewish quarter of Boston. I am familiarly acquainted with a very large number of the residents of the slums.

These men have made me a confidant in nearly everything that concerns. them, and now that I have been absent for a few months from the work my mail is constantly burdened with letters written in the queer scrawling hand of Russian Jews. Hence, however faulty my philosophy may be, its errors are not founded on an ignorance of the conditions.

In attempting to answer the question as to how to cleanse the slums I am reminded of the remark of General Grant, "That the best way to do a thing is to do it." The Christian army, like that of General McClelland, is forever waiting for proper equipment. Jesus said, take neither purse nor scrip, neither two staves, but simply go. Perhaps the general principle of this command, expressed in modern English, would be, "When Christ sends you on a mission wait not for money or facilities, or for an appropriation from a missionary society, but begin." And the command that follows immediately after would also suggest that you should be quick about it; for the disciples were to salute no man by the way. A special delivery stamp was on their message. When Jesus saw the blind man by the way he did not tell the man to wait while he went to the apothecary's for some magic healing salve. He spat on the ground and made clay of the spittle and anointed the eyes of the blind. That is to say he infused his own life into the common clay beneath his feet and gave it a healing efficacy. And so every man is to take the common means at hand and trust to the supernatural to give it power. Prof. Richard Moulton said one day, that he defined the obvious as that "which was so near to us that we never saw it." The obvious way of cleansing the slums is so natural, so simple and so entirely at our command that we often do not see it at all.

God keeps saying to the Christian trembling before the great work that he is called to do and lamenting his lack of means, as He said to Moses, "What is that in thine hand?"

Let me describe to you the foundation of a mission which in a modest way illustrates the principle of which I have been speaking. In the Spring of '93 there were three young men about to conclude their course in the Boston University School of Theology. They felt called to begin mission work in Boston. But how was it to be done? The city missionary society of their church was painfully crippled for funds. In the great slum portion of the city there was not a single church, mission or other philanthropic institution belonging to the denomination to which they were attached. Two months before they graduated these young men, by the help of the Dean of the school persuaded the Boston City Missionary Society to hire them at the rate of $400 per year. Before the end of the year two of them were each offered four times that amount but preferred to remain at their posts. They went down among the tens of thousands of Russian Jews, Portuguese and Italians in the great foreign quarter of the city. They had no hall, no church, no appropriation for rent. They were landed on the curbstone and told to found a mission, and warned not to expect a single cent of appropriation in so doing. Well, to make a long story short, they did it. If you will go there today you will find an Italian Church of some hundreds of members, a Portuguese Church, a Medical Mission, an Evangelistic hall, and thirteen professional missionaries paid to give their lives to that work. If those young men had waited until a reasonable salary had been guaranteed to a single one of them, I doubt if the work would ever have been begun.

I was talking with Bishop Thoburn, the Bishop of India, and Malaysia, some months ago, and he informed me that a few minutes before a mission property worth several thousand dollars had been transferred to his hands. "That," said he, "would look like a very good thing, wouldn't it? But now hear the other side of the question," said he, "I have just assumed the support of two missionaries in connection with this property, and I haven't the remotest idea where the money is coming from." "And that," he continued, "has been the history of the India Mission from the beginning." Step after step in the dark. If there are any qualities needful in missionary work, they are the qualities of faith and humility. Faith to go without a complete path-finder in our pockets; humility to use the means at hand. For younger workers, however, this faith is not one which allows us recklessly to incur financial obligation. Let me illustrate the beginnings of certain phases of the work with which I was connected in Boston.

The beginning of our boys club.

A Russian Jew comes to repair a broken light in a window in the Settlement House. This is our chance. We cultivate his acquaintance as he cuts away at the hardened putty, and when he finally melts into confidence, we say: "Have you any children Mr. Baker?"

"Yes, I have a boy named Solomon."

"Ah, indeed. How old is he?"

"Thirteen."

"That is just the right age. Tell him I want to see him."

Tuesday night, at the appointed time, a quiet, black-eyed little Jew rang the door-bell, and the worker, who had him in charge, exerted himself to his utmost to make that a delightful evening for Solomon. They talked, they drummed on the piano, they played checkers, they looked at picture books. That night was the critical time in the history of the boys' club. The next week it was organized, and that without a single additional stroke of work from the University Settlement worker. He had captured little Solomon, and little Solomon captured his playmates.

THE MASTER'S METHOD

Did not this in a small way illustrate the method of the Master? He had undertaken the conversion of the world, and yet he found time to talk with the poor woman at the well. That he did so, shows that he considered such a course to have been the swiftest way to bring the teeming millions of earth to his feet.

I have lived in one of the densest slums on the Continent for three years, and yet I have never had anything to do with the masses. All my dealings have been with the Italian, Antonio or Gaetano, with the Jewish, Mordica or Abraham.

It has been found in our Boston work largely impracticable to use many of the theological students because they are willing only to sit upon the platform and address the multitude. It is but now and then that a man comes along who is willing to devote himself unreservedly to the common unromantic work of dealing with the individual.

BY THE PEOPLE AS WELL AS FOR THE PEOPLE.

This brings us to another important principle, namely, that most of the work for the salvation of the lower classes is to be done by those who are only a grade above them in the social scale.

The Samaritan woman brought the whole town out to hear Jesus. Attention to this one person proved to be the quickest way to get the ear of the multitude. So it is ever. You remember after Jon. G. Paton had worked and suffered for years on an island of the New Hebrides, the whole people were converted as by a Divine compulsion through the fiery sermon of a half-naked chief. Bishop Thoburn says that in India more people are converted by the poor and illiterate Hindustani preachers who sit down on the door step of a native hut and sing and talk to the people than by the educated missionaries from Europe and America. Jesus spent a very large part of his time training twelve fishermen. And they, according to his prophecy, were to do greater things than He. The training of lay workers is one of the great questions before us today. Prof. Huxley said that there ought to be a ladder from the gutter to the university upon which every lad might climb as far as he was worthy to climb. Certain it is, there ought to be a ladder from the common walks of life reaching upward to the best training in Christian work, upon which every man and woman who has leisure or talent or love might climb as far as he or she was worthy to climb.

In London, New York, Chicago, Boston and many other cities there are these training schools for lay workers, taught much as our medical schools are, by busy men who each give one or two hours a week to this work, without compensation.

It is amazing what capacities for religious work there are in the common people. One of the enthusiastic women in our Settlement suggested to a club, consisting mostly of Italians, ranging in age from fourteen to sixteen, that she organize, out of the younger boys of the neighborhood, an "Anti-Cigarette League." The plan appeared to me very impracticable. "Why, woman," thought I, "these slum boys capable of doing missionary work. You may be thankful if you succeed in getting them to be fairly decent themselves." One week from that time that same little group of Italian boys brought forty somewhat overawed youngsters into the Settlement House; and had them sign a pledge to keep themselves from various gross forms of vice to which the boys of that section were addicted. The Settlement missionaries, mind you, had little or nothing to do with the affair. I was permitted to be a spectator. The boys came up one-by-one and sat down by the master of ceremonies, a young Italian named Liveroni. With unfeigned seriousness he read the pledge to them. He then had the boy read it himself. Next he asked him whether he was sure he wanted to sign it. "Because," said he, "we want none of the boys who sign the pledge to be seen doing the very things they have promised not to do." One boy wavered a little in his faith as to his ability to keep the pledge, and withal showed a tendency to frivolity; and was accordingly set aside as unworthy to be enrolled. I could not have gotten those boys together by weeks of work, unless I had hired them, to sign that pledge. What a minister, who flattered himself that he was a trained missionary, could not do, eight boys from the slums successfully accomplished. The young boys whom they organized into this club had previously been turned out of the Settlement as incorrigible by a very skillful worker, who, by the way, was for some years a successful professor in your own high school. Some nights after, the same lads kept an audience of seventy young boys still while a gentleman lectured to them on the evil effects of nicotine.

I worked for nearly a year to organize a Jewish night school, and succeeded only in getting half a dozen young men to attend the class. In the middle of the summer, however, a young Hebrew by the name of Schwartz, became interested, and in a short time he filled every available room in our Settlement House with eager students, and that, too, on the very hottest night in July.

What an example of the utilization of lay effort do we find in the Salvation Army. Every member, you know, sits on the platform and feels the weight of responsibility in conducting the meeting. All the church in the pulpit-that is the Salvation Army method.

A JOYFUL MESSAGE

This brings us to notice another element of the Salvation Army's success, and of all success among the poor, disconsolate children of the alley and the slum. The Salvation Army always have a "good time" at their meetings. No minister there that reminds you of an undertaker! The dispensation of the Holy Spirit began by the necessity on Peter's part of explaining that the Apostles were not intoxicated. "These men are not drunken, as you suppose, seeing it is but the third hour of the day." In like manner the doings of the Salvation Army give occasion to the mockers to say that these men are "full." They are full. But they are "not drunken with wine, but filled of the Spirit." The poor addled headed victims of intemperance, with brains soaked in whiskey, are not able to follow a sermon. They must have a religious appeal to their emotions and a constantly varying program, such as we find in the cheap theaters. The Salvation Army meetings are said to be modeled on the cheap variety theaters of London.

DISCIPLINE

And not only are the common people to co-operate in this work for the poor, and to have this spiritual efflatus that gives them liberty and unction, but they are to be subject to discipline. And this brings us to say that the first necessity in this work is to find your Gideon who has power of faith and personality to say "Look on me and do likewise; and behold when I come to the outside of the camp it shall be that as I do, so shall ye do."

A VOLLEY

The common folk are profoundly impressed by what we call "a demonstration." The Midianites were put to flight by a pitcher and lantern demonstration quite similar to the "volleys" which are fired in some of the meetings of General Booth's followers. Paul says that the unity of Christians is to the forces of evil "an evident token of perdition." There is something about the united tread of a body of soldiers, and the sudden and simultaneous leveling of their rifles that strikes terror to the mob. In like manner the disciplined unity of Christians puts sin to the route. I was in the Settlement during the great Christian Endeavor Convention last July, and as the historic part of Boston is now the slum region, these Endeavorers for nearly a week, by the tens of thousands, kept pouring down into the Italian and Jewish quarters. The effect of their kindly words and bright smiles upon the poor of our district was simply indescribable. We explained to these people how that the Endeavorers were made up of representatives from nearly all Protestant denominations, and that they were united in a determination to love Christ and spread his kingdom. You know the idea of the "trades" union is very strong among the working people. In some of our cities they will not eat a loaf of bread that does not have the union label on it, and if we can persuade them that our form of belief and practice is "union made" we acquire great influence. I have often told mission audiences that I was a walking delegate for the union started by Jesus, the Carpenter of Nazareth, and I was urging them to join so that we might all stand shoulder to shoulder and back to back to protect ourselves against the forces of evil. And their attention was always aroused by the figure. During this same Christian Endeavor Convention a number of Italian boys came to the House with a supply of bunting under their arms which they had borrowed; and after an hour's work we found their club room beautifully decorated. "Boys," said I, "what did you do this for?"

"Oh." was the answer, "we thought we would leave it up during the Convention."

What a prophecy of the future, that these young foreigners should be so impressed by the glad fervor of our Christian young people. What an illustration of the fact that the slums are to be reached by the co-operation of all Christians. That evening I had a class of Russian Jews in rhetoric. They were usually eager to learn and impatient of a digression, but this evening they absolutely refused to give attention to the subject. They were full of questions about the Christian Endeavorers. The query seemed to have suggested itself to one as to whether the denominations were not pretty much at one after all. "How is this," said he, "I go to the Methodist, the Congregational and the Presbyterian churches and I hear about the same thing?"

When I explained the difference they were evidently surprised that I did not run down all sects but my own. There is no doubt whatever that one of the principal reasons why Protestants do not succeed in evangelizing the unreached masses is their lack of unity. This unity does not at present at least mean giving up of denominational responsibility for individual missions, but rather in the careful repression of the denominational spirit when making our appeal to the masses.

But, you say, that I have made the poor responsible for a large part of the work among the poor. What are the so -called upper classes to do? Must they retire to their elegant homes, like the twenty and three thousand whom the Lord separated from Gideon's band as poor material for such fierce fighting? By no means. No man who is not more refined than Jesus Christ is above this work. The point that I would emphasize is this: that like the Master, the educated and refined leaders should give a great deal of attention to the training of humbler men for the work.

At many of the mission meetings in which I worked we had the presence of the professor of Hebrew of the Boston University. He did not say much or do much, but the fact that the professor would honor our meeting with his presence gave me increased influence with the audience. In continental Europe few persons of any consequence have anything to do with the poor. Hence they despise the missionary as a plebeian, and for any one of acknowledged social position to give the prestige of his presence is very helpful. Again the upper classes can investigate the conditions of the poor. "Blessed is he that considereth the poor." It is written in the Scripture that when Elymas the sorcerer withstood Paul and Silas, "seeking to turn away the deputy from the faith." "Then Saul, who is also called Paul, filled with the Holy Ghost, set his eyes on him." That is what many other men, full of the Holy Ghost need to do in our great cities.

In the north end of Boston there is a street which for a generation has been filled with the lowest dance houses. Deputations from the Rescue Home have been, during the last year or so, going nightly into these places and simply "setting their eyes on" the conditions that there existed. A decided impression has been made. The sailor boys did not care to indulge in such orgies at the risk of looking up at any moment to find the calm eyes of a pure woman fastened upon them.

In closing, let me say with all possible emphasis, the man Christ Jesus is the picture that most easily secures the attention of the masses. The deeds of this Man and His wonderful work will bring a look of interest to the face far more quickly than any argument that may be presented. Over and over again have I seen the look of indifference or contempt turn to one of interest and sympathy at the telling of the stories of the evangelists in modern English -of how Christ defended the woman of the town who washed his feet in the house of the proud Pharisee; of how he ate with publicans and sinners.

It is no mere theory, but the solid experience of every man who comes in close touch with the sunken masses, that more than any ingenious instrumentalities it is the uplifted Christ Himself who will draw all men unto Him.

DISCUSSION

MR. C. S. HUBBARD: If we can't do anything else let us get up in the morning with the determination to do something to make the world better -to speak kindly to a dog, or do some kind act for something or somebody. Let us make it a rule every morning to start out to do something good that day.

REV. FRANK DOTY: I have been a city missionary in this city for two years. I have never found it as difficult to transfer these people from the slums to the church as it is to keep them there; they don't find the people in the church that care to fellowship with them; they feel as if they were not wanted there; no one bids them welcome, and they come out with a determination never to return. I have had several of these people from the mission join the church, and it has only been a few weeks when they came to me and said, "Mr. Doty they don't treat us as well in the church as you do." I say, "Why yes they do." They say, "No they don't; they don't even shake hands with us, and when they do they act as if they were afraid we would contaminate them." Do you want to reach the people in the slums of the city? Then you must come in contact with them. Bring your good clothes and culture, let them associate and come in touch with the "salt," bring them in touch with these Christians and you will do more for this work than you can do in any other way.

* * *

Topic for Thursday, Dec. 5-"Entire Consecration."

"Up, Sanctify yourselves, for tomorrow the Lord will do wonders among you."

MORNING

After the devotional services, which were conducted by Rev. John H.

Murray, Rev. Andrew Dunlap, pastor of First Christian Church, read an address on "The Scriptural Theory of Entire Sanctification."

The Scriptural Theory of Entire Sanctification

Rev. Andrew Dunlap

B ut in what does consecration consist?

First and preliminary to all else, it is to "set apart," to "dedicate." This is separation, self surrender and recognition that we are God's. In the Old Testament times consecration was known by specific acts and ceremonies that fitted and delivered the offering. In the consecration of the Aaronic priesthood there was a closet of meditation and prayer, an anointing with holy oil, the offering of sacrifice, and the putting on of new suits prepared in reference to the priestly office. The Disciples of Jesus tarried in Jerusalem, in the upper chamber, at the altar of prayer, in gracious waiting for the endowment of the Holy Spirit. In all cases of consecration the spirit of it is this, to make fit for the Lord's use. We can see something of the realty of the sacrifice in the words of Dunbar's song:

> *"My life, my love I give to thee,*
> *Thou Lamb of God who died for me."*

Second, consecration consists in a divine quality to be attained. What is the quality? There is only one that fits the case, that is "holiness." When Aaron and his sons were consecrated, "they made a plate of pure gold and grave upon it, like the engravings of a signet, HOLINESS TO THE LORD." That was a key-note, and a not to be forgotten one. Some of the words used for consecration in the original signify to make holy. The word is somewhat interchangeable with the word sanctify, and especially is this root quality of holiness borne out in both. Holiness is the vital point in God-ward religion. It means wholeness, completeness, and soundness of moral character. Its spirit lies in the demand for the subjugation of the thought, word and actions all to the Christ ideal of life. In shortest terms it is love in the heart and in the life, for that is to be like God, for God is love.

This grace is a gracious attainment; it is indeed an endowment quality, but very practical withal, and clear above the sentimental thing conceived in the lapsing condition of overwrought nerves resulting from high emotional excitement. Dr. Huntington says: "Holiness was meant, our New Testament tells us, for every-day use. It is home-made and home-worn. Its exercise hardens the bone and strengthens the muscle in the body of character. Holiness is religion shining. It is the candle lighted, and not hid under a bushel, but lighting the house. It is religious principles put into motion. It is the love of God sent forth into circulation, on the feet, and with the hands of love to man. It is faith gone to work. It is character coined into actions, and devotions breathing benedictions on human sufferings, while it goes up in intercessions to the Father of all piety."

The third thing in consecration is service. Consecration is not half consecration until it has vitalized energy, and equipped us full handed for blessed work. The everlasting saints rest is not yet. This is the time for duty. If there is any body in this universe who should be thoroughly alive and full of gracious activities it is the re-born child of God.

Christians need tools to work with, and they need energy to use them, and I do not believe that God will allow any to go unfurnished who desire equipment for what they can do. Christ's religion is not a sofa chair religion, but an up-and-at-it religion. All that the go-easy religionists need to enable them to realize their ideal is that somebody with more energy than themselves should put rockers under their sofa, and then sing a sweet lullaby for them, and they would quickly pass off into the sleep of oblivion for time; but of course they would want some angel of mercy to wake them up in the bright morning of eternity that they might share in the glorious song of the redeemed, but it is doubtful if they would not be too lazy to sing the song even then. If we all could only get rid of the disposition to pose as some sort of ornamental thing in Christ's kingdom we would soon get a better idea of what Christ wants in service.

It is no use for us to say that we cannot be useful, for we have both tools and opportunity if we would not dissipate them. Christ gave his disciples truth, "sanctify them through thy truth" and he will give us the same weapon. If we will take it and learn how to use it the victory is half won before the battle begins. What an irresistible force for God is the armory of truth.

One of the Hebrew words for consecration means to fill the hand. That is the point to which our consecration must bring us all. Hands full for Christ, hands full for humanity, Christians loaded for service, is God's way, and it is of no avail for us to pass our lives away in a dreamy sleep. Three words may express the scriptural theory: Recognition, communion and service. Service for the kingdom of God in this world, communion with God in holiness by love, and complete recognition that we are his. Let this grace be in us all and tomorrow God will show us his wonders in answer.

W. T. Perkins, General Secretary of the Young Men's Christian Association, then made an address on "Scriptural Illustrations of Entire Sanctification"

Scriptural Illustrations of Entire Sanctification

Sec. W. T. Perkins

The speaker cited Enoch, Abraham, Joseph, Moses. Nehemiah, Daniel, Paul, and above all, Jesus, the son of God, as cases of complete consecration. Fixing the eyes on these typical cases he exclaimed:

"Is not this consecration, to give our life, not up to ease and self-gratification, but to the deliverance and the leading out into a larger life those about us who are in the bondage of sin? Is not this consecration, to abstain from that which will in any way weaken our health and strength, to pray to God continually despite the opposition of men, and to determine to be right with God rather than be popular with men? Is not this consecration, to righten municipal wrongs; to turn people to God; to unify the church, and to magnify God and His holy Word."

Speaking of Jesus, he said: "Finally let us withdraw our attention from these remarkable men, who were not at all times blameless, and let us turn our eyes to the exemplary character; to the blameless, spotless life of the Son of God. He is the supreme example; He is the highest type of perfected manhood; He is the acme of true consecration. His meat and drink was to do the will of His Father, and to die for the world He wished to help and for the people He desired to save. He gave the best He had; He gave Himself. For He so loved the world, that He gave Himself, that whosoever believe in

Him should not perish but have everlasting life.

Oh, that we all might have the Christ spirit of consecration, so, like Him, we could say at the end of this earthly life, 'I have finished the work Thou gavest Me to do.' "May this be our experience, and may the following words be embraced in the prayerful resolve of each one of us:

> *"My life, my love, I give to thee,*
> *Thou Lamb of God, who died for me;*
> *I consecrate my life to thee,*
> *My Savior and my God."*

> -*"I'll live for Him"* Author: R. E. Hudson

Discussion of the subject followed the address.

Rev. W. J. Coulston, pastor of the Baptist Church at Washington C. H., O., then read a paper on "Characteristics of Consecration."

Characteristics of Consecration

Rev. W. J. Coulston

C onsecration is the act of a saved man. In conversion we receive from God. Being converted we may give to God. The giving of the saved life to God in Christ, in self-surrender, is consecration. Consecration is a recognition of personal obligation under the gospel. "I am debtor, I am debtor," cried Paul. A man will not pay a debt until he feels his indebtedness. The recognition of indebtedness under the gospel is a fundamental principal in Christ, in self-surrender, is consecration.

Paul believed he owed men the gospel and confessed the debt. His sense of indebtedness did not rest, however, upon the basis common in our thought - favors received. Men so measure obligation, and express the measure in dollars and cents.

Paul's gift was himself. He had received much from God, but little, save hurt, from man. Yet he was debtor to man. He measured his obligation by the law of Christian stewardship, by which he was bound to give according to his ability and his fellow-man's need.

These two - my ability and man's needs - determine my debt. And my ability is of least consequence. What does my fellow-man need? That is the question. Furthermore, the Christian is able to supply the man's need, for he has his own experience and God's inexhaustible fulness to draw upon.

The second element in Christian consecration is a personal commitment to the service of Christ and the gospel. "I am ready," said Paul. "Ready," calls the Captain, as He stands by His company's line, and every musket is in position and every soldier is intent upon the next command. The volley is fired as from one gun because all were ready.

"Ready," shouts the starter upon the athletic field, and every runner is at the scratch, with body bent and muscles tense, expectantly waiting the signal to start.

What God in His Church, now militant, most needs is soldiers-not guerrillas or bushwhackers, but soldiers, men and women loyal and obedient.

A third element of consecration is a personal sense of power with the gospel, and of the power of the gospel. "I am not ashamed of the gospel, for it is the power of God unto salvation."

Christ does not send us into work without equipment. "Ye shall receive power after that the Holy Ghost is come upon you." "Go, and lo I am with you alway." In relation to the Holy Spirit and the abiding Christ, yet apart from these, peculiar to itself, the gospel has power. There is a "preparation of the gospel."

Paul knew the saving power of Christ. The story of it is the gospel. He had seen thousands come under its blessed power as he told the story. The gospel was the power of God unto salvation. He knew it, gloried in it, was in no sense afraid to try it anywhere, was ready and not ashamed to preach it in Rome.

Given a specific work and a perfect implement with which to do it, and there is no room for doubt or hesitation. Such is exactly the case with the Christian and his work. Before us is the world under the curse of the law and the power of sin. Unto it we are sent with the story of Him who "Hath redeemed us from the curse of the law being made a curse for us," and "Who is able to save to the uttermost all who come to God by Him."

The gospel of Christ is the sufficient answer to every question, and the satisfaction of every longing of the human soul and life. How can a man who has experienced its blessed power help telling the glad story? Believe it, and in it, and you will tell it with an impassioned earnestness that will be irresistible to men!

This is consecration, self-surrender to God in Christ, with the consciousness of personal obligation to Christ and to those for whom He died; exhibiting itself in personal commitment to the service of Christ, with an unreserved confidence in the power of the gospel and of personal power with the gospel.

The last address of the forenoon was delivered by Rev. J. C. Jackson, Sr., D. D., pastor of Wesley Chapel, on "The Need of Consecration."

The Need of Consecration

Rev. J. C. Jackson, Sr., D. D

There is a type of so - called consecration which is about as cheap as it is worthless. I do not know whether much or anything is made of it in other denominations than my own-the Methodist Episcopal-but I do know much is made of it by some ministers and some members among us. It consists substantially in first preaching to a lot of so-called Christians, assembled in some congregation for revival services, about certain imaginary, transcendental, religious experiences that are located in the emotions. They are then called upon to come forward and bow at an "altar" and "consecrate themselves, their time, talents, property, all they have and are, to God," and to ask Him to "accept the sacrifice," and to "bless" them, and to "get the blessing" is the great objective point. To be wrought up to a great emotional fervor, and then to pass into a state of natural reaction of quietness or peace, which is simply the relaxing of over-wrought nerves, is supposed to be the sign that God has "accepted the sacrifice." Then the people have been "blessed." Then they are in high favor with God, and are entitled to look down from the height of a certain superiority upon their fellow church members. The others are not so "spiritual" as they so "unworldly"-so "deep" in their experiences. The others have not got so much "power." But in twenty-five years' observation of people who are frequently going through this kind of "consecration," I have never been able to find that they have any less of the "old Adam" afterward in them than anybody else. They will lie as quick as anybody else; they will get mad as quick; and they are just as hard, upon the whole, to get money out of for any good cause as anybody else. If you go to them with the story of some poor widow who is starving, or some orphan child who needs clothing, or some discouraged laboring man who ought to have his rent paid in order to help him through a tight place, you will not get it any quicker than from people who do not claim to be "consecrated" at all. In fact, in my experience as secretary of a rescue mission, having many thousands of needy cases pass through its hands yearly, I found I stood just as good a chance, if not better, of getting aid from infidels, Jews, agnostics, atheists and saloon keepers, as from this type of "consecrated" people. They seemed to imagine that their so-called "experiences," which were but the spasms and reactions of an over-wrought self-produced, nervous excitement, somehow brought them into special favor with God, and absolved them from any special duty of love or service to God's poor children. The less we have of this kind of consecration, the better. It is a farce, a delusion, and a snare. It has, in many, supplanted the idea of any true consecration, which means sacrifice of ease, sacrifice of pleasure, sacrifice of money. We had better, it seems to me, consider ourselves as publicans and sinners; we will be in a more hopeful state for getting into right relations with God and man, if we do not befool ourselves and others with any such nonsense.

The only kind of "consecration" I care one rap for, or believe in-the only sort that is not a stench in the nostrils of any practical, common-sense, blood-earnest Christian, is the consecration that is willing to lay its heavenly experiences on the shelf, and take off its coat, and get down to the often disagreeable work of making this world better. It means being willing to associate with folks who are not interesting; it means going to places where you will get the pauper smell. It means sacrificing, if need be, the junketing trip to Florida, in order to save money to take some poor girl out of the store to send her to school. It means staying home from the Melba concert in order, first, that you may pay your honest debts to the grocer around the corner, and in the second place, that you may have something to give the sick shoemaker's family. This is what I understand to be Christianity. It is the consecration of a tender heart, of a helping hand, of a pitiful soul. And I thank God, there are some Christians who have this idea of consecration. As I have waded chin-deep during the last few years in the miseries and wretchedness's of darkest Paterson, in New Jersey, and the darkest corner of Jersey City, and darkest homes in New York I have been cheered to find many good people-some of them in very humble circumstances - and others-thank God-rich, who put aside the weekly amount for charity, and who didn't reckon their church expenses in as charity, either-as one rich man who showed me his accounts, not long since, did-people whom I could send to the case of need-who bought cheaper clothes, and denied themselves, sometimes, of excursion trips, and who didn't get as often to lectures and concerts as they otherwise would have done, in order that they might have wherewith to give to the poor and help good causes. That, I perceive, to be the kind of consecration needed, and I can find it among Universalists, and Unitarians, and Jews; and in Felix Adler's Ethical Society, and I have found it there as well as among orthodox Christians; and I call such people brethren in the essential Christ just as quickly as any other sort. But for any type of religion which plumes itself on its orthodoxy; which is awfully keen in its scent for heresy; which titillates itself with the semi-exotic fervor's of so called "consecration" meetings, with its kid gloves in its hands, and its scent of Yhlang-Yhlang in its sanctified nose; which sits in its ceiled houses and its warm churches, and around its turkey dinners and champagne suppers; which heeds not the cry of the perishing, nor stretches out its hand to the poor at its gate. I, for one, loathe and abominate it; I spit upon and hate it, and I believe it is the very chief anti - Christ against which the true Church of God has to contend today. Sooner than that such a type of Christianity should come to prevail in the Church, it would be better that all our churches and creeds, and commentaries, and theologies, should be swept away, and God's Holy Spirit of love and Christly helpfulness, which is now, in these last years, being poured out in unusual measure upon God's true children should be left to work its work, and organize itself a new body in this earth wherein to dwell. Better, if they get in the way-I fear-better, if they puff people up with the vain conceit of their own holiness-abolish our denominations and make a fresh start with all those who are of the Christ spirit. It is getting too late in the nineteenth century for the world to stand humbug much longer. It wants fruits, and if it does not find them, it will cut down the tree that does not bear them, and plant another in its place.

The consecration which is willing to go to work for the city's welfare, is especially needed among the rich and well-to-do, who have leisure to take office, to be secretaries of societies, to be aldermen and health inspectors, and in general to devote themselves to the public service. It is a burning shame to rich men who have the social influence, and the money, and the time, to let a few preachers and women beard the lion of licentiousness, and rum-selling, and oppression of the poor, in his den, alone. It has been my duty in another city to stand, every council meeting night, by the year, with a few other preachers, resisting the granting of illegal liquor licenses. We needed money to hire detectives and legal counsel to do the detective and lawyer work necessary; and we continued to need it to the end. We needed men of social standing and recognized power and influence in that city to stand up and back us as we struggled, like Paul, with the wild beasts. We had some, but the men we needed, as a rule, were at Lake Mohawk, spending money; or off on six-months' trips to Europe, delectating themselves among the art galleries of Florence, and bringing home artificial parrots and cuckoo clocks from Geneva.

I hold that a man who makes his money in a town, who, by means of that money arrives at a condition of affluence and leisure, owes something more to that town than to pack his grip-sack and go to Europe. I hold that the only justification he has for having $200,000, or $500,000, or $1,000,000 more than his toiling, equally worthy fellow-men, to whom God has not given quite so much brains or so good a chance, is that he use his leisure and his fortune for the benefit of his fellow-men. I hold that a reign of terror and the blotting out of all idle, luxurious plutocracy, were better, in the long run, than the quiet acceptance of the doctrine that when a man has made his pile he has a right to do with it what he pleases, and spend his leisure in idleness and self-indulgence. It is a matter for devout thanksgiving to God and the Holy Spirit of enlightenment that we have in this city, and many cities, a growing, glorious class of the rich, who love their fellow-men; who administer their wealth as a trust from God; who feel that they are here for something else than to have a good time in the world, and who, with their accumulated, baptized capital, are the strong right hand of the true Christian Church, the community's hope; they have brains; they have the power to get wealth, and they use it for the glory of God and man. God bless the rich Christians and multiply them a thousandfold. But for the idle rich, the selfish rich, the luxurious rich, God has no use in this country, and the people themselves are not going to have any use much longer.

I am not very well "up" in my notions of the exact relations of capital and labor; I have not very clearly defined ideas about socialism, and all that-the subject is a big one, and I've been too busy as a preacher in other departments to go into it as much as I wish I had time to do-and as much as some very wise friends tell me I ought to do. I don't know that I fully endorse our Brother Mills's preaching of the doctrine of an unqualified altruism, if I rightly understand him; but this one thing I am perfectly clear about-we need a vast amount more altruism than we have, and the Church ought to have that kind of preaching for about two hundred years now, till it got out of its foolish notion of hugging itself in its holy raptures, and letting the world go to the devil. And we need a vast amount more of altruism among the well-to-do, and the leisurely, and the cultivated, or the devil will soon foreclose His mortgage upon them, and hell will break loose. I have a sort of general notion, after all, that what is needed is not so much, possibly, a change in the system of doing business by competition-I can hardly see how our average human laziness can get along without that I have not much faith in the commercial utopias of Bellamy all that sort of a thing may be all right as an ideal, and may come after a while. But it seems to me that if our rich men go on making money on this present competitive plan, it is all right if they will only regard themselves as making it for the general good of all. If they regard their talent and their opportunities as a God-given capacity, bestowed for the making of money to help the lame, and less gifted. I am perhaps a very poor Socialist. But I am clear that what will save the rich, will be to make a true consecration of themselves to God.

Let these, and let us all, make a practical consecration of ourselves to God and His kingdom of righteousness, and let the Thomas A. Kempis's and the Madame Guyon's, and their modern successors, have a monopoly of the other kind, and settle accounts with God and man for themselves at last.

The need of entire consecration. If any of us think that the devil cares a brass farthing for the cheap emotionalism of Christian piety; if anybody cherishes the nonsense that rum shops and bawdy houses and tenement rookeries, and dirty streets, and dirty water, and dirty politics, are going to be prayed out of Columbus, the sooner we drop such humbug the better. The best kind of praying and the best kind of consecration I know of is the prayer and consecration of hard work. The Lord helps those that help themselves.

When we in New Jersey, yonder, consecrated ourselves to get out of our prayer meetings and into political meetings; when we went by the thousands to our weak-kneed legislators and took them by the nape of the neck and held them to their sworn duty; when we literally bulletined the names of the men who would not help us on the part of our churches and swore holy war upon them, then it was that New Jersey downed the race-track gamblers, and railroaded ballot-box stuffers to the penitentiary by the score, and redeemed that State from a worse political thralldom than Washington broke the power of when he whipped the Hessian's at Trenton.

The prayer meeting is all right in its place, but faith without works is dead. This is a practical age and cares only for practical things.

* * *

AFTERNOON

The first address of the afternoon was by Rev. Thomas Winfield Booth, pastor of Russell Street Baptist Church, on "Helps to Consecration."

Helps to Consecration

Rev. Thomas Winfield Booth

He spoke in part as follows:

First among the things that should help us to make a perfect consecration is the great need of consecrated lives in our city. The Mills meetings have served us as a kind of looking glass. We have been looking at ourselves and have found, to some degree what manner of city we are. That was a dark picture we looked upon last Tuesday, when we drew back the curtain and saw the sin and poverty and crime in Columbus. It was such a sight as moved our Saviour with compassion and should stir the Christian consciousness to its deepest feeling.

Another fact that should draw us into a full surrender of ourselves to Christ is that the laborers are so few. I do not mean to say that there are not consecrated men and women in our churches. There are many who have left all and followed Him. But the number is too small. It is small, indeed, when compared with the work to be done. This is not the saddest side of it all. The hardest thing for me to say is this, that the consecrated laborers are few when compared with the number of professed followers of Christ.

It will be easier for us to devote ourselves entirely to the service of Christ if we remember whose we are. Men forget this. The Christians at Corinth forgot it. They were fast becoming the slaves of sin, and Paul wrote to them: "What, know ye not that your bodies are the temples of the Holy Ghost, in you, which ye have of God, and ye are not your own? for ye have been bought with a price; therefore glorify God in your body and in your spirit, which are God's."

Wendell Phillips once heard Lyman Beecher preach on this theme, and after the sermon he went to his room, threw himself on his face, saying, "Lord, I belong to Thee; take what is Thine own." If it be a difficult thing to devote ourselves wholly to Christ, let us pray the Holy Spirit to deepen in our hearts the appreciation of the fact that we are not our own; we belong to Christ. Then shall we be able to say from our hearts, "Lord, I belong to Thee; take what is Thine own."

I mention, as a last help to a life of consecration, this: That we ourselves were saved by the self-sacrifice of others.

A stranger was seen one day going up to a neglected grave in the cemetery at Nashville, Tenn. He had a flower in his hand which he laid upon the grave. The warden stepped to his side and asked if his brother or father was buried there? "No," said the stranger, "he was not a relative. But I will tell you who. When the war broke out I was living in Illinois. I wanted to enlist, but I was poor and had a wife and seven children. At last I was drafted. I had no money to hire a substitute; so I made ready to go, leaving my family to live as best they could. Just then a young man came to me and said, 'You have a large family. Your poor wife cannot clothe and feed them. I will go in your place.' He went in my place. He was wounded at Chickamauga and was taken to the hospital in Nashville, and here he died. Ever since that day I have wanted to come and see his grave, but was not able to pay the car fare. At last I saved up enough and have come to see my dear friend's grave." Tears streamed down his cheeks as he stooped down and set up a little slab by the grave on which were cut the words, "He died for me."

If the self-sacrifice of man for man will beget such deeds of grateful devotion, what shall we say of this: "While we were yet sinners, Christ died for us?" "Who, then, is willing to consecrate his service this day unto the Lord?"

* * *

The next address was by Rev. W. J. Russell, pastor of Central Christian Church, on "The Results of Consecration."

The Results of Consecration, Rev. W. J. Russell

What are the results of consecration? In other words, what will follow a life that has renounced allegiance to the world and earnestly and believingly surrendered heart and soul to the will of Christ?

1. There will be peace. This is the outflow of a consecrated life. It is languid indecision, desperate sullenness, anything which keeps a man away from Christ, that prevents peace. Do we want the picture of a restless heart? Infinite duty, infinite transgression, infinite woe-that is the restlessness of man. God's remedy to heal this restlessness is to write His law by the Spirit upon the heart, so that we love Christ, and then we have what Christ commands. It has been well remarked, it is not said that after keeping God's commandments, but in keeping them, there is great reward. God has linked these two things together, and no man can separate them-obedience and peace. The heart of consecration is devotion to the will of Christ. And the last step in a Christian's progress toward peace is the attainment of a spirit of active obedience. The Lord Jesus cannot give you peace whilst there is one point of controversy between you and Him. The lack of peace so manifest in the lives of many who profess to be the children of God is due to the fact that there has been but a partial surrender to Christ. I ask you to pause here for introspection. How is it with you? You read and pray and go to church, and endeavor to maintain a respectable position among religious people, and yet your heart is cold, your soul is barren. You realize that you

have the form of godliness without its power. Why is this? Is it the lack of wholeness of purpose? Some act of obedience not complied with? Some idolatry? Supreme selfishness? Is not your life, after all, one of practical atheism-God not entering into your plans, your labors, or your enjoyments? What is needed is a complete consecration. When that point is reached, the clouds of doubt and despair will depart, the joyous sunbeams of God's love will beam upon the heart, and peace will visit the soul; yes, peace in the soul which faith lifts above the storm-cloud, and which bathes in the calm sunlight while the tempest breaks beneath it.

2. There will be joy. Peace is passive, but joy is active. The consecrated soul has more than an inner glow; it has an outward beaming. It rises above mere peace into that "morally glad frame of heart," in which we not only peacefully acquiesce in the ways of righteousness, but delight and exult in them as ways of pleasantness. There is a joy of the world, but, like gathered flowers, though fair and sweet for a season, it must soon wither and become offensive. But the joy that is the result of a consecrated life is like smelling the rose on the tree; and it is lasting-immortal. The joy of the world is like the brilliancy of the bubble, that bursts at the touch of the finger of sorrow, or sickness, or loss, or a thousand sharp fingers besides; but the joy of a consecrated soul is like the brilliancy of a sapphire, that can pass through the furnace without losing a single ray.

Has the Divine Master touched the heartstrings of your soul? If not, He is waiting to do so and cause it to swell and break with a pulse divine.

"In the still air the music lies unheard;
In the rough marble beauty hides unseen;
To make the music and the beauty needs
The master's touch, the sculptor's chisel keen.
Great Master, touch us with Thy skillful hands;
Let not the music that is in us die!
Great Sculptor, hew and polish us; nor let,
Hidden and lost, Thy form within us lie!"

3. "In the still air the music lies unheard; In the rough marble beauty hides unseen; To make the music and the beauty needs The master's touch, the sculptor's chisel keen. Great Master, touch us with Thy skillful hands; Let not the music that is in us die! Great Sculptor, hew and polish us; nor let, Hidden and lost, Thy form within us lie!" Another result of consecration is the power for doing Christian service. It was the spirit of consecration that enabled the apostles to labor and suffer for their Master. It kindled the life into a calm, steady flame of zeal and devotion. It enabled them to face all dangers and hardships; and gave them that Christian heroism which helped them to suffer and die as good soldiers of the cross. He, then, who has entered into the beautiful palace of consecration, is strong to do the work of Christ. He will have a love that will labor to save the fallen and degraded. Those who believe shall have power given to do works, in some respects greater than any Christ did, not greater miracles, but to effect greater moral and spiritual revolutions-works that shall take in a magnitude of results beyond anything that belonged to Christ's earthly ministry. The beauty of holiness belongs to an infinitely higher realm than the finest grace or mightiest power of physical display. A miracle may split the hardest rock, but holy volition s are not born of force. A hand of power may write on the wall a nation's fate, but faith alone can paint Christ on the soul. "Because I go away," says Christ, "that is, because your life shall be a life of faith, a life of devotion to My service, your 'works' will be 'greater' than all My miracles."

This thought needs to be impressed upon every heart. Let us realize the exalted position which we occupy. Christ has called us into service. If we are His, we must be powerful. In the ever-deepening desire for complete surrender to the will of Christ, lies a wonderful enlarging of outer power for Him. The constant practice in the small prepares us for the large. We are not called to look for service in prominent places. Barnes says: "One Niagara is enough for a continent." We need tens of thousands of little streams to meander through our fields to make them fertile and fruitful. In the Church we need consecrated, tongues that will speak, consecrated hands that will work, and consecrated hearts that will sympathize. It is the little deeds of love that make the great ocean of Christian influence. And God prepares His workers by giving them an absorbing fidelity in the unseen inner life, which spreads through all the soul and at last brings the whole round of being in unity, and the soul is ready for any task, large or small. Then comes that noble, transcendent hour, when God's command to do some high behest for Him finds the soul ready, girt for action and full of power.

The truth is, dear hearers, we do not half live up to our privileges. Hence we fail of exercising that power which we might. It is ours to live in a much higher sphere; then would the primitive power of the Church be felt, and thousands crowd to its portals. It is ours to walk in constant communion with God, and if we did, we should conquer the world. This should be the ruling purpose of our lives. God's love is the point from which to move the soul. When this is realized and experienced you will move as an angel of goodness on earth. Your influence, living after your death, will remain *"A rill, a river, a boundless sea,"* upon whose waters numberless trophies shall be borne, to adorn your triumph when you take your place among the victors in the kingdom of God.

* * *

The next address was by Rev. A. D. Hawn, D. D., pastor Presbyterian Church, Delaware, Ohio, on "How to Consecrate One's Self to God."

How to Consecrate One's Self to God

Rev. A. D. Hawn, D. D

An eminent English writer says: "We consecrate ourselves by the response of our faith; by our obedience to the divine law; by subjecting our judgment and our will to the truth; by giving full play to all godly emotions; by the formation of habits of thinking and feeling which consolidate into holy character and build up a holy life." There appears to be this difference between consecration and sanctification: The former belongs to us, the latter to God. While it is true that the two are inseparably linked together in the individual Christian; still the work of consecration is that which specially belongs to us. I shall therefore consider it mainly from the human standpoint.

Genuine consecration requires a willing mind. Its whole value is in its voluntariness. Of our own free will and consent we must yield soul, mind and body to our Lord. Since the will is the chief power of our nature, it must deliberately and determinedly purpose to love and serve the Lord before there can be any real consecration. The Lord cannot accept a dedication that is not wholly and freely made.

As there is nothing in Christ that may be refused, so there must be nothing in us from which He must be excluded. We must feel it no sacrifice to renounce any whim, passion, habit, friendship or amusement of which He would not approve.

Pericles said to the Athenians: "I would have you day by day fix your eyes upon the greatness of Athens, until you became filled with the love of her;

then you will freely give your lives to her, as the fairest offering which you can present at her feet." So we need, day by day, to fix our eyes upon the greatness and excellencies of Christ, until we are so filled with love and devotion to Him that we will unreservedly lay our whole life at His feet and be thoroughly consecrated to Him; and that will be the fairest offering we can present.

Then consider, also, the many and glorious manifestations of earnest, persistent efforts to an ever-increasing consecration that we have in the history of the Christian Church: A Paul, the long list of early martyrs for the faith, the Christian missionaries, such as Brainerd and Elliott, the Moravian brethren, Williams, Judson, Carey, Morrison, Livingstone, Martyn, and hundreds of others. Talk of consecration! There it was not talked about, but lived out in daily lives of ceaseless devotion to Christ Jesus and His work. O, my friends, if, in sight of such consecrated and persevering labors, we realize that we are not wholly given to Christ, and to an ever-increasing devotion, then let us place ourselves hard by the cross of Christ, where we can see His wounds still bleeding for us, see His body still quivering in pain for us, and that will surely incite us to renew our consecration, and to henceforth press on from one degree of perfection to another. Not only from the walls of pastors, but from the walls of every home, shop, office, counting room, where Christians are found, there should be an imaginary picture of the Crucified One looking down and saying, "Live for Me! Live for Me!"

Topic for Friday, Dec. 6-"The Holy Spirit."

"Ye shall receive power, after that the Holy Ghost is come upon you. "

MORNING

The last day of the Convention opened with a devotional meeting, conducted by Rev. W. L. Lemon, pastor of Memorial Baptist Church.

The first address was given by Rev. A. J. Hawk, pastor of Gift Street

Methodist Church, on "The Holy Spirit in the New Testament."

The Holy Spirit in the New Testament

Rev. A. J. Hawk

H e spoke, in part, as follows:

In the work of personal salvation it is the Holy Spirit that comes into direct contact with the soul, convincing it of sin, reproving, warning, striving, and producing that feeling of unrest and sorrow for sin common to all awakened persons. Then the Holy Spirit woos and draws toward Christ, and thus helps the soul, in its infirmities, to offer acceptable prayer for mercy. As faith takes hold of Christ the Spirit applies the blood, agreeable to Paul's words when he speaks of "the washing of regeneration and the renewing of the Holy Spirit." Hence, the Holy Spirit is the author of the new birth, and not only so, but also the witnesser to the blessed fact that the work is done. "The Spirit beareth witness with our spirit that we are the children of God."

God ever stands in a gracious attitude toward the children of men, if they will only turn to Him in His own appointed way for help. And whenever Christian people feel their need of the baptism with the Holy Spirit to better qualify them for work in His cause, and meet the requirements of prayer, faith and obedience, then it is they may, and do, receive the larger and fuller manifestation of the power of the Holy Spirit in their hearts and lives. There was another Pentecost after Peter and John were forbidden by the Jewish rulers to preach any more in the name of Jesus Christ, under threats of the severest penalties, when the entire Church betook itself to prayer. Then it was we read, "And when they had prayed, the place was shaken where they were assembled together; and they were all filled with the Holy Ghost, and they spake the word of God with boldness." And still another, at the home of Cornelius, when Peter preached to a Gentile congregation, and, as he himself describes the scene, "And as I began to speak, the Holy Ghost fell on them, as on us at the beginning." Now, if three Pentecosts, why not three hundred? And if to a large and then to a small congregation, why not to the individual believer? Shall we not each and all be encouraged to seek this great blessing, especially as our Saviour says, "How much more will your Heavenly Father give the Holy Spirit to them that ask Him?"

* * *

Following are extracts from the address by Rev. P. A. Baker, pastor of Third Street Methodist Church, on Cleansing."

Cleansing

Rev. P. A. Baker

That man in his unregenerate state is entirely out of harmony with the ethical character of his Maker and Judge, is well nigh an accepted doctrine of the universal Church; hence, the practical redemption of the soul consists in its emancipation from its own base and evil nature, and in the transformation of the spiritual nature from sin to holiness - the effacing of the earthly and the restoration of the image of God.

There is no state of grace or purity to which man may attain and pronounce himself free from danger and beyond the reach of temptation; and whoever goes, for present inspiration, back to some tree, fence corner or altar, as the place where they received the so-called "second blessing," goes too far after fire to be of much assistance, either to God or humanity. The grace of today will not supply the need of tomorrow any more than the breakfast you ate this morning will answer the need of tomorrow morning.

"Ye shall receive power after that the Holy Ghost is come upon you." Power to resist evil and power to do good. It makes men honest in the face of temptation, pure when surrounded by evil, hopeful when the way seems dark and hedged in-helps us to think right, talk right, and act right. It is the very essence of the true kingdom.

Men have usually all of this power that they want. "They ask and receive not, because they ask amiss." Others want it until they see the responsibilities and required devotion that comes with it, and then they don't want it. There are many people willing to be wholly the Lord's, if being His would require no sacrifice of time, ease, or means. Hence, they want religion as they want contagious diseases that they must have-in a light form.

We have abundance of splendid machinery, churches fine enough, congregations rich enough, preachers eloquent enough, choirs that sing sweet enough - if not quite plain enough, but we seem to lack the power-what our fathers were fond of calling "Holy Ghost power."

If what we have heard during the past few days be true, may it not be that our churches need to be cleansed of a few golden images and Babylonish garments? If this be true, the first need is a few earthquake shocks of conviction, such as unhinged the gates of that old Philippian prison, set Paul and Silas at liberty and made the jailer cry, "What must I do to be saved?"

A little of Paul's type of pulpit ministration might be helpful as a forerunner. I am aware that some may be in the condition of the old artilleryman, who said he was afraid to fire off his cannon for fear it might kick over the gun carriage. It may be that before the "Word of the Lord can have free course and be glorified," it may be necessary to smash a few gun-carriages.

The fact is, we do not plan for great things. We are too easily satisfied. If our churches hold their membership and we come out at the end of the year with ten or a dozen of an advance over and above deaths and removals, we think we have done well; but as a rule such a record is a confession of great spiritual leanness. The Lord cannot bless nothing, and many of us have not done anything that He can bless, hence, we are unblessed, so far as any real spiritual vitality is concerned.

Work for the Master is easy when the spirit of the Master is in us, and we become Christ-like by doing what Christ would do, and saying what Christ would say. There is no royal road to spiritual favors by which one may receive more than another. There is a light that lighteneth every man, and whoever is willing to pay the price may possess the power. The price is self-renunciation-a willingness to let Christ have His way in us and with us. Then it is that we learn that Christ's way is the easy way, and the safe and satisfactory way.

Not by some frenzied struggle after holiness, but by daily obedience to the will and the commandments of God, which so keeps us before Him, and in His presence, that we are changed unconsciously from character to character by the very reflection of His holy nature.

* * *

The last address of the morning session was delivered by Rev. W. C. Stinson, pastor of First Presbyterian Church, Chillicothe, Ohio, who spoke in part as follows on The Holy Spirit in Daily Life."

The Holy Spirit in Daily Life

Rev. W. C. Stinson

May we have the spirit of God in the practical affairs of life? Yes, we not only may, but must have Him, if we are to overcome the besetting sins and resist temptation, and if we are to be agencies for the development of the kingdom of God on earth. We must have the spirit of God in the times of temptation. There is no chapter more real and intense than the chapter on temptation, sinful appetites and tendencies, temptation to impurity, to dishonesty, and temptation to neglect the duties of ordinary life. Now, we must have the spirit of God within us to enable us to overcome these temptations. Why is it that one man succeeds in overcoming temptation and another man does not? It is because one man has within him the pledge of victory and the other the pledge of defeat. When you see a young fellow who refuses to go out at night because be fears the temptation upon the street, you have pity for his moral weakness. It is not that we shall keep ourselves from these various places of temptation in the world, but that we shall take into them the personality that is secured to us by the Holy Spirit, and after man with his soul is entirely surrendered to the spirit of God, the spirit of God will keep him secure. If we possess the spirit of the life of Christ, then we are dead unto trespasses and sins. The only sure safeguard against temptation is to give ourselves over completely to the keeping of the Holy Spirit and to reckon these natures of ours as the temples of the Holy Ghost and then trust the Holy Spirit to keep what properly belongs to Him. The temptation of Christ was the greatest temptation that has ever come to man, first to selfishness, then to presumption, and lastly to blasphemy; but He was kept secure in the hour of His awful temptation by the Spirit within Him, and he who trusts in this Spirit shall become a prince in Israel.

The very slow progress of the kingdom of God on earth is due to the fact that it is not set up in the shop and store, and in the railway office, in the bank and upon the farm, in the school house and in the home, and in all of the secular pursuits of life, and the time has come for Christian men and women to break down this false distinction between the secular and the spiritual.

What we need on the earth today is not more preachers, but preachers who are filled with the spirit of God. Not more money, but money consecrated to Almighty God. Not more churches, but the membership of our churches so wrought upon by the spirit of God that whatever they say or do, shall promote the kingdom of righteousness in the earth, and that man who has failed to consecrate his business to Almighty God will be under just as great condemnation as the minister of the gospel who uses his profession for the sake of personal emolument.

How the spirit of God would dignify all the labor of love, take away all its drudgery, and then give us the sublime consciousness that we are associated with Christ Himself in the development of His kingdom on earth, so that preachers and school teachers, and jurists and statesmen, and mechanics and bankers, and tailors and all of us, might exclaim together, "We are workers together with God in the bringing in of the kingdom of righteousness in the earth."

* * *

AFTERNOON

The first paper of the afternoon was by Rev. R. S. Lindsay, pastor of Eastwood Congregational Church. He spoke in part as follows, on "Knowledge."

Knowledge

Rev. R. S. Lindsay

The fact that Christ was not able to impart all the truth about the things of the kingdom teaches us the duty of aiming after a rich spiritual life in order to win the world to Christ. For the world is carnal, and is not able to discern the things of the Spirit of God. It cannot receive Him because the Spirit and the things of the spirit must be spiritually discerned. This is Paul's interpretation of Christ's words to the disciples. The world may possess the gift of other knowledge, the result of investigation and research and criticism; but this cannot lead the unspiritual man to the possession of the Spirit of Truth. Spiritual knowledge, a knowledge of the things of the kingdom of God, a knowledge which puts us into fellowship with the life and teaching of Jesus is not the fruit of intellectual attainment, or mental grasp of the sciences and philosophies or histories of the world, but can be ours only by possessing the Christ-spirit of humility, dependence and love.

> *"Thy home is with the humble, Lord!*
> *The simplest are the best;*
> *Thy lodging is in Christ-like hearts;*
> *Thou makest there Thy rest."*

-Thomas Hornblower Gill

No man by searching can find out God; no man by study can discover spiritual things. All our knowledge of Him in relation to our spiritual life must be communicated to us by His spirit." The doctrine of Paul is in exact accord with the authoritative teaching of Christ. It is this: The unspiritual man is incompetent to know spiritual truth. And this is by no means a strange, unreasonable doctrine. It comes under the same law which governs us in acquiring knowledge in any branch of learning. Only one with music in his soul can enter into the delights of the masters. A lover of nature alone is able to interpret nature. What is art to the unartistic eye is deformity to the artistic eye. In natural things the eye and ear need to be educated in order to see and hear the sights and sounds of the world. We cannot apprehend the truth of any subject until we have developed our minds on the line of that subject. Knowledge of any kind comes to us by contact with it. And when Paul says, in his first letter to the Corinthian Church, that "The natural man receiveth not the things of the spirit of God; for they are foolishness unto him; and he cannot know them because they are spiritually judged," he is uttering one of the commonest truths of life. The Pentecostal blessing was nothing remarkable when we recall that, for ten days, the disciples were together in prayer, lifting up their hearts and thoughts and affections to God, and thus coming in contact, by communion of spirit with spirit, with the divine life.

This doctrine of the sources of our spiritual knowledge is a most important one, yet it is often misapprehended. Spirituality needs a new definition by the Church. To be filled with the Holy Spirit frequently means an awakened emotional life, and a deadening of the moral and ethical perceptions. But surely no one was less emotional than Christ, who seemed to pass quietly over Palestine doing good as He went about, and yet sending out such a mighty spiritual power from Himself that at a touch from His garments the sick were healed.

The real secret, after all, of a baptism of the spirit of God lies in our willingness to be used for God. Entire consecration-presenting ourselves as living sacrifice a humble dependence upon the divine spirit, a recognition of cur spiritual needs, a sincere yearning for better things-frequent meditation upon that which is lovely and of good report; this will quicken our spiritual life and bring us into communion with the Father.

* * *

There being no discussion of the preceding paper, Rev. J. W. Icenbarger, pastor of Central Baptist Church, Dayton, Ohio, was introduced, and spoke on "Joy in the Holy Spirit."

Joy in the Holy Spirit

Rev. J. W. Icenbarger

Following are some choice extracts from his address:

The word joy means exalted. It is rejoicing, it is excitement, the pleasurable feeling flowing from the spirit in a believer, after the love of God is shed abroad in the heart. It is the second fruit of the Spirit. (See Romans v. 5; Gal. v. 22.) The Spirit came on the day of Pentecost to take the place of Jesus Christ, and to show many things unto the believing, obedient disciples.

There are distinct aspects of this joy, as there are different aspects of truth that the Spirit uses in producing this joy.

First. There is the joy of salvation flowing from Jesus as the salvation of God, revealed by the Holy Spirit to our hearts. The angels said to the shepherds: "Behold, I bring you glad tidings of great joy, which shall be to all people, for unto you is born this day, in the city of David, a Saviour who is Christ, the Lord."

Secondly. There is the joy of knowing what we have in Jesus Christ as believing ones. In John xv. 11, the Saviour says: "These things have I spoken unto you that my joy may remain in you, and that your joy might be full."

Thirdly. There is the joy of doing what Jesus wants us to do, the joy of obedience. In John 13:17, He said to His disciples, just after that memorable event of feet washing: "If ye know these things, happy are ye if ye do them." Then the cleansing of the defiled, by applying the water that is in the Word, or the restoring of the wandering who have gotten out of the path and into

248

defiled ways, will bring joy to the heart of the one who thus follows the example of Jesus in cleansing the defiled.

Again, there is the joy of winning souls to Jesus. In 1 Thessalonians 2:19, the apostle says: "What is our hope or joy or crown of rejoicing? Are not even ye in the presence of our Lord Jesus Christ at His coming? For ye are our glory and joy. "Oh, the joy of winning a soul to Jesus! Some of you know the joy that flows into your heart when a soul that you have been laboring with consciously receives Jesus as the Saviour, and penitently confesses Him as such. There is a flow of joy, seemingly unspeakable, into the heart of the successful soul winner.

Again, there is joy when I fall into manifold temptations. James 1:2 says: "My brethren, count it all joy when ye fall into manifold temptations."

Then, lastly there is the joy of hope, of confident expectation, the promise of good things.

Beloved, we cannot have any aspect of this joy except through the power of the Holy Ghost. And now in conclusion, let me ask, are we full of this joy? If not, why not? What aspect of truth are you not believingly, prayerfully drinking in so that you may be filled with this joy of the Holy Ghost? There is a deficiency somewhere if we are not full of it. How am I to be full of the Holy Ghost joy? I answer, by coming believingly, prayerfully, obediently to, and drinking of the fulness that there is in Jesus Christ. You remember that last day, that great day of the feast, Jesus said, "If any man thirsteth, let him come unto Me and drink. He that believeth on Me, out of his belly shall flow rivers of living water." Oh, that it may come today in fulness, into our hearts to flow out in streams of blessing to others!

* * *

The last address of the Convention was delivered by Rev. W. E. Biederwolf. He spoke as follows on "The Power of the Holy Spirit."

The Power of the Holy Spirit

Rev. W. E. Biederwolf

A mong the last things that the Saviour said to the disciples were these words: "Tarry ye in Jerusalem until ye be endued with power from on high." As they looked upon the cold and unbelieving world and realized something of the service they were to render and the task that they were to accomplish, and the almost irreconcilable barriers they were to encounter, they felt insufficient for these things, and felt the need of some power other than their own, if they were to accomplish any great thing for God. Welcome, indeed, then must have been these words of the Saviour falling in rich promise upon their hearts, that they were not to be left alone. But against the power of an unbelieving world was to be matched a power from on high, and against wisdom and human belief and judgment was to be placed the Holy Spirit of God. "Tarry ye in the city of Jerusalem until ye be endued with power from on high." As one of our brothers informed us, "power" comes from a word in the Greek, which, when translated, means dynamite. And the power of the Holy Ghost is the dynamite of the Holy Ghost, the power by which the kingdom of heaven is to be perfected upon this earth through human instrumentality. And I am quite sure that if those disciples who stood for three years at the feet of the great Teacher, the best theological seminary this world has seen, and who had witnessed miracles, seen His power and witnessed His resurrection, if they were not allowed to stir one step in the way of active service until they had received this power from on high, I am sure it is the greatest folly and presumption for us to hope for any kind of success if we enter the Master's work without feeling sure of this power, and we have no reason to doubt, and every reason to believe, that all the power of the Holy Ghost did fall upon them. The task that they were to accomplish was next to impossible. Yea, it was impossible, but the touch of the Holy Spirit of God was making the impossible possible, and when the Holy Spirit came it filled them like mighty rushing wind, coursing through every fibre of their being like an uncontrollable fire and created in them an intense desire to see the kingdom of God made perfect in the earth, and fired them with a Jesus-like passion for souls and filled them with all the fulness of God's power, and sent them out into the world to stand for their Master. The strength of the Master had fallen upon them. The mantle of one far greater than Elijah had indeed fallen upon the sons of men, and they went out to accomplish greater things than the Master Himself had done, because He had said, "They that follow after Me shall do greater works than I have done." It was the power of the Holy Spirit upon them.

Now, this power we have been speaking about today is a thing to be appreciated, rather than defined. But that we have the promise of this power for service is the testimony of the Word of God, and that this power has rested upon God's people in all ages is the testimony of individual experience and observation. What was it that made D. L. Moody a mighty man of God and power? Is it his college and theological education, or the power of God working in and through that man, and the power of God resting upon him? Mr. Mills tells in his excellent book, "Power From on High," of a young student at Phillips' Academy, at Andover. The student was a stupid individual and while he prayed there in that academy the rest of the students graduated from the academy and passed through the college course and came back to enter the theological seminary, and still the poor fellow was unable to pass the examination. He had more power for God and righteousness and more influence on the people than all the other students of that academy, and at last the professors sent him on to the seminary, and when he got into the seminary, poor fellow, it was all Hebrew to him. He could not make any better progress. While there he had some power for

God, and he did more work for righteousness than all the students of the seminary, and all the professors and the Christian people of the town. He went down to a factory village and started a Sunday school with twenty men in it, and many people yielded themselves to Christ, and he went over to the little city of Lawrence and started a Sabbath school there, and in that place there is a powerful and efficient church as the result of his efforts, and when the time for the summer vacation came there was a message received from a lady in New Hampshire who said, "There is only one person in this place that believes in God. Can't you send a young man down from the seminary to preach to us the word of God?" There was not a man among them who would go, but this young man, and he wanted to go; and he went and laid the matter before the professors about going to that place, but the professors were in doubt about licensing him, but finally they concluded that he could not do very much harm in six months, and they gave him a six-months' license. He went down there and went to work. He did not live down there very long until the poor fellow died. But before he died every man. woman and child in that township, with the exception of one man, had been brought to Christ, and that man moved away.

It is the power of God working through our lives that makes us effective workers for God. We may ask, "Are these exceptional cases, or are they given to us for examples?" Both; I think they are exceptional cases. It is not the experience of the average Christian to be filled with such power as that; but there is no reason why every Christian should not be filled with such power. Let me ask this question this afternoon: What have you been doing during the past years for Christ? You have had no burning passion for souls, and what you have said or done is simply without power and is of little or no consequence. You have worked? Yes; and you have had faith, too; but not a single soul for Christ. You speak, but there is no power that follows. You cry, "Awake! Arouse! Arouse yourselves!" And the sleeper only turns in his bed. Says Mr. Arthur, "When the powerless powder and the powerless cannon ball are put into the powerless cannon, and the spark of fire enters it, and that powerless powder flashes like the lightning, then the powerless thundering ball smites as if it had been sent from heaven." And six-months, there is a power that can take the things of God and burn them in the hearts of men until they shall cry in deep concern, "Men and brethren, what shall we do?" And this power is yours by promise and lies within your reach.

Child of God, it is not more work that you need. All of our work will mean only a row of ciphers if we do not work in the power of the spirit of God. It is not more learning we need. The most learned philosopher in the land, without the Holy Ghost, is of less consequence to the kingdom of God than the most ignorant slave with that baptism. When learning and education is put as a substitute for the power of the Holy Spirit, it is indeed without avail. It is not this we need. It is the power of the Spirit resting upon us. I have no sympathy with that spirit which derides the Church as a miserable failure. If the Church is an imperfect organization, it is not unlike every other thing with which man has to do; but I believe that the Church of God is the most perfect thing in itself that this world has ever seen, except the perfect life of the Son of God Himself, and the most perfect of many of the saints composing the Church, and I believe that in the heart of the hopeful Christian there is no room for any such deadly pessimism, but the heart must be filled with hope born of the spirit of God that expects to see the Church ride on in glorious triumph from victory unto victory, until the kingdoms of this world shall become the kingdom of our Lord and His Christ, and whatever failure we have made in the past, either as individuals or as a Church, is because we have not worked in connection and conjunction with the mighty power of God. You have doubtless heard that beautiful description of the light of the Holy Sepulchre in Jerusalem on Easter day. The church is crowded by more than a thousand people who sit enveloped in darkness, and in the hand of each one is an unlighted torch. The venerable father comes and passes through their midst. He passes into the tomb where the dead body of Jesus is supposed to have lain. In breathless suspense the great crowd wait anxiously until a spirit appears at the door, and the father comes forth with a lighted torch from the tomb of the Saviour, and instantly the thousands of hands are reaching for that torch, and instantly the thousand torches are lighted from the light of that one torch, and they go into the lanes and alleys and streets and homes of the city of Jerusalem with the light that comes from the Saviour's tomb. Do you want your torch lighted by the light of Christ? Are you thirsty for the baptism of power? "They that hunger and thirst after righteousness shall be filled." The prophet said, "I will pour out my spirit upon him that is thirsty." Do you want the Holy Spirit's power? Do as the woman that cried out in her great agony, "I will die if I do not receive this blessing." Are you willing to go up to Jerusalem, stretch yourself out upon the cross and ask God to drive deep the nail that shall forever crucify every selfish ambition? Are you willing to ask God for the spirit today, and if you are, before we leave shall we not go into the place of the death of our Christ and there let the light of His spirit burn everything un-Christ-like out of our lives and then touch our dead torch with the light that burns with Christ's love? Let us go from this place out into the alleys and streets and homes and in all the dark places of this city, lighting other torches with our own and kindling such a fire as shall never cease to burn until the whole city is glowing with the light that comes from the tomb of our Christ and our God. This power is for you. It is the promise of God. Shall we claim it? And shall we lift our souls up today and cry, "Come, Holy Spirit, Heavenly Dove, with all Thy quickening powers; kindle a flame of sacred love in these cold hearts of ours?"

Oh, spirit of God, uplift our faith until this precious love shall fill our souls and the shining of our faces declare that we have seen the face of God.

* * *

After the singing of a song, and some announcements, Mr. Mills preached a sermon upon the subject of "Power," and closed the meeting with a consecration service, at which scores of people gave earnest testimonies for God and the power of the Spirit as made manifest in their hearts, throughout the whole series of meetings, and especially during the Christian Convention. The Convention then adjourned sine die.

IV

Part Four

Endorsements by Pastors

How Pastors Were Impressed by the Great Awakening

I have been asked to write a few lines as to the Mills meetings in Columbus. The meetings have been grand from the first to the last day. The Gospel was given to us with great power, and we have never known so much about love and the Kingdom of God before.

Sin in all its forms has been condemned regardless of the position or opinion of men. Mr. Mills does not count numbers; neither does he make any charge for his work, but, his whole heart goes out after lost souls that they may be saved. The midweek Sabbath, when the stores and many saloons were closed to attend the Mills meetings, made us feel that Columbus herself had been converted. It is impossible to express in words the good Mr. Mills has done in this city, and he will never know until he enters the beautiful city and crown upon crown is placed upon his head.

Ministers and laymen have been revived, sinners saved, and a great harvest is already ripe for reaping.

-**W. L. LEMON**, Pastor of Memorial Baptist Church

One of the first striking features of the wonderful revival campaign, is the perfection of the preliminary arrangements. Nothing was left to go at random. Every detail was arranged, and the whole plan showed the masterly hand of an able general.

Another remarkable feature of the movement was the practical unanimity of all connected with it, and the hearty co-operation of the ministers and Christian workers. The spirit of love was manifested from the very first. Then the work of Mr. Mills and his assistants was so earnest and able, that there was a rising tide from the very first service. There was a directness in the preaching and an earnestness in the appeals that could not fail to lead men to decision.

The noon day sermons on the Kingdom of God in its relation to the burning questions of the day, were simply revelations of a new world of thought and interest. Such great thoughts and such mighty presentation of the Scriptures will doubtless bring in a new era in the Church and in the world. The establishment of the "Kingdom of God" in the world in all its glory and power is a new interpretation of the many precious promises of the Bible. Such a view enlarges the conception of this age and this dispensation, and thrills the heart with new hope and courage for humanity.

The great climax of the meetings was the great gathering of men at the Rink on the last Sunday night. The presence of the Holy Spirit was manifested in a holy hush that made the place solemn as eternity. Columbus has never had in all its history such a mighty movement toward God and righteousness.

-**ADDISON E. DAVIS**, Pastor Grace United Brethren Church

When I came to Columbus as pastor two months ago, I was glad to learn that a part of the Mills meetings were to be held in my church. I had long desired to have a good opportunity of studying Mr. Mills's methods in revival work. I confess to some prejudice against evangelists in general, and, possibly a little against Mr. Mills in particular. But after careful observation and co-operation in the union meetings, I desire to say that the methods employed by Mr. Mills and his associates are not objectionable in any particular. The system and generalship displayed are marvelous. Mr. Mills is always master of the situation. His genial and kindly bearing is winning.

The spirited congregational singing conducted by capable Christian leaders, the able preaching by Messrs. Mills and Beiderwolf, and their strong appeals both to Christian and sinner to do what Christ would have them do, all result in good. The cards are not signed thoughtlessly. Almost every one that I have followed up gives promise of the genuine beginning or renewal of the Christian life. The fellowship of the churches is glorious. But the strongest feature of the work is the noonday sermons by Mr. Mills on applied Christianity. His theology is intensely practical, but well sustained by Scripture, and it is likely to result in the reconstruction of more than one old sermon by his clerical hearers. His great theme is the religion of love for humanity as an evidence of love for God, and the bringing about through love of the Kingdom of God on earth.

-**A. J. HAWK**, Pastor Gift Street M. E. Church

The history of Columbus can not be written after 1895 with "Mills Meetings" left out. As a religious movement this revival stands unparalleled to date, within our city. Young people and children will speak of it half a century hence as a Mahanaim, a gathering of the "Hosts or Companies of God." It was a season of heavenly visitation to multiplied thousands. It arrested the universal public attention, and compelled the respect of opposers and unbelievers. No sensational methods were used. The Gospel was preached in its simplicity and sweetness, and it proved the power of God unto salvation to hundreds. Never before, in this city, did so many Churches, with their pastors and adherents, come into such close and harmonious touch with one another. Denominational lines were temporarily obliterated, and will henceforth be less distinct. If the day of organic union seems still far away, the more desirable era of spiritual union is nearer than it was before. Perhaps greatest, among the many great and good effects, is the blessed realization of the Kingdom of God now on earth, in the minds of the multitudes who heard the wonderful noon-day sermons of Brother Mills on that subject.

Great and lasting will be the fruits of this revival, and to God be the glory.

-J. C. JACKSON, JR., Pastor of Third Avenue Methodist Episcopal Church

Mr. Mills is a man who lives in God's great to -day. He does not believe that the Holy Spirit said his final word to those saints of blessed memory whose bones now molder in the dust. He respects what the spirit of God gives to living men. The methods of business of one hundred years ago are not the successful methods of today. So, in the business of religion, the methods of presenting God's unchanging truth vary with age and environment.

The first great result achieved, worth all the effort if nothing else had been accomplished, is the splendid unification of our churches in the single object of presenting Jesus Christ as the Redeemer of the world. Protestantism is one in the Lord Jesus and one in her desire to save the souls of men.

To my mind the strong emphasis laid upon the fact that the Christian life is a giving up of some things one might naturally wish to do, a denying of self, and a service for humanity in the Master's name, a rising up into the very atmosphere of the Redeemer's life stamps it as crowned with the approval of Him, who came into the world not to be ministered unto, but to minister.

The many who are coming into the kingdom of God declare too, that the power of the Cross, the old, old story of a Savior's love, has not lost its attractiveness for the human heart. I rejoice with joy unspeakable that amid the many absorbing themes that occupy the minds of men, the coming of this evangelist to our city, has given the Kingdom of God so large a place in thought and heart.

And may it be the harbinger of an awakened and redeemed city wherein shall dwell righteousness, and whose citizens shall serve its interests political, business, educational and benevolent in the loving, self-sacrificing spirit of the Man of Calvary. And if the Church of God only realizes the throne of her power why may not we see such things come to pass?

-**FRANCIS E. MARSTEN, D. D.**, Pastor of Broad Street Presbyterian
Church

Editorial Comments

The sermons of Mr. Mills are intensely practical. They are directed right to the men and women in front of him. They go so straight to the work, that one in his audience may see persons dodging to miss his arrows. There is no mincing of words. Full of zeal and conscious of an upright motive, he speaks the hard truth without masquerade. There are ministers in Columbus of equal ability and eloquence, but few, very few, with equal energy, and burning with equal zeal to expose wrong. He wastes no time about theology or dogmatic questions. He deals with men and women and their relations to these passing days, and uses the Bible and its heroic characters only to illustrate and fortify his thought. His intense zeal and utter unconcern for social distinctions, and his denunciation of worldly meanness wherever found, and his courageous recognition of humanity, even in the dust and foulness of life, makes him a preacher for the wilderness of civilization. No man of our time sees more clearly the folly and madness of the modern hurly-burly we call the civilized life we are living. He knows it is utterly wretched, and is getting worse and worse in its eviler aspects. His clear voice is sounding the key that would make a joyful, helpful chorus, if the world were to join in with it.

There is but little cant or dogma in his current as it floats along, and but little air of superstition blowing from the high level of his rational thought. He believes in God and in the kinship and even brotherhood of all men. He thinks the world sad and filled with sorrow, because the brothers and sisters of the human family are estranged from each other. There would be harmony as divine as that of heavenly choirs if men and women would see and know each other in loving and unselfish sympathy. The deeper the sympathy, the loftier the nature of man. Religion, according to his thought, is not a formula or mathematical quantity, but a vital energy and impulse impelling toward whatever is best, least selfish and most kind. Religion is not for one day of the week or month or year, but the companion and guide for life and every moment of it. It is impossible for it to inhabit a selfish or ignoble body. The temple where it dwells must be pure. That member of a Church who grinds the life out of the poor and makes their days long with pain in search of money to pay his usurous interest is not a Christian in his way of thinking, but he has a Christian's spirit and inspiration, who nobly resolves that there shall be no poor and needy, if out of his store he can minister to their want.

There can be no doubt of the sanity and high standard of his teaching. His words, like rosemary, are for remembrance. "Let us not wait till our lives are over," said he, "in expectation that at death we shall be wafted into a heaven of oriental splendor which we do not merit, but let us make a paradise here while we are waiting among the joyless children of men." He is a preacher of profound conviction, and too nobly courageous to temporize with any form of wrong. He is no doubt engaged in the task for which he is best fitted. It is doubtful if his ringing, truthful words could long be endured from the same pulpit Sunday after Sunday to a city church congregation. They would fester in the minds of too many members of the church, and they would seek escape from the torture of their conviction by absence. But to arouse a religious sense and to lead the selfish to think of the vanity of riches, and the folly of fashion, no diviner voice has ever been heard preaching in the wilderness of this community, calling men and women to nobler, juster lives. Let every citizen of Columbus hear him before his ministry is done among us.

-**De Witt C. Jones**, in the Columbus Press.

A New Era in Evangelism

The evangelism of Paul, Wesley, Whitfield and Finney was a sublime illustration of the power of one man over his own generation when filled with God consciousness.

They wrought mightily because they were impelled in their arduous labors by an all-consuming zeal for God and man. The message which these men delivered and which turned multitudes toward righteousness, was in every case best adapted to move those who heard it. But today is by no means the same as yesterday. If Wesley should preach the very same sermons once delivered to the eager multitudes in the fields and commons, it is not at all likely that the same effects would follow. He that would speak effectively to this generation must be a child of today; he must enter deeply into the struggles through which the men of to -day are passing. And the problems of our day are different from those which confronted the thoughtful in other ages. Whatever changes have been wrought in human nature and in society, man is still a sinner and God is still willing and able to save. It still remains true that religion is the best aid to morality. The unselfish life is the only worthy and finally triumphant life. And we are beginning to see more clearly than ever before that it is the function of religion to furnish the motive to an unselfish life. Only religion is sufficient to do this. The stone which the social builders have rejected is about to become the head of the corner. What is needed just now more than anything else is not a more complete mastery of the physical forces, but a general diffusion of the the spirit of unselfishness, which shall insure the right use of the forces already discovered. In fact we have come to a point in our material development where great wealth will prove a curse to multitudes, unless there comes with the enlarged power which it brings, also a great inspiration to large-mindedness and benevolence.

It has become evident that politics, commerce and business must repent and accept Christ or be lost. But the must painful feature of the situation is the fact that the majority of those who manage the affairs of the state and the business of the world do not want what they need.

How shall we persuade those who do not believe in Christ to accept Him?

Revivals of religion have proved to be a very effective means of reaching the careless and hardened and turning them to righteousness. And yet the revival that aims exclusively at the salvation of the individual is felt to be inadequate to the demands of the day. The new evangelism differs from the old, mainly in the fact that to conviction of personal sins and effort to save men from them, is added conviction and sorrow for social sins and a practical effort to improve the material, political and social environment in which the individual lives. One of the marked features of the great awakening in this city is the widening of the sacred sphere so as to include the whole of life. A great stride has been made toward removing the artificial and hurtful distinction between the sacred and the secular, as any one will see by reading the foregoing pages. This is due to the fact that men perceive as never before the relation between the things that surround a man and his conduct and character. Multitudes of men born of the spirit of the times are now giving themselves joyfully to the work of saving society in order that the units of which it is composed may have a chance for an abundant life. And if it is reasonable to be concerned about the salvation of one man and to labor for that end, how much more should we pray and sacrifice for the saving of the great social body!

The Mills meeting in this city has shown clearly that the old-time revival, with its intense fervor and power, has developed into a great interdenominational all-inclusive religious movement, touching life at every point, quickening in all men whatever makes for personal and social righteousness, and rebuking all persons and institutions that dare to array themselves against God and the true interests of men. The great awakening in Columbus is another name for a great revival, modernized, enlarged and greatly improved.

Appendix

Since the first pages of this work went to press the great meeting closed. The last service, which was a most wonderful one, was held in the Park Rink, and will never be forgotten by the 5,000 persons who were present. After the benediction was pronounced, about 2,000 people, including the choir of 500, accompanied Mr. Mills to the Union Station and bade him an' affectionate farewell by singing "God be with you till we meet again."

The number of cards signed during the meeting, by those who thereby expressed a desire to lead a Christian life, was 2,467.

On Sunday, December 8th, special cards were distributed in the Sunday Schools of all the co-operating churches, and probably 1,500 of these were signed by the scholars on that day; making thus a total of about 4,000 expressions of desire to follow Christ.

A great many of the churches are at this date holding services in order to help those now interested into a definite Christian experience.

One of the many good results of the meeting is a real union of feeling, plan and purpose on the part of the pastors and members of all the churches. As a direct result of this, a Civic Federation has been formed, at the head of which is Dr. Washington Gladden, the well known author and preacher. Roman Catholics and Israelites have been invited to join in this great movement to promote the common welfare in this city, and have cheerfully expressed their willingness to co-operate with their Protestant brethren in every possible way.

The pastors of the city have announced that they will preach on "The

Enforcement of Law" on Sunday, December 29th.

As these pages go to press, there is some probability that Mayor Allen will close the gambling places, so high has the tide of righteous indignation against the non-enforcement of law risen.

The Kingdom of God has come with prevailing power. Men are now working under the inspiration of new hope, new assurance and love. Never in the history of this city has the word "wonderful" been used as frequently as during the last month.

The germs of measureless moral possibilities are sprouting vigorously.

> "We are living, we are dwelling
> In a grand and awful time,
> In an age on ages telling,
> To be living is sublime."

DECEMBER 19, 1895

V

Scans of Original Publication Pages

Drawn Map of Meeting Locations

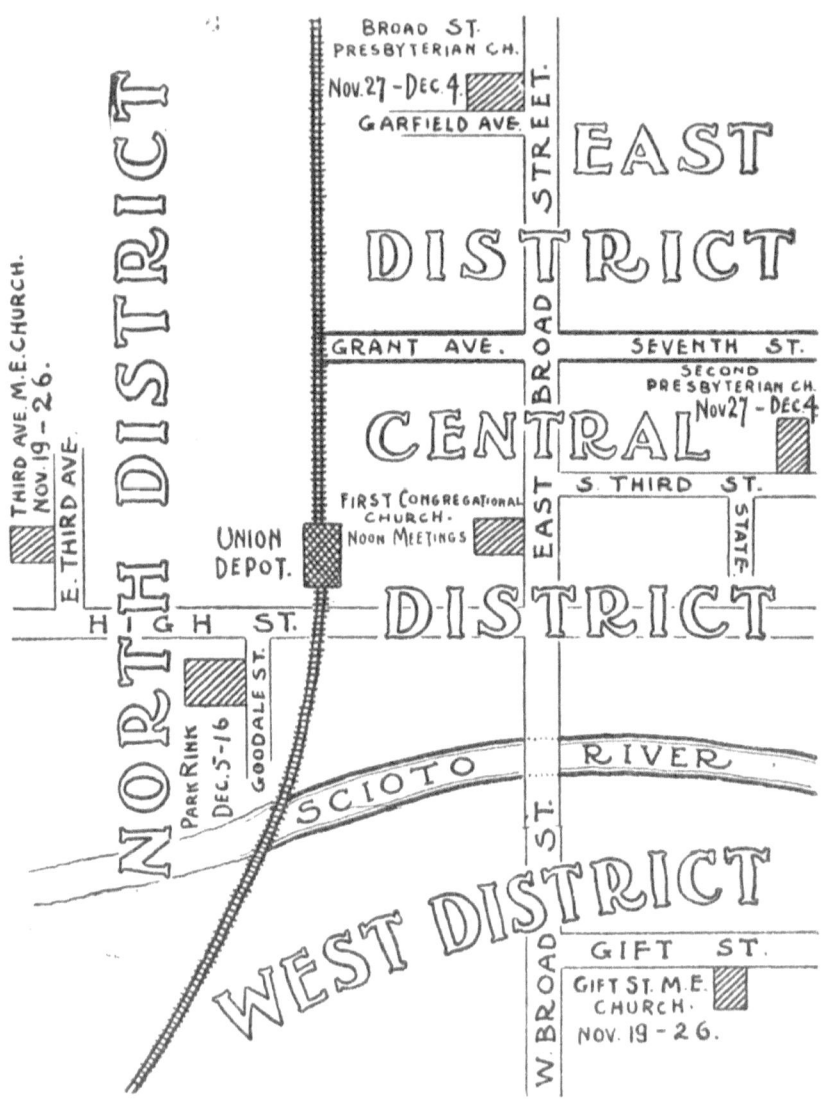

"This cut shows in part where and when the meetings were held. From November 19th to 26th, inclusive, meetings were held in the North and West Districts. From November 27th to December 4th, inclusive, meetings were held in the East and Central Districts, and also in the South District in the German Methodist Church and Turner Hall. The noon meetings were held daily except Saturday in First Congregational Church until November 29th, after which it became necessary on account of the large attendance to use the Board of Trade Auditorium."

Names of Ushers, Students, & Choir Members

Committee on Ushers and Assistants.

W. T. PERKINS, Chairman.

J. E. HUFF,   W. H. HUGHES.

NORTH DISTRICT.

J. H. SELLS,   J. R. SHRUM,

H. A. NUNEMACHER.

EAST DISTRICT.   WEST DISTRICT.

C. O. TRACY,   H. E. RAWSON,   A. W. McPEAK,   G. W. BRADFORD,

W. G. HARRINGTON.   CHAS. McCOY.

CENTRAL DISTRICT.

L. D. MYERS,   J. W. ESTILL.

Names of Doorkeepers, Ushers and Lady Assistants.

Ackley, Miss Ada	Bennett, J. N.	Burrington, P. V.
Ackley, Miss Alice	Beller, H. C.	Bulkley, Mrs. Ralph
Aikin, Miss Stella	Bean, A. W.	Carson, J. C.
Agnes, Miss Eula	Behmer, Miss Effie C.	Candy, Mrs. Robert
Allen, B. M.	Bell, Miss Nettie	Castle, Mrs. F. O.
Allison, J. M.	Bliss, Mrs. M. W.	Carr, Miss Marian
Anderson, John M.	Blackford, Miss Jean	Chapman, Miss Hannah
Anderson, John	Blake, Monroe	Clevenger, Miss Anna
Andrix, John	Bowers, James S.	Clark, Miss Maggie
Armstrong, Miss Jessie	Bond, Miss Blanche	Conrad, John,
Arnold, Miss Amy	Boesel, Oliver H.	Coen, Samuel F.
Arnold, Charles L.	Bowne, Mrs. Mary	Copeland, Miss Fannie
Aukerman, Burtt	Brown, W. H.	Coates, Mrs. A. D.
Ault, Mrs. John	Bradford, George W.	Courtney, Miss Mary
Babbitt, C. H.	Brown, J. K.	Cole, George N.
Babbitt, Miss Alice	Brook, Miss Ella	Copeland, Foster
Bartram, C. E.	Brewer, J. W.	Cornell, Mrs. C. R.
Bartram, Mrs. C. E.	Bradfield, Abner W.	Conklin, Mrs. B. F.
Bauman, Earl E.	Brown, J. Findley.	Cole, F. F.
Bancroft, Miss Allie	Broadfoot, David	Connell, Mrs. D. R.
Bane, R. R.	Broes, A. B.	Cook, Demmie
Barnes, Clyde F.	Brown, Mrs. S. C.	Crouse, Edward
Beck, J. W.	Bunker, Miss Abbie	Crawford, Miss Sadie
Beery, Dr. J. E.	Butler, James	Crain, George W.

Cratty, Joseph
Crippen, H. C.
Cubbige, Mrs. Ella
Culp, Miss Dora
Curtis, Edna A.
Crooks, James
Davidson, G. W.
Ditrick, S. B.
Dunham, J. Dudley
Dann, J. Lyman
Dunham, Mrs. J. M.
Davies, John
Davies, John L.
Davies, Miss Mary C.
Dudrow, J. S.
Dean, Miss Ella
Donham, Morice
Doty, E. M.
DeVore, Miss Vitia
Deahl, Miss Lucy
Deaver, Mrs. Wm.
Dann, E. W.
Deardurff, Orrin
Dickinson, Mrs. J. F.
Doe, Miss Carrie E.
Dowdell, Miss Ruth E.
Davis, Miss Ivy Bell
Evans, Mrs. James
Edwards, David
Evans, Miss May
Everett, C. D.
Evans, Walter
Ebright, Miss Elsie
Edwards, Miss Jennie
Earl Robert
Ewing, Milan C.
Evans, Miss Mame
Fisher, J. D.
Frankenberg, F.
Ford, Stanley
Fouty, Charles
Funk, J. M.
Fay, Mrs. H. D.
Fisher, Mrs. E. E.
Fowler, C. H.
Fohrman, Miss Lizzie
Fisk, Miss L. V.

Fix, Mrs. George M.
Fritter, Lincoln
Gordon, Charles
Gerneinhardt, Frank F.
Griffiths, Miss Mary
Griffiths, Miss Kate
Good, Miss Nellie
Giesy, Mrs. H.
Goddard, Loring H.
Graves, Dean
Gill, Miss Alice
Griggs, Julian
Hanna, J. C.
Herbert, C. T.
Howell, Miss Virginia
Howald, Fred
Hartley, J. A.
Hartley, R. A.
Haines, Clyde O.
Hutton, Miss Rebecca
Hughes, F. M.
Hutchins, R. G.
Holmes, Miss Mary G.
Hopper, Miss Florence
Harrison, J. O.
Hester, Mrs. E. H.
Heyl, Mrs. Wm.
Harrison, Mrs. J. O.
Hannum, John C.
Hunter, George
Hutton, John E.
Humphrey, Mrs. C. F.
Horne, Lewis
Hubble, Miss Clara
Holmes, Mrs. J. T.
Hammond, Miss Jennie
Harris, E. L.
Harris, Mrs. E. L.
Hoffman, C. S.
Henry, John K.
Henry, Mrs. John K.
Houseman, C. H.
Heimberger, H. J.
Hardman, Ralph
Huddleson, Carlos
Huntington, A.
Horne, Miss Ottora

Huddleson, Miss Mabel
Hoyer, W. E.
Hersheiser, W. A.
Hamilton, George W.
Hutchinson, Miss Jessie
Hamming, Miss Iva
Howard, E. D.
Irwin, Miss Alice
Immel, Alex.
Johnson, Charles
Judd, Miss Helen
Jones, David
Jones, Miss Anna
Johnson, William
Jones, Miss Lulu
Jones, Miss Ada
Jeffrey, J. A.
Jeffries, C. W.
Jones, David
Jones, John
Jones, W. E.
Kuhn, Miss Grace
Kerns, Mrs. M. J.
Killian, S. D.
Kauffman, Mrs. F. B.
Kirkpatrick, W. A.
Kibby, G. N.
Kerr, Frank
Kinsell, Miss Katharine
Kersey, W. R.
Kail, Harry
Lippitt, Mrs. Dr. B. F.
Lieb, Miss Gertrude
Lowe, Miss Maude
Lawrence, Dr. F. F.
Lanman, Mrs. J. T.
Little, Mrs. W. P.
Lovell, Ray E.
Lonnis, Mrs. H. C.
Lonnis, H. C.
Lloyd, Homer A.
Lilley, J. W.
Ledman, O. S.
LaMonte, Charles L.
Lewis, Mrs. James
McMillen, John
McCoy, Charles B.

McManigal, N. F.
McKinstry, Miss May
McKee, Miss Mame
McCarty, J. E.
McGinnis, H. A.
McKinney, W. D.
McKee, H. N.
McLaughlin, C. R.
Mull, Miss Lizzie
Moorehead, Albert L.
Moorehead, Miss G. M.
Morriss, W. H.
Mead, Miss Laura
Munson, C. E.
Maxwell, Mrs. F. C.
Mellon, George S.
Maynard, B. L.
Main, jr., Rufus
Merriman, Miss Elsie A.
Mills, Miss Harriet A.
Masters, Miss Anna
Morlan, Miss Ida
Mills, W. T.
Moon, Miss Agnes
Neereamer, A. L.
North, Miss Mary H.
Noble. W. H.
Nesbitt, Mrs. J. C.
Norris, Miss Mamie
Nesbit, Hugh
Naftel, John
Nitschke, James
Olwine, Miss Gertrude
Orvis, W. S.
O'Brien, E. H.
Overall, Mrs. Jessie
Osgood, R. H.
Plaisted, E. W.
Payne, Mrs. A. C.
Pickett, W. F.
Payne, Henry
Peake, Mrs. Albert
Plimmer, Richard
Pancake, Jesse C.
Powell, Mrs. T. E.
Price, Mrs. Dr.
Park, W. D.

Platt, Miss Maggie
Pace, Vinton
Pickering, W. S.
Pickering, C. C.
Parks, Miss Julia
Price, William
Phillips, Carl T.
Pomeroy, A.
Robinson, Mrs. John
Ross, Miss Lizzie
Rawson, Mrs. H. E.
Rownd, R. M.
Raymond, Mrs. Ida
Runyan, Miss Cora
Raymond, Mrs. Ida
Rownd, Mrs. R. M.
Rexer, Miss Anna L.
Rankin, Miss Nettie
Rhoades, Mrs. John A.
Rodgers, Miss Estella
Ridenour, Frank
Rodgers, Pearl
Rowand, Charles
Roderick, Mrs. Thomas
Rector, Fred C.
Rhoades, John B.
Schneider, J. C.
Sigler, B. R.
Steward, Mrs. Dr. S. H.
Slyh, Charles J.
Sherman, Chris.
Shull. C. B.
Souder, Miss Roxanna
Seeds, E. W.
Shawan, Prof. J. A.
Smith, Oliver
Stimmel, George
Snell, Miss Ada
Sells, F. A.
Scott, Miss Emma
Sherman, Miss Alice B.
Slyh, Miss Emma
Smith, J. C.
Schooley, Walter
Sheldon, Theodore
Steele, J. G.
Smith, A. C.

Syfert, Harry R.
Smith, Miss Alice
Smith, Miss Laura
Strayer, Mrs. Emma
Strayer, C. S.
Smalley, F. A.
Shriver, Russel B.
Shepherd, James G.
Stoddard, Dr. Wm.
Thomas, Morgan
Timmons, Nicholas
Thomas, Mrs. Morgan
Taylor, W. J.
Tremaine, H. H.
Taylor, Mrs. C. M.
Timmins, Mrs. S.
Taylor, E. M.
Thompson, E. F.
Talbott, Herbert
VonGerichten, Ludwig
Vittum, J. E.
Weller, S. N.
Wilcox, Mrs. Jonas
Watt, A. F.
Walker, W. R.
White, Z. L.
Wood, E. F.
Williams, Henry A.
Walton, Edwin
Winters, Dr. S. B.
Wolcott, Prof.
Wright, Miss M A.
Wolfley, Jesse T.
Williams, Miss May
Willson, L. C.
Whitney, William E.
Wood, Miss Lillian
Wynkoop, Miss Estella
Winn, Miss Ella
Walker, F. C.
Wilson Mrs. A. W.
Williams, Miss Elizabeth
Watts, Frank
White, Hiram S.
Willard, Mrs. Chas.
Woollard, Miss Ollie
Zealer, Wm. H.

Students from the Ohio State University.

Allaman, W. E.
Adamson, R. E.
Abbott, A. G.
Brand, H. F.
Burkett, D. V.
Baker, C. W.
Baer, Philip
Birdsall, J. W.
Cratty, J. M.

Cunningham, J. F.
Enos, E. E.
Forgy, R. W.
Huddleson. D. C.
Henderson, F. A.
Landacre, F. L.
Pabodie, R. J.
Persing, M. J.
Randolph, F. N.

Sprague, C. F.
Scott, Ernest
Snow W. A.
Steeb, C. E.
Shuck, C. L.
Travis, F. L.
Warden, Leo

Names of Members of the Grand United Choir.

Amerman, Mark
Allison, Louise
Anderson, Minnie
Arthur, Will A.
Ayers, Alice
Allen, C. N.
Anderson, Cora
Aiken, Miss
Ames, Eva S.
Barrows, Madge
Blaugher, Ida
Boyle, Emma
Bean, Harry
Bartlett, E.
Brown, Ernest E.
Brelsford, Mrs.
Bookman, Bertha
Barnes, Millie
Bradford, O.
Biven, Lutie
Biven, Birdie
Brooke, Ella A.
Baker, Anna
Burner, May E.
Benbow, Jane
Bown, S. J.
Bryson, James
Blankinship, M. W.
Boggs, Louvilla
Bauman, E.
Bunch, May

Brown, O. T.
Bauman, Mrs. Minnie
Brown Effie
Bowen, D. J.
Beany, Mrs.
Bennett, Carrie
Brandt, Anna
Bowman, Della
Bethel, C. R.
Bryan, Daisy
Bainter, Lydia
Bloos, Wm.
Browning, F. H.
Colmer, C. W.
Culbertson, Stella
Capell, Ella
Calvert. James M.
Crippen, Mrs.
Cook Chester
Crippen, Frank
Cummins, Rosa
Copeland, Maude
Clevenger, Mrs. E. H.
Copeland, Nellie, H.
Conwell, Ollie
Conwell, Mary
Clevenger, E. H.
Colvin, Sadie
Cook, Mrs. F. W.
Case, Flora May

Carpenter, George
Castle, Mrs. T. O.
Clemens, H. E.
Culp, Dora
Culp, Emma
Colmery, Miss L. J.
Colton, W. R.
Cummins, Chas. J.
Conrad, L.
Davis, Iva, Belle
Danner, Louise
Daniels, Mrs.
Dempsey, Harriet
Drew, Minnie
Dickey, Mrs. M. C.
Davis, Mamie
Denny, Meda
Dempsey, Miss
Deahl, Vena
Deahl, Lucy
Dempsey, Alberta
DeWitt, J. W.
Denny, Jessie
Davies, Martha A.
Davies, Jennie C.
Davies, John T.
Dutcher, Charley W.
DeBruin, Chas. E.
Everitt, Etta
Eagleson, Bert

277

Evans, Mamie
Evans, Mrs. J. A.
Edgington, Jennie
Edgington, W. J.
Ensign, Geo.
Ensign, Mrs. G.
Eagleson, S. B.
Edwards, Fannie
Edwards, Ollie
Edwards, Goldie
Earls, James
Earls, Belle
Eaks, John M.
Evans, David C.
Everett, C. D.
Fassig, Elizabeth
Fisher, E. E.
Fisher, Mrs. E. E.
Francis, Jessie B.
Fenner, Mrs. M. B.
Fleming, Clara
Fippin, Samuel
Fox, Grace
Frey, Emily J.
Fox, Evangeline
Fix, G. Louis
Fisher, Gertrude E.
Grimm, May
Gilbert, Edna
Griffin, C. L.
Grube, Eda C.
Gunning, Helena
Guest, Lettie
Gates, Emma M.
George, Wm.
Grimm, Anna M.
Grimm, Sue
Gasber, Roxie E.
Glenn, Minnie
Gorham, O. S.
Halley, Martha
Halley, Mary
Hershiser, Wm A.
Harris, J. Edwin
Hennis, Carl
Hagans, Maggie S.
Hinkle, W. L.

Hinkle, Jessie
Henry, Mae
Henry, Lou
Horne, Bertha
Harris, Lena
Hobensach, Etta
Hare, Claude H.
Howard, Zelotes
Hosper, E. J.
Hubbard, Margaret
Hance, Ada B.
Huddle, Clara
Hill, Maude A.
Hall, Mattie E.
Heimberger, M. L.
Heimberger, C. E.
Hughes, Elizabeth
Henderson, Mrs. Cora D.
Hamilton, A. D.
Hartsook, E.
Hartsook, Mrs. E.
Harman, T. A.
Hillery, E. Myrtle
Hillery, Beatrice
Hancock, J. C.
Horne, Ottora M.
Hafford, Helen F.
Hoffman, H. Louis
Hemphill, Frank
Hunt, C. Al.
Huntley, Sarah
Hartman, Josie
Herrman, Gracia E.
Henderson, Ruth
Herbert, E. J.
Humphrys, C. B.
Henderson, Lizzie M.
Hillery, Mrs. J. S.
Innis, Chas. L.
Jones, Ira M.
Jones, Anna E.
Jones, Lulu B.
Jones, Jeannette
Jones, Katherine
Jones, Jennie R.
Judd, W. O.
Jackson, L. P.

Johnson, Bly
Johns, Jessie
Johns, Alice
Knox, W. E.
Kraner, Charles E.
Kilbourne, Carrie
Kilbourne, Maude
Knell, Fred H.
Knoderer, H. G.
Knoderer, Minnie
Knoderer, Nettie
Kyner, E. Dell
Kuhn, Lizzie M.
Kadel, M. George
Latham, Lizzie
Lippert, O. G.
Lafayette, Mrs.
Long, Myrtle
Longenecker, Chas.
Lewis, C. H.
Lortz, Carrie
Lynn, Mrs. C. C.
Laisure, Belle
Lemon, Mrs. W. L.
Lloyd, Minnie C.
Lewis, Marie
Lott, Maybelle
Lippitt, Zudie
Lott, Maureen
Meikle, Marion
Meikle, Helen B.
McKown, F. L.
McBride, Cora
McKinley, Leone
McKee, Nell
McDowell, John A.
McClintock. Chas.
McKinney, Ida
McKinney, Cora
McElroy, Martha
McCoy, Robert
Meyer, Cynthia
Moon, Agnes
Miner, Cora A.
Miller, Ira,
Malone, Cora
Martindell, Madge

Marshall, Mrs. M. M.
Meeks, C. E.
Morley, A. D.
Moorhead, Gertrude
Morley, Ida May
Marshall, W. S.
Miller, C. H.
Morgan, Ed J.
Madden, Lily Belle
Marshall, W. O.
Mayfield, Nancy
Murray, Grace
Mangold, Katherine
Marshall, Mrs. Maude
Miller, Pearl
Morin, Anda
Madox, Miss Lou
Mayo, Mrs. E.
Mayo, Marcellite
Markel, A. R.
Neel, H. N.
Neel, Clara
Neel, Sadie
Norris, Nina
Nelson, W. W.
Nonemacher, Henry L.
Nurnberger, Mrs. Wm.
Osburn, R. C.
Propst, J. D.
Propst, Hattie
Propst, Mrs. J. D.
Phillips, Laura
Phelps, Adelaide
Pierson, Celia
Pontius, J. W.
Patterson, Anna
Price, Anna
Patton, Elizabeth
Pugh, Mrs. T. D.
Peters, Mamie
Propst, Emma
Plaisted, Mrs.
Peake, Mrs. A.
Payne, Alice
Payne Myrtle M.
Peake, A.
Powell, Mary A.

Pressler, Carrie
Pengelly, Emily J.
Paramore, C. D.
Ross, C. M.
Reinkens, Chas. L.
Ruth, Lillian
Roberts, Margaret
Robberts, Laura
Reed, Mr.
Rexer, Emma D.
Reese, Grace K.
Reichard, Wm. H.
Rees, John
Roderick, Thomas
Randolph, F. M.
Reedy, Dolores
Reedy, Sylvia
Rhoades, Maude A.
Rhoades, Mrs. H. V.
Rogers, Daisy
Stevenson, Mrs. B. S.
Stevenson, W. P.
Shelton, Mrs. C. L.
Shroyer, C. T.
Spencer, Mrs. Laura
Smith, R. Easter
Swartz, A. H.
Stevenson, C. S.
Shaw, Mr.
Sage, Edith W.
Sage, F. K.
Smith, Gertrude M.
Smith, Minnie
Smith, Cora
Snow, W. A.
Skinner, W. E.
Slyh, Emma R.
Strong, Mary
Scobie, Katie
Slyh, Edwin M.
Scott, H. B.
Starbuck, Lulu
Starbuck, J. S.
Sill, Ella M.
Swartzell, Mrs. S. K.
Starr, Hetta B.
Starrett, Fanny

Starrett, J. C.
Simmons, Ollie Maude
Smith, Chas. J.
Smith, Laura
Scott, Bennett M.
Stutson, Mrs.
Taylor, L. M.
Taylor, Sarah F.
Teaff. Mrs. Celeste
Teal, Mayme
Thibault, Anna
Thibault, Mrs. P.
Thomas, Annie M.
Thomas, Lily M.
Thompson, Alice K.
Thompson, Kate
Thompson, Lewis P.
Thrall, F. Raymond
Tomkinson, Mrs. C.
Torrey, Ada
Trew, Emma
Tufts, Cora
Turney, Miss C.
Turney, Tesa
Tuttle, Chas. B.
Tuttle, S. S.
Twigg, Mary G.
Twigg, Stella
Ulen, C.
Ustick, Mrs. E. E.
Ustick, Faye S.
Ustick, R. E.
Van Siever, Mae
Wall, Miss
Wallis, F. W.
Wallis, Mrs. F. W.
Walters, Minnie R.
Walton, Dora
Walton, Wilber J.
Watson, Emma
Watson, Kate
Watson, Margaret
Watson, Martha
Weare, Walter B.
Weaver, Frank
Weaver, Mrs. Frank
Weaver, W. B.

279

Wells, Mrs. C. N.
White, Clark S.
Wiggins, Arthur M.
Williams, Mrs. Bentz
Wills, Mrs. Chas.
Wilson, Ada
Winn, Miss A.

Winn, Ella
Wiswell, Jerusha
Wolf, Anna
Wolfley, O. A.
Wood, Bessie
Woodin, Grace
Worley, Lelah

Wright, Mary
Wynkoop, Stella
Young, F.
Zarbaugh, L. L.
Zeigler, Helen

Pianists.

Fenimore, Miss Ruth
Freeman, Miss Sarah

Humphrys, Miss Carrie
Blake, Miss Ora K.

Torrey, Miss Viva